ABOUT THE AUTHOR

Colly Aleksander, was born in 1986 in Novi Sad, Republic of Serbia. He graduated Psychology from faculty of Philosophy in Novi Sad and Started his Ph.D. Studies. He worked at Children's Hospital where his main tasts were psychological evaluation in order to identify psychosomatic diseases, Psychological support from parents, and child and adolescent psychotherapy.He has many scientific articles written and published in academic journals. He is focused, deligent, fair, ambitious, able to make decisions and determine priorties, focused on achieving results, competitive spirit, intersted in the individual and teamwork, dedicated and reliable.

ABOUT THE BOOK

Industrial organization is a field of economics that studies the strategic behaviour of firms, the structure of markets and their interactions. The study of industrial organization adds to the perfectly competitive model real-world frictions such as limited information, transaction cost, of adjusting prices, government actions, and barriers to entry by new firms into a market. It then considers how firms are organized and how they compete. Organizational behaviour is a relatively new, interdisciplinary field of study. Although it draws most heavily from the psychological and sociological sciences, it also looks to other scientific fields of study for insights. One of the main reasons for this interdisciplinary approach is because the field of organizational behaviour involves multiple levels of analysis, which are necessary to understand behaviour within organizations because people do not act in isolation. That is, workers influence their environment and are also influenced by their environment. Industrial psychology is a relatively new branch of psychology that was created for corporations and organizations that needed more structure. Industrial psychology is able to provide this structure by evaluating employee behaviour for the good of the company. It is often referred to as organizational psychology because of its emphasis on analysing individuals who work for various organizations. The book is designed to help the students and professionals to quickly acquire the knowledge and skills they need for this subject.

Ethics and Value in Industrial Organization Psychology

Colly Aleksander

AMIGA PRESS. INC
Delhi -110051

AMIGA PRESS. INC
H.O :- 28-A, Indra Park, Chander Nagar
Delhi :- 110051 (India)
Tel :- 011-22504028, +91-98736-57000
Email :- info@amigapress.co.in
amigapub@gmail.com
Website :- www.amigapress@co.in

This edition is published by Amiga Press.Inc

ISBN : 978-93-87295-20-9

First Published 2019

Printed and bound by Amiga Press Inc. New Delhi-India

Preface

Industrial and organizational psychology is applies psychology to organizations and the workplace. Industrial-organizational psychologists contribute to an organization's success by improving the performance and well-being of its people. An I-O psychologist researches and identifies how behaviours and attitudes can be improved through hiring practices, training programs, and feedback systems.

Organizational Psychology is a subject which applies the principles of psychology into one of the most important areas of people's life-work. Specifically, we work with the human aspects of the workplace and aim at improving people's efficiency, and hence organizational effectiveness, through our knowledge about human functioning. There exist a group of professionals who share a similar aim and are working closely with us, the human resource professionals. Despite the close relationship with HR professionals, Organizational Psychologists are distinctive professionals. Unfortunately, there is always some confusion among the general public that people just cannot tell who is who. More importantly, even some HR professionals do not know what we are doing and what can we offer them.

When we tell them we are Psychologists, a frequent reply is "but we don't have any mental problems"! As Organizational Psychologists, we work with a wide range of domains that are related to people's everyday work life. We design work activities, schedules and workplaces; we design reward principles that are based on human motivation theories; we develop training principles and train the trainers; we develop selection procedures and tools; we formulate performance appraisal systems; and we advise on organizational development issues as well as career development decisions.

Organizational Behaviour scientists have conducted extensive studies on job definitions and the tasks a job comprises. They have looked at how each job fit into different groups within the organization, a process called departmentalization. The researchers have studied managerial spans of control, i.e., the number of people an individual manager can manage most effectively. The process required that researchers reduce to its most basic level each task performed and then find ways to perform jobs more efficiently and effectively.

Many researchers have suggested viable ways that organizations could restructure jobs and relationships to stimulate job satisfaction and productivity simultaneously. They have devised better communications programs, identified the elements that create stress, and explained how it could be better managed.

Organizational Behaviour scientists performed extensive studies on company cultures and climates with an eye to upgrading employees' quality of life in the workplace. They have sought ways to include more people in the managerial and decision-making processes. Their suggestions have included such techniques as quality circles and participative management programs.

Employees in future will demand the management for hike in wages and benefits. The management will also respond positively to the employees demand. Some employees will be satisfied with the increased in wages and benefits and adjust their expenses with the level of wages and benefits from time to time willingly. Some employees will not be satisfied with the level of wages and benefits and will not go for second job in future because of their in ability in getting a second job. Such type of employees will have a conflict with the organizational wage level as this category of employees need a second job for additional income and it will not be available to them. Thus, their efforts to earn additional income through second job will not bear any fruit. Such type of efforts and the consequent result may be called Blue Moon Lighting by employees.

Industrial development cannot be at the cost of the environment. Alongwith strictly implementing the pollution and environment protection measures, the State would be striving to set right the irregularities in this regard, which has taken place in some industrial clusters. The State would also like to confine the development of highly polluting industries to the zones and designated estates specifically set up for industries so that the pollution control measures can be managed economically and the standards in this regard can be met adequately.

This is a reference book. All the matter is just compiled and edited in nature, taken from the various sources which are in public domain.

The book is designed to help the students and professionals to quickly acquire the knowledge and skills they need for this subject.

—*Editor*

Contents

1

Introduction

Industrial and organizational psychology (I-O) applies psychological concepts and methods to optimize human potential in the workplace. Personnel psychology, a subfield of I-O psychology, applies the methods and principles of psychology in selecting and evaluating workers. I-O psychology's other subfield, organizational psychology, examines the effects of work environments and management styles on worker motivation, job satisfaction, and productivity.

INDUSTRIAL AND ORGANIZATIONAL PSYCHOLOGY

Industrial and organizational psychology (also known as *I-O psychology, industrial-organizational psychology, work psychology, organizational psychology, work and organizational psychology, industrial psychology, occupational psychology, personnel psychology* or *talent assessment*) applies psychology to organizations and workplaces. These organizations and workplaces include for-profit businesses, non-profits, government agencies, colleges, universities, and graduate and professional school programs. Industrial-organizational psychologists contribute to an organization's success by improving the performance and well-being of its people. An I-O psychologist researches and identifies how behaviours and attitudes can be improved through hiring practices, training programs, and feedback systems. In the academic context, an I-O psychologist's research might similarly focus on improving admissions systems, learning outcomes, academic achievement, degree completion, and teaching and assessment methodologies.

Guion (1965) defines I-O psychology as "the scientific study of the relationship between man and the world of work:... in the process of making a living" (p. 817). Blum and Naylor (1968) define it as "simply the application or extension of psychological facts and principles to the problems concerning human beings operating within the context of business and industry" (p. 4). I-O psychology has historically subsumed two broad areas of study, as evident by its name, although this distinction is largely artificial and many topics cut across both areas. It has roots in social psychology; organizational psychologists examine the role of the work environment in performance and other outcomes including job satisfaction and health. I-O psychology is also represented by Division 14 of the American Psychological Association. Sometimes, I-O psychology is considered a sister field or branch of organizational studies, organizational science, organizational behaviour, human resources, and/or management, but there is no universally accepted classification system for these related fields. Common research and practice areas for I-O psychologists include:

- Job performance
- Job analysis/competency modeling
- Personnel recruitment and selection
- Student/educational selection and assessment
- Judgment and decision making
- Performance appraisal/management
- Individual assessment (knowledge, skills, and ability testing, personality assessment, work sample tests, assessment centres)
- Psychometrics
- Compensation
- Training and training evaluation
- Employment law
- Work motivation
- Job attitudes (e.g., job satisfaction, commitment, organizational citizenship, and retaliation)
- Occupational health and safety
- Work/life balance
- Human factors and decision making
- Organizational culture/climate
- Organizational surveys
- Leadership and executive coaching
- Ethics
- Diversity
- Job design
- Human resources
- Organizational development (OD)
- Organizational Research Methods
- Technology in the workplace
- Group/team performance

I-O psychologists are trained in the "scientist-practitioner" model. The training enables I-O psychologists to employ scientific principles and research-based designs to generate knowledge. They use what they have learned in applied settings to help clients address workplace needs. I-O psychologists are employed as professors, researchers, and consultants. They also work within organizations, often as part of a human resources department where they coordinate hiring and organizational development initiatives from an evidence-based perspective.

History

The "industrial" side of I-O psychology has its historical origins in research on individual differences, assessment, and the prediction of performance. This branch of the field crystallized during World War I, in response to the need to rapidly assign new troops to duty stations.

After the War the growing industrial base in the US added impetus to I-O psychology. Walter Dill Scott, who was elected President of the American Psychological Association (APA) in 1919, was arguably the most prominent I-O psychologist of his time, although James McKeen Cattell (elected APA President in 1895) and Hugo Münsterberg (1898) were influential in the early development of the field. Organizational psychology gained prominence after World War II, influenced by the Hawthorne studies and the work of researchers such as Kurt Lewin and Muzafer Sherif.

Research Methods in I-O Psychology

As described above, I-O psychologists are trained in the scientist-practitioner model. I-O psychologists rely on a variety of methods to conduct organizational research. Study designs employed by I-O psychologists include surveys, experiments, quasi-experiments, and observational studies. I-O psychologists rely on diverse data sources including human judgments, historical databases, objective measures of work performance (e.g., sales volume), and questionnaires and surveys. I-O researchers employ both quantitative and qualitative research methods. Quantitative methods used in I-O psychology include both descriptive statistics and inferential statistics (e.g., correlation, multiple regression, and analysis of variance). More advanced statistical methods employed by some I-O psychologists include logistic regression, multivariate analysis of variance, structural equation modeling, and hierarchical linear modeling (HLM; also known as multilevel modeling).

HLM is particularly applicable to research on team-and organization-level effects on individuals. I-O psychologists also employ psychometric methods including methods associated with classical test theory (CTT), generalizability theory, and item response theory (IRT). In the 1990s, a growing body of empirical research in I-O psychology was influential in the application of meta-analysis, particularly in the area of the stability of research findings across contexts. The most well-known meta-analytic approaches are those associated with Hunter and Schmidt, Rosenthal, and Hedges and Olkin. With the help of meta-analysis, Hunter and Schmidt advanced the idea of validity generalization, which suggests that some performance predictors, specifically cognitive ability tests have a relatively stable and positive relation to job performance across all jobs.

Although not unchallenged, validity generalization has broad acceptance with regard to many selection instruments (e.g., cognitive ability tests, job knowledge tests, work samples, and structured interviews) across a broad range of jobs. Qualitative methods employed in I-O psychology include content analysis, focus groups, interviews, case studies, and several other observational techniques. I-O research on organizational culture research has employed ethnographic techniques and participant observation to collect data. One well-known qualitative technique employed in I-O psychology is John Flanagan's Critical Incident Technique, which requires "qualified observers" (e.g., pilots in studies of aviation, construction workers in studies of construction projects) to describe a work situation that resulted in a good or bad outcome. Objectivity is ensured when multiple observers identify the same incidents. The observers are also asked to provide information about what the actor in the situation could have done differently to influence the outcome.

This technique is then used to describe the critical elements of performance in certain jobs and how worker behaviour relates to outcomes. Most notably, this technique has been employed to improve performance among aircraft crews and surgical teams, literally saving thousands of lives since its introduction. An application of the technique in research on coping with job stress comes from O'Driscoll and Cooper. I-O psychologists sometimes use quantitative and qualitative methods in concert. For example, when constructing behaviourally anchored rating scales (BARS), a job analyst may use qualitative methods, such as critical incidents interviews and focus groups to collect data bearing on performance. Then the analyst would have SMEs rate those examples on a Likert scale and compute inter-rater agreement statistics to judge the adequacy of each item. Each potential item would additionally be correlated with an external criterion in order to evaluate its usefulness if it were to be selected to be included in a BARS metric.

Motivation in the Workplace

Understanding what motivates an organization's employees is central to the study of I/O Psychology. A number of various theories and topics define employee motivation within the discipline of I/O Psychology: Motives and Needs, Expectancy Theory, Equity Theory, Goal-Setting, Cognitive Evaluation Theory, Work Design, Reinforcement Theory, creativity, groups, and culture.

Motives & Needs: Most recently, research in motives and needs in I/O Psychology has concentrated on two areas: Job attributes and Need for Achievement. Job attributes: It is impossible to discuss motivation and job attributes in I/O Psychology without crediting Herzberg's Motivation Hygiene Theory (also referred to as Herzberg's 2-Factor Model). As the first job-based theory, Herzberg's Motivation Hygiene Theory argued the content of a person's job was the primary source of motivation. In other words, he argued money was not the most effective form of motivation to an employee. Essentially, Herzberg argued high levels of hygiene factors (pay, job security, status, working conditions, fringe benefits, job policies, and relations with co-workers) could only reduce employee dissatisfaction (not create satisfaction). Motivation factors (level of challenge, the work itself, responsibility, recognition, advancement, intrinsic interest, and opportunities for creativity) however, could stimulate satisfaction within the employee. Shortly after Herzberg's 2-Factor Model, Hackman and Oldham contributed their own, more refined, job-based theory; Job Characteristics Theory. JCT attempts to define the association between core job dimensions, the critical psychological states that occur as a result of these dimensions, the affective outcomes, and growth need strength. Core job dimensions are the characteristics of a person's job. The core job dimensions are linked directly to the critical psychological states. According to JCT, an organization that provides sufficient levels of skill variety, task Identity, and task significance to its employees will in turn deliver experienced meaningfulness. Sufficient levels of autonomy will inspire felt responsibility for the employee, and proper feedback will provide the employee with knowledge of results.

The combined effect of these psychological states results in a desired affected outcome: Internal motivation, job satisfaction, performance quality, low absenteeism, and low turnover rate Lastly, the glue of this theory is the "growth need strength" factor which ultimately determines the effectiveness of the core job dimensions on the psychological states, and likewise the effectiveness of the critical psychological states on the affective outcomes.. Further analysis of Job Characteristics Theory can be found in the Work Design section below. Need for Achievement: Atkinson & McClelland's Need for Achievement Theory is the most relevant and applicable need based theory in the I/O Psychologist's arsenal. Unlike other need-based theories, which try to interpret every need, Need for Achievement allows the I/O psychologist to concentrate research into a tighter focus. Studies show those who have a high need for achievement prefer moderate levels of risk, seek feedback, and are likely to immerse themselves in their work Achievement motivation can be broken down into three types: Achievement; seeks position advancement, feedback, and sense of accomplishment, Authority; need to lead, make an impact and be heard by others, and Affiliation; need for friendly social interactions and to be liked. Because most individuals have a combination of these three types (in various proportions), an understanding of these achievement motivation characteristics can be a useful assistance to management in job placement, recruitment, etc.

Work Design

Job based theories of motivation in Organizational Psychology rely on the proposition that the content of one's job is the most significant source of motivation. Based on that assumption, several approaches to work design have been researched and applied, including Hertzberg's Motivation-Hygiene theory and Job Characteristics Theory. Each theory has informed the evolution of work design approaches. The following work design approaches to motivation illustrate this evolution: the Humanistic Approach which then led to the Job Characteristics Approach to job design.

Humanistic Approach

The Humanistic Approach to job design was a reaction to the "worker dissatisfaction over Scientific Management" and focused on providing employees with more input and an opportunity to maximize their personal achievement as referenced by Jex and Britt. The two approaches used in the Humanistic Approach to job design are job rotation and job enrichment. Job rotation allows employees to learn new skills and provides them with greater variety.

According to Jex and Britt this would be most effective for simple jobs that can become mundane and boring over time. Job enrichment is based on leveraging those aspects of jobs that are labeled motivators, such as control, intellectual challenge, and creativity. The most common form of job enrichment is vertical loading where additional tasks or discretion enhances the initial job design.

Job Characteristics Approach

The Job Characteristics Approach to job design relies on how core dimensions affect motivation. These dimensions include autonomy, variety, significance, feedback, and identity. Jex and Britt highlight several interventions related to enhancing these core dimensions:

1. Vertical Loading – similar to the intervention used in the Humanistic Job Enrichment approach. This intervention is designed to enhance autonomy, task identity, task significance, and skill variety.
2. Task Combination – by combining tasks into larger units of work and responsibility, task identity may be enhanced.

3. Natural Work Units – is a form of task combination that represents a logical body of work and responsibility that may enhance both task significance and task identity.
4. Establishing Client Relationships – designs interactions between employees and customers, both internal and external to enhance task identify, feedback, and task significance by improving the visibility of beneficial effects on customers.
5. Feedback – by designing open feedback channels this intervention attempts to increase the amount of feedback received.

In the same way that job based theories to motivation have evolved over time, the approach to designing work for motivating employees have evolved. The Humanistic Approach attempted to improve the effectiveness on motivation by focusing on design from the workers perspective, with an eye towards input and personal achievement. The Job Characteristics Approach attempts to enhance motivation by focusing on improving the core dimensions of autonomy, variety, significance, feedback, and identity.

Expectancy Theory

According to Vroom's Expectancy Theory, an employee will work smarter and/or harder if he believes his additional efforts will lead to valued rewards. Expectancy Theory explains this increased output of effort by means of the equation F = E (Ó I x V), whereas:

F (Effort or Motivational Force) = Effort the employee will expend to achieve the desired performance;

E (Expectancy) = Belief that effort will result in desired level of performance;

I (Instrumentality) = Belief that desired level of performance will result in desired outcome;

V (Valence) = Value of the outcome to the employee.

There are three key considerations in applying Expectancy Theory to the workplace:

Performance-Outcome Expectancy Employees believe that if they perform as desired by their employer, they will be rewarded with certain outcomes.

Outcome Attractiveness Each individual employee is motivated by different kinds of rewards. A precursor to motivation is that the employee finds the reward(s) attractive. Effort-Performance Expectancy The employee internally considers how likely it is that he will achieve the performance desired by the employer. In order for the employee to be motivated by the reward, the employee must believe that he is capable of achieving the desired performance. Expectancy Theory posits employee satisfaction to be an outcome of performance rather than the cause of performance. However, if a pattern is established whereas an employee understands his performance will lead to certain desired rewards, an employee's motivation can be strengthened based on anticipation.

Equity Theory

Equity Theory provides a framework for understanding the dynamic give-and-take scenarios that play out between employee and employer. The Theory examines the value proposition the employee forms when he considers the value that he provides to his employer relative to the value that his employer provides to him. In particular, Equity Theory research has tested employee sentiments regarding equitable compensation. Employee inputs take the form of work volume and quality, performance, knowledge, skills, attributes and behaviours.

The company-generated outcomes include rewards such as compensation, praise and advancement opportunities. The employee compares his inputs relative to outcomes; and, then, extrapolating to the social context, the employee compares his input/outcome ratio with the perceived ratios of his peers to determine if he is being under-compensated, over-compensated or equitably compensated.

While it has been established that Equity Theory provides insight into scenarios of under-compensation, the Theory has generally failed to demonstrate its usefulness in understanding scenarios of overcompensation. In the late 1990s and early 2000s, equity theory research was superseded by research using an organizational justice framework.

Goal Setting

An I/O psychologist can assist an employer in designing task related goals for their employees that are 1) attainable, 2) specific, 3) appropriately difficult, and 4) feedback providing, in hopes of rousing tunnel vision focus in the employees. Studies have shown both feedback from the employer and self-efficacy (belief in one's capabilities to achieve a goal) within the employee must be present for goal setting to be effective.

However, because of the tunnel vision focus created by goal setting theory, several studies have shown this motivational theory may not be applicable in all situations. In fact, in tasks that require creative on the spot improvising, goal setting can even be counterproductive.

Furthermore, because clear goal specificity is essential to a properly designed goal setting task, multiple goals can create confusion for the employee and the end result is a muted overall drive. Despite its flaws, Goal Setting Theory is arguably the most dominant theory in the field of I/O Psychology; over one thousand articles and reviews published in just over thirty years.

Cognitive Evaluation Theory

Cognitive Evaluation Theory (CET) is a subset of Self-Determination Theory (SDT) as proposed by Deci and Ryan. CET attempts to determine whether the employee's source of motivation is derived from internal, external or a combination of internal and external sources. CET was proposed for examining conditions in which both internal and external factors contribute to motivation, in particular the impact of external factors on intrinsic motivation. CET theorizes that external factors including rewards and managerial oversight can make an employee experience less autonomy, which can result in decreased intrinsic motivation.

Reinforcement Theory

Among the various theories of motivation, the reinforcement theory has received great attention within the past few decades. In short, this theory highlights the relationship between behaviour and its consequences. At the most pedestrian level, reinforcement was first brought to the forefront by Skinner when he shared findings on pigeons pressing buttons (behaviour) to receive food (consequence).

When translated into motivation in the workplace, the reinforcement theory certainly has its applications. At a systematic level, employee behaviours are identified, measured, and analysed in terms of their functional consequences, and then an intervention is implemented to encourage an increase in motivation.

The studies which used this framework showed an improvement in performance after the intervention. Further, Sama, Kopelman, and Manning found that use of a reinforcement strategy called Premack's principles improved employees' productivity twofold. Punishment is also part of the reinforcement theory in that it attempts to decrease undesired behaviours. While studies have shown that punishment may produce an overall behaviour change, it decreases employee morale and intrinsic motivation and should thus be avoided.

Creativity

On the cutting edge of research pertaining to motivation in the workplace is the integration of motivation and creativity. Essentially, according to Ambrose and Kulik, the same variables that predict intrinsic motivation are associated with creativity. This is a helpful conclusion in that organizations can measure and influence both creativity and motivation simultaneously. Further, allowing employees to choose creative and challenging jobs/tasks has been shown to improve motivation. In order to increase creativity, setting "creativity goals" can positively influence the process, along with allowing more autonomy (i.e. giving employees freedom to feel/be creative). Other studies have found that team support may enable more creativity in a group setting, also increasing motivation.

Groups and Teams

As the workplace is changing to include more group-based systems, researching motivation within these groups is of growing importance. To date, a great amount of research has focused on the Job Characteristics Theory and the goal-setting theory. While more research is needed that draws on a broader range of motivation theories, research thus far has concluded several things; a)semi-autonomous groups report higher levels of job scope (related to intrinsic job satisfaction), extrinsic satisfaction, and organizational commitment; and c) developmentally mature teams have higher job motivation and innovation. Further, voluntarily formed work teams report high work motivation. Though research shows that appropriate goal-setting influences group motivation and performance, more research is needed in this area (group goals, individual goals, cohesiveness, etc.).

There are inseparable mediating variables consisting of group cohesiveness, commitment, and performance. As the workplace environment calls for more and more teams to be formed, research into motivation of teams is ever-pressing. Thus far, overarching research merely suggests that individual-level and team-level sources of motivation are congruent with each other. Consequently, research should be expanded to apply more theories of motivation; look at group dynamics; and essentially conclude how groups can be most impacted to increase motivation and, consequently, performance.

Culture

Kotter and Heskettcategorize cultures into three groups: Strong, Strategically Appropriate, and Adaptive. Each has been identified with high performing organizations and has particular implications on motivation in the workplace. *Strength:* According to Kotter and Heskett, the most widely reported effect of culture on performance is that strong cultures result in high performance. The three reasons for this are goal alignment, motivation, and the resulting structure provided. Goal alignment is driven by the proposed unified voice that drives employees in the same direction. Motivation comes from the strength of values and principles in such a culture. And structure is provided by these same attributes which obviate the need for formal controls that could stifle employees. There are questions that concern researchers about causality and the veracity of the driving voice of a strong culture.

Strategically Appropriateness: A strategically appropriate culture motivates due to the direct support for performance in the market and industry: "The better the fit, the better the performance; the poorer the fit, the poorer the performance," state Kotter and Heskett. There is an appeal to the idea that cultures are designed around the operations conditions a firm encounters although an outstanding issue is the question of adapting culture to changes in the environment.

Adaptability: Another perspective in culture literature asserts that in order for an organization to perform at a high level over a long period of time, it must be able to adapt to changes in the environment. According to Ralph Kilmann, in such a culture "there is a shared feeling of confidence: the members believe, without a doubt, that they can effectively manage whatever new problems and opportunities will come their way." In effect, the culture is infused with a high degree of self-efficacy and confidence. As with the strong culture, critics point to the fact that the theory provides nothing in the way of appropriate direction of adaptation that leads to high performance.

Competing Values Framework

Another perspective on culture and motivation comes from the work of Cameron and Quinn and the Competing Values Framework. They divide cultures into four quadrants: Clan, Adhocracy, Market, Hierarchy, with particular characteristics that directly affect employee motivation.

- "Clan" cultures are collaborative and driven by values such as commitment, communication, and individual development. Motivation results from human development, employee engagement, and a high degree of open communication.
- "Adhocracy" cultures are creative and innovative. Motivation in such cultures arises from finding creative solutions to problems, continually improving, and empowering agility.
- "Market" cultures focus on value to the customer and are typically competitive and aggressive. Motivation in the market culture results from winning in the marketplace and creating external partnerships.
- And finally, "Hierarchy" cultures value control, efficiency, and predictability. Motivation in such a culture relies on effectiveness, capability, and consistency. Effective hierarchy cultures have developed mature and capable processes which support smooth operations.

Culture has been shown to directly affect organizational performance. When viewed through the lens of accepted behaviours and ingrained values, culture also profoundly affects motivation. Whether one looks at the type of culture – strong, strategically appropriate, or adaptive – as Kotter and Heskett do, or at the style of culture – Clan, Adhocracy, Market, or Hierarchy – as Cameron and Quinn do, the connection between culture and motivation becomes clear and provides insights into how to hire, task, and motivate employees.

Motivation Summary

The effects of motivation are fundamental to organizational and employee performance and thus I/O Psychology. As Jex and Britt. Organizational Psychology; Scientist-Practitioner Approach. New Jersey: John Wiley & Sons</ref>. point out "organizations that are armed with a clear understanding of motivation are in a better position to influence employee behaviour than are organizations that lack this knowledge." As described, some of the important theories in this discipline cover Motives and Needs, Expectancy Theory, Equity Theory, Goal-Setting, Cognitive Evaluation Theory, Work Design, and Reinforcement Theory.

Remuneration and Compensation

Compensation includes wages or salary, bonuses, pension/retirement contributions, and perquisites that can be converted to cash or replace living expenses. I-O psychologists may be asked to conduct a job evaluation for the purpose of determining compensation levels and ranges. I-O psychologists may also serve as expert witnesses in pay discrimination cases when disparities in pay for similar work are alleged.

Training and Training Evaluation

Most people hired for a job are not already versed in all the tasks required to perform the job effectively. Similar to performance management, an I-O psychologist would employ a job analysis in concert with principles of instructional design to create an effective training programme. A training programme is likely to include a summative evaluation at its conclusion in order to ensure that trainees have met the training objectives and can perform the target work tasks at an acceptable level. Training programs often include formative evaluations to assess the impact of the training as the training proceeds. Formative evaluations can be used to locate problems in training procedures and help I-O psychologist make corrective adjustments in the while the training is ongoing.

Individual Assessment and Psychometrics

Individual assessment involves the measurement of individual differences. I-O psychologists perform individual assessments in order to evaluate differences among candidates for employment as well as differences among employees. The constructs measured pertain to job performance. With candidates for employment, individual assessment is often part of the personnel selection process. These assessments can include written tests, physical tests, psychomotor tests, personality tests, work samples, and assessment centres. Psychometrics is the science of measuring psychological variables, such as knowledge, skills, and abilities. I-O psychologists are generally well-trained in psychometric psychology.

Productive Behaviour

Productive behaviour is defined as employee behaviour that contributes positively to the goals and objectives of an organization. When an employee begins a new job, there is a transition period during which he or she is not contributing positively to the organization. To successfully transition from being an outsider to a full-fledged member of an organization, an employee typically needs job-related training as well as more general information about the culture of the organization. In financial terms, productive behaviour represents the point at which an organization begins to achieve some return on the investment it has made in a new employee. There are three common forms of productive behaviour in organizations: job performance, organizational citizenship behaviour (OCB), and innovation.

Organizational Citizenship Behaviour

Organizational citizenship behaviour (OCB) refers to productive behaviours that are not part of an employees' formal job description. There are five categories of organizational citizenship behaviours: (1) altruism, (2) courtesy, (3) sportsmanship, (4) conscientiousness, and (5) civic virtue. There are three different explanations for why employees engage in organizational citizenship behaviour. The first has to do with positive affect, an overall positive mood increases the frequency of helping behaviour. The second explanation, which stems from the equity theory, is that employees reciprocate fair treatment that they have received from the organization. The third explanation is that some employees have personality traits that predispose them to participate in organizational citizenship behaviour. There are also employees who will perform organizational citizenship behaviour to influence how they are viewed within the organization. While these behaviours are not formally part of the job description, performing them can certainly influence performance appraisals.

Innovation

Innovation is a form of productive behaviour that employees exhibit when they come up with novel ideas that further the goals of the organization. Innovation at an individual level is dependent on task-relevant skills (general mental ability and job specific knowledge), creativity-relevant skills (ability to concentrate on a problem for long periods of time, to abandon unproductive searches, and to temporarily put aside stubborn problems), and task motivation (internal desire to perform task and level of enjoyment).

There are things that organizations can do in order to breed innovation in the workplace. Some of these items include providing creativity training, having leaders encourage and model innovation, allowing employees to question current procedures and rules, seeing that the implementation of innovations had real consequences, documenting innovations in a professional manner, allowing employees to have autonomy and freedom in their job roles, reducing the number of obstacles that may be in the way of innovation, and giving employees access to resources (whether these are monetary, informational, or access to key people inside or outside of the organization).

ORGANISATION OF INDUSTRY: MANAGERIAL STRATEGIES AND PROBLEMS

In this section we shall attempt to review the researches relating to industrial organisation and structure. In 1982, the Sri Ram Centre for Industrial Relations and Human Resources undertook a survey of 51 organisations in order to understand the nature of industrial organisations in the country and to analyse their influence on labour management relations, more specifically supervisory-management relations. The report of this study was written by Baldev R. Sharma (1987A). The study was significant in the sense that for the first time such a large sample of industrial organisations was taken for study and quantitative data on them were collected. The report stated that both private sector and public sector organisations believed that safety, security (at work) and monetary benefits constitute the most important needs of the employees. However, there are important dimensions of the organisational climate such as participation in decision making, redressal of grievances, training and advancement. Sharma also refers to the theoretical controversy between human relations and scientific management approaches, more specifically on the tendency to separate mental work from physical work in the latter approach. In trying to resolve this controversy, he suggests that monetary benefits alone cannot overcome workers' alienation, as the title of the book, *Not by Bread Alone* suggests.

Four years later, in 1986, Sharma conducted a restudy of one of the organisations covered by the survey (Sharma 1987B). He found that all the variables remained unchanged expect one, namely, monetary benefits. However, he found that though it now ranked higher, increase in emoluments did not affect production. He concluded that perceptions of organisational reality are intimately related to the action and inaction of management.

A. V. Subharao (1987) selected two steel plants for studying co-operation and conflict between labour and management. One of these plants was in the private sector (Tata Steel in Jamshedpur) and the other in the public sector

(Bokaro Steel Plant). Subharao found that industrial relations at Jamshedpur were better than at Bokaro. This difference was primarily because there was only one recognised union at Jamshedpur and it was possible to have joint consultations between union and management. In Bokaro, on the other hand, there were a number of recognised unions and each tried to compete with the others in trying to get more benefits. The author's reasoning appears to be somewhat simplistic.

The Industrial Disputes Act has always had mixed reactions. While trade unions and labour have supported it, managements have been critical of it. C. K. Johri's paper on industrial relations (Johri 1990) deals with this issue. He strongly advocates that the industrial relations system must be reformed to permit greater freedom to managements. He feels that the Industrial Disputes Act hinders such a process. Hence he suggests that the Act should be repealed and labour should be provided with social insurance as a form of protection. This would pave the way for more effective management on the one hand, and ensure some security to labour on the other.. Johri's suggestions seem unrealistic. Social insurance for workers is a very difficult proposition. We will deal with the dimensions of this problem in a later section on social security.

C. S. Rangarajan (1997) studied how workers, supervisors and executives perceive their work. The author holds that role conception is an important aspect of one's participation in the work organisation as role performance depends upon role conception. He examines the organisational dimensions of the bureaucratic structure. The study also attempts to understand the problems of migrant labour while adjusting with urban-industrial order and their traditional values.

K. Mamkoottam (1994) discussed the changes in labour management relations after the reforms of 1991. He notes that after liberalisation, there was a need for changes in technology and manpower planning so that industry could compete in the global market. Initially, the employers insisted on a deregulated environment with a flexible labour force, while the workers and trade unions resisted these moves. However there is a gradual process of change taking place in both the manpower strategies adopted by the employers and the response to the imperatives of change on the part of the employees and unions. He concludes that a development of professionally oriented human resources management strategies and positively oriented collaborative employee/union strategies are beginning to emerge. Mamkoottam's predictions may now look like wishful thinking because, ten years after he published his article, the divide between labour and management seems to have hardened. In most of the large formal sector organisations, the employees are more interested in holding on to their jobs as these are being reduced in large numbers. These moves leave very little option for building positively oriented collaborative strategies. Pradip Khandwala's study of innovative corporate turnaround (Khandwala 1992) produces an enquiry on how 'sick' organisations go about regaining health and shape. Of the 65 cases taken, 16 belong to India. The main findings show that turnarounds are caused by a variety of factors. These include change in the helm of affairs in the corporation, change in organisational structure, change in product mix, change in market focus—from domestic to international are some of them. We shall deal with the problem of recovery of 'sick' industries in the section on labour where we will look at studies on worker co-operatives. These represent how turnaround was possible with the help of those at the bottom of the organisational hierarchy.

The problems of unionisation of the managerial cadre is the focus of a study by Baldev R. Sharma (1993). His study deals with how managerial staff are forming their own associations known as Officers' Association (OA). The book has an exhaustive survey of the existing literature in the field and has a vast amount of data on managerial unionism. He finds that the OAs are found only in the public sector and their main objective being welfare of their members. Though Sharma tries to show

Strategic management as a technique is new in India and there is hardly any research on it. E. A. Ramaswamy (1994) notes that this is precisely because industrial management in India comprises largely knee-jerk responses to crises. His study of a rayon factory in Coimbatore addresses several important issues in the contemporary industrial relations scenario. It is the outcome of over twenty years of research of the author. The study examines the role of the state in management of industrial relations has not been positive. The author also discusses other issues such as the relevance of collective bargaining and bilateral negotiations, the nexus between unions and political parties and the relations between unions, workers and management. This longitudinal study shows how brittle the union-worker relationship can be and how easily the workers shift their loyalties from one union to another and the irrational attitudes of the management towards the unions.

Debi S. Saini has edited a volume on different aspects of labour and law (Saini 1995). The papers offer a critical examination of the existing labour laws in the country. These are divided into four sections. The first section examines the existing labour laws and finds that they provide protection to only the organised sector. The second section provides descriptions of the pathetic working conditions of migrant, bonded and agricultural labour. The third section discusses the issues of globalisation, industrial restructuring and industrial relations laws while the fourth section has papers dealing with alternatives in labour justice dispensation.

Though Multi-National Corporations have made their mark in India and there have been heated debates on their functioning, there are hardly any significant studies of the conglomerates. We found only two such studies during this period. Jairus Banaji and Rohini Hensman, the first one, studied industrial relations in two major Dutch MNCs operating in India, namely, Philips and Hindustan Lever Limited. The study provides a comparison on industrial relations in the establishments of the same MNC in India and Europe. The authors find that foreign companies in Mumbai have created a section of workers whose consciousness is dominated by the fact that they are employees of international organisations. These workers are also unionised but their unions are not linked with any of the national federations. The authors see merit in this as the national federations are politicised and ruled by political parties. The internal unions have greater stake in the working class in the concerned organisations.

A major problem with such an argument is that it fails to take into account the political conditions at the time of independence, in 1947, that gave rise to these internal unions in MNCs. In 1948 there were mainly three trade union federations, namely All India Trade Union Congress of the communists, Indian National Trade Union Congress of the Congress and Hind Mazdur Sabha of the socialists. These federations were arch rivals of each other but they had one thing in common. They were all against the indiscriminate role of foreign capital. This made them inherently anti-MNC. Hence it can be argued that the MNCs themselves encouraged their workers to form internal unions (instead of joining a federation) as these organisations were less likely to be against foreign capital. On the contrary, these workers were very proud of their employment in foreign owned companies. They felt superior to the run-of-the-mill workers in other factories or mills. One must also consider the fact that most of the MNCs did not have unions under colonial rule. These company unions came up only after independence. Hence, one needs to raise the question why the same employers, who were reluctant to allow their workers to unionise before independence, suddenly allowed them this right at a time when unions were becoming increasingly against foreign capital.

V. Janardhan's (1997) article on MNCs examines the manner in which companies, especially in Asia, are globalising and the strategies they tend to follow. The paper provides an analysis of the strategies adopted by a leading multinational corporation, British American Tobacco and its Indian affiliates.

ORGANIZATIONAL CULTURE

Organizational culture can be described as a set of assumptions shared by the individuals in an organization that directs interpretation and action by defining appropriate behaviour for various situations. There are three levels of organizational culture: artifacts, shared values, and basic beliefs and assumptions. Artifacts comprise the physical components of the organization that relay cultural meaning. Shared values are individuals' preferences regarding certain aspects of the organization's culture (e.g. loyalty, customer service). Basic beliefs and assumptions include individuals' impressions about the trustworthiness and supportiveness of an organization, and are often deeply ingrained within the organization's culture.

In addition to an overall culture, organizations also have subcultures. Examples of subcultures include corporate culture, departmental culture, local culture, and issue-related culture.

While there is no single "type" of organizational culture, some researchers have developed models to describe different organizational cultures. Organizational culture has been shown to have an impact on important organizational outcomes such as performance, attraction, recruitment, retention, employee satisfaction, and employee well-being. Also, organizations with an adaptive culture tend to perform better than organizations with an unadaptive culture.

Group Behaviour

Group behaviour is the interaction between individuals of a collective and the processes such as opinions, attitudes, growth, feedback loops, and adaptations that occur and change as a result of this interaction.

The interactions serve to fulfil some need satisfaction of an individual who is part of the collective and helps to provide a basis for his interaction with specific members of the group. A specific area of research in group behaviour is the dynamics of teams. Team effectiveness refers to the system of getting people in a company or institution to work together effectively. The idea behind team effectiveness is that a group of people working together can achieve much more than if the individuals of the team were working on their own.

ADVERSE WORKING CONDITIONS LINKED TO PSYCHOLOGICAL DISTRESS AND JOB SATISFACTION

A number of well-designed longitudinal studies have adduced evidence for the view that adverse working conditions contribute to the development of psychological distress. Before turning to those studies, the reader should note that psychological distress refers to feelings of demoralization that are aversive to people, and often drive them to seek professional help, without the individuals necessarily meeting criteria for a psychiatric disorder. Psychological distress is often expressed in affective (depressive) symptoms, psychophysical or psychosomatic symptoms (e.g., headaches, stomachaches, etc.), and anxiety symptoms.

The relation of adverse working conditions to psychological distress is thus an important avenue of research. Job satisfaction is included in this chapter because it is a key variable in a great deal of research on organizations and is related to a host of health outcomes.

Parkes (1982) conducted one of the methodologically soundest studies of the relation of working conditions to psychological distress in British student nurses. She found that in this "natural experiment," student nurses experienced higher levels of distress and lower levels of job satisfaction in medical wards than in surgical wards; compared to surgical wards, medical wards make greater affective demands on the nurses. In another methodologically sound study, Frese (1985) showed that objective working conditions give rise to subjective stress and psychosomatic symptoms in blue collar German workers. In addition to the above studies, a number of other well-controlled longitudinal studies have implicated work stressors in the development of psychological distress and reduced job satisfaction.

There is also increasing interest in the OHP community in (a) understanding the impact of the latest economic crisis on individuals' physical and mental health and well-being and (b) calling attention to personal and organizational means for ameliorating the impact of the crisis.

Work and Mental Disorder

Using data from the Epidemiologic Catchment Area (ECA) study, Eaton, Anthony, Mandel, and Garrison (1990) found that members of three occupational groups, lawyers, secretaries, and special education teachers (but not other types of teachers), showed elevated rates of *DSM-III* major depression, adjusting for social demographic factors. The ECA study involved representative samples of American adults from five cities, providing relatively unbiased estimates of the risk of mental disorder by occupation; however, because the data were cross-sectional, no conclusions bearing on cause-and-effect relations are warranted. Evidence from a Canadian prospective study, however, indicates that individuals in the highest quartile of occupational stress are at increased risk for an episode of major depression.

Another study based on the ECA found high rates of alcohol abuse and dependence in the construction and transportation industries as well as among waiters and waitresses, controlling for socio-demographic factors. Within the transportation sector, heavy truck drivers and material movers were at especially high risk. A prospective study of ECA subjects who were followed one year after the initial interviews provided data on newly incident cases of alcohol abuse and dependence. The study found that workers in jobs that combined low control with high physical demands were at increased risk of developing alcohol problems although the findings were confined to men.

In a case-control study, Link, Dohrenwend, and Skodol found that, compared to depressed and well control subjects, schizophrenic patients were more likely to have had jobs, prior to their first episode of the disorder, that exposed them to "noisesome" work characteristics (e.g., noise, humidity, heat, cold, etc.). The jobs tended to be of higher status than other blue collar jobs, suggesting that downward drift in already-affected individuals does not account for the finding. One explanation involving a diathesis-stress model suggests that the job-related stressors helped precipitate the first episode in already-vulnerable individuals. There is some support for the finding from the ECA data.

Workplace Interventions

OHP interventions often concern both the health of the individual and the health of the organization. Adkins (1999) described the development of one such intervention, an organizational health center (OHC) at a California industrial complex.

The OHC helped to improve both organizational and individual health as well as help workers manage job stress. Innovations included labour-management partnerships, suicide risk reduction (there had previously been elevated suicide risk at the complex), conflict mediation, and occupational mental health support. OHC practitioners also coordinated their services with previously under utilized local community services in the same city, thus reducing redundancy in service delivery.

Hugentobler, Israel, and Schurman (1992) detailed a different, multi-layered intervention in a mid-sized Michigan manufacturing plant. The hub of the intervention was the Stress and Wellness Committee (SWC) which solicited ideas from workers on ways to improve both their well-being and productivity. Innovations the SWC developed included improvements that ensured two-way communication between workers and management and reduction in stress resulting from diminished conflict over issues of quantity versus quality. Both the interventions described by Adkins and Hugentobler et al. had a positive impact on productivity. OHP has played a role in interventions employed in very difficult work-related circumstances. The Mental Health Advisory Teams of the United States Army employ OHP-related interventions with combat troops. OHP also has a role to play in interventions aimed at helping first responders.

Schmitt (2007) described three different highly focused and modestly scaled, successful OHP interventions that helped workers abstain from smoking, exercise more frequently, and shed weight. Other, even less expensive, yet successful OHP interventions include a campaign to improve the rates of hand washing, an effort to get workers to walk more often, and a drive to get employees to be more compliant with regard to taking prescribed medicines. The interventions tended reduce organization health-care costs.

Currently there are efforts under way at NIOSH to help reduce the incidence of preventable disorders (e.g., sleep apnea) among heavy-truck and tractor-trailer drivers and, concomitantly, the life-threatening accidents to which the disorders lead and improve the health and safety of workers who are assigned to shift work or who work long hours.

Workplace Incivility and Violence

Workplace incivility has been defined as "low-intensity deviant behavior with ambiguous intent to harm the target....Uncivil behaviours are characteristically rude and discourteous, displaying a lack of regard for others" Incivility is distinct from violence.

Examples of workplace incivility include insulting comments, denigration of the target's work, spreading false rumours, social isolation, etc. A summary of research conducted in Europe suggests that workplace incivility is common there. In research on more than 1000 U. S. civil service workers, Cortina, Magley, Williams, and Langhout (2001) found that more than 70% of the sample experienced workplace incivility in the past five years. Compared to men, women were more exposed to incivility; incivility was associated with psychological distress and reduced job satisfaction.

OHP is also concerned with work-related violence. According to figures from the United States Bureau of Labour Statistics, in 1996 there were 927 work-associated homicides, in a labour force that numbered approximately 132,616,000. The rate works out to be about 7 homicides per million workers for the one year.

Although one work-related homicide is too many, work-related homicide is *relatively* rare. Workplace assault is much more prevalent. Assaultive behavior in the workplace often produces injury, psychological distress, and economic loss.

One study of California workers found a rate of 72.9 non-fatal, officially documented assaults per 100,000 workers per year, with workers in the education, retail, and health care sectors subject to excess risk. A Minnesota workers' compensation study found that women workers had a twofold higher risk than men, and health and social service workers, transit workers, and members of the education sector were at high risk compared to workers in other economic sectors. A West Virginia workers' compensation study found that workers in the health care sector and, to a lesser extent, the education sector were at elevated risk for assault-related injury.

Another workers' compensation study found that excessively high rates of assault-related injury in schools, health-care, and, to a lesser extent, banking.

In addition to the physical injury that results from being a victim of workplace violence, individuals who witness such violence without being directly victimized are at increased risk for experiencing adverse effects, as found in a study of Los Angeles teachers. Although the dimensions of the problem of workplace violence vary by economic sector, one sector, education, has had some limited success in introducing programmatic, psychologically-based efforts to reduce the level of violence.

OHP research suggests that there continue to be difficulties in successfully "screening out applicants [for jobs] who may be prone to engaging in aggressive behavior," suggesting that anti-aggression training of existing employees may be an alternative to screening. There have not, however, been enough rigorously evaluated studies of the effectiveness of training programs aimed at reducing workplace violence. The reduction of workplace incivility and the curtailing of job-related violence are fertile areas for further OHP research.

PSYCHOLOGY IN BUSINESS MANAGEMENT

Business Strategy/The Psychology of Business Management

Several psychologists have conducted studies to determine the psychological patterns involved in strategic management. Typically senior managers have been asked how they go about making strategic decisions. A 1938 treatise by Chester Barnard, that was based on his own experience as a business executive, sees the process as informal, intuitive, non-routinized, and involving primarily oral, 2-way communications. Bernard says "The process is the sensing of the organization as a whole and the total situation relevant to it. It transcends the capacity of merely intellectual methods, and the techniques of discriminating the factors of the situation. The terms pertinent to it are "feeling", "judgement", "sense", "proportion", "balance", "appropriateness". It is a matter of art rather than science."

In 1973, Henry Mintzberg found that senior managers typically deal with unpredictable situations so they strategize in *ad hoc*, flexible, dynamic, and implicit ways. He says, "The job breeds adaptive information-manipulators who prefer the live concrete situation. The manager works in an environment of stimulous-response, and he develops in his work a clear preference for live action."

In 1982, John Kotter studied the daily activities of 15 executives and concluded that they spent most of their time developing and working a network of relationships from which they gained general insights and specific details to be used in making strategic decisions. They tended to use "mental road maps" rather than systematic planning techniques.

Daniel Isenberg's 1984 study of senior managers found that their decisions were highly intuitive. Executives often sensed what they were going to do before they could explain why. He claimed in 1986 that one of the reasons for this is the complexity of strategic decisions and the resultant information uncertainty.

Shoshana Zuboff (1988) claims that information technology is widening the divide between senior managers (who typically make strategic decisions) and operational level managers (who typically make routine decisions). She claims that prior to the widespread use of computer systems, managers, even at the most senior level, engaged in both strategic decisions and routine administration, but as computers facilitated (She called it "deskilled") routine processes, these activities were moved further down the hierarchy, leaving senior management free for strategic decision making.

In 1977, Abraham Zaleznik identified a difference between leaders and managers. He describes leaders as visionaries who inspire. They care about substance. Whereas managers are claimed to care about process, plans, and form. He also claimed in 1989 that the rise of the manager was the main factor that caused the decline of American business in the 1970s and 80s. Lack of leadership is most damaging at the level of strategic management where it can paralyse an entire organization.

According to Corner, Kinichi, and Keats, strategic decision making in organizations occurs at two levels: individual and aggregate. They have developed a model of parallel strategic decision making. The model identifies two parallel processes both of which involve getting attention, encoding information, storage and retrieval of information, strategic choice, strategic outcome, and feedback. The individual and organizational processes are not independent however. They interact at each stage of the process.

Human Resource Management

Human resource management (HRM) is the strategic and coherent approach to the management of an organization's most valued assets-the people working there who individually and collectively contribute to the achievement of the objectives of the business. The terms "human resource management" and "human resources" (HR) have largely replaced the term "personnel management" as a description of the processes involved in managing people in organizations. In simple sense, HRM means employing people, developing their capacities, utilizing, maintaining and compensating their services in tune with the job and organizational requirement.

2

Industrial Organizational Psychology

Job analysis is often described as the cornerstone of successful employee selection efforts and performance management initiatives. A job analysis involves the systematic collection of information about a job. Job-analytic methods are often described as belonging to one of two approaches. One approach, the task-oriented job analysis, involves an examination of the duties, tasks, and/or competencies required by a job. The second approach, a worker-oriented job analysis, involves an examination of the knowledge, skills, abilities, and other characteristics (KSAOs) required to successfully perform the work. These two approaches are not mutually exclusive. Various adaptations of job-analytic methods include competency modeling, which examines large groups of duties and tasks related to a common goal or process, and practice analysis, which examines the way work is performed in an occupation across jobs. Job-analytic data are often collected using a variety of quantitative and qualitative methods. The information obtained from a job analysis is then used to create job-relevant selection procedures, performance appraisals and criteria, or training programs. Additional uses of job-analytic information include job evaluations for the purpose of determining compensation levels and job redesign.

Performance Appraisal/management

Performance appraisal or performance evaluation is the process of measuring an individual's work behaviours and outcomes against the expectations of the job. Performance appraisal is frequently used in promotion and compensation decisions, to help design and validate personnel selection procedures, and for performance management. Performance management is the process of providing performance feedback relative to expectations and improvement information (e.g., coaching, mentoring). Performance management may also include documenting and tracking performance information for organization-level evaluation purposes. An I-O psychologist would typically use information from the job analysis to determine a job's performance dimensions, and then construct a rating scale to describe each level of performance for the job. Often, the I-O psychologist would be responsible for training organizational personnel how to use the performance appraisal instrument, including ways to minimize bias when using the rating scale, and how to provide effective performance feedback. Additionally, the I-O psychologist may consult with the organization on ways to use the performance appraisal information for broader performance management initiatives.

Personnel recruitment and Selection

I-O psychologists typically work with HR specialists to design (a) recruitment processes and (b) personnel selection systems. Personnel recruitment is the process of identifying qualified candidates in the workforce and getting them to apply for jobs within an organization. Personnel recruitment processes include developing job announcements, placing ads, defining key qualifications for applicants, and screening out unqualified applicants.

Personnel selection is the systematic process of hiring and promoting personnel. Personnel selection systems employ evidence-based practices to determine the most qualified candidates. Personnel selection involves both new hires and individuals who can be promoted from within the organization. Common selection tools include ability tests (e.g., cognitive, physical, or psychomotor), knowledge tests, personality tests, structured interviews, the systematic collection of biographical data, and work samples. I-O psychologists must evaluate evidence regarding the extent to which selection tools predict job performance, evidence that bears on the validity of selection tools.

Personnel selection procedures are usually validated, i.e., shown to be job relevant, using one or more of the following types of validity: content validity, construct validity, and/or criterion-related validity. I-O psychologists adhere to professional standards, such as the Society for Industrial and Organizational Psychology's (SIOP) *Principles for Validation and Use of Personnel Selection Procedures* and the Standards for Educational and Psychological Testing. The Equal Employment Opportunity Commission's *Uniform Guidelines* are also influential in guiding personnel selection although they have been criticized as outdated when compared to the current state of knowledge in I-O psychology.

Individual Assessment and Psychometrics

Individual assessment involves the measurement of individual differences. I-O psychologists perform individual assessments in order to evaluate differences among candidates for employment as well as differences among employees. The constructs measured pertain to job performance. With candidates for employment, individual assessment is often part of the personnel selection process. These assessments can include written tests, physical tests, psychomotor tests, personality tests, work samples, and assessment centres.

Psychometrics is the science of measuring psychological variables, such as knowledge, skills, and abilities. I-O psychologists are generally well-trained in psychometric psychology.

Motivation in the Workplace

Motivation is a positive drive that forces a person to reach the goal. In a workplace the manager or supervisor has to know the needs or drive of individual and motivate according to it. In an organization, when an employee is doing good job or production is increased by him, he must be rewarded with respect to his needs.

Organizational Culture

Organizational culture can be described as a set of assumptions shared by the individuals in an organization that directs interpretation and action by defining appropriate behaviour for various situations. There are three levels of organizational culture: artifacts, shared values, and basic beliefs and assumptions. Artifacts comprise the physical components of the organization that relay cultural meaning.

Shared values are individuals' preferences regarding certain aspects of the organization's culture (e.g. loyalty, customer service). Basic beliefs and assumptions include individuals' impressions about the trustworthiness and supportiveness of an organization, and are often deeply ingrained within the organization's culture.

In addition to an overall culture, organizations also have subcultures. Examples of subcultures include corporate culture, departmental culture, local culture, and issue-related culture. While there is no single "type" of organizational culture, some researchers have developed models to describe different organizational cultures. Organizational culture has been shown to have an impact on important organizational outcomes such as performance, attraction, recruitment, retention, employee satisfaction, and employee well-being. Also, organizations with an adaptive culture tend to perform better than organizations with an unadaptive culture.

Group Behaviour

Group behaviour is the interaction between individuals of a collective and the processes such as opinions, attitudes, growth, feedback loops, and adaptations that occur and change as a result of this interaction. The interactions serve to fulfil some need satisfaction of an individual who is part of the collective and helps to provide a basis for his interaction with specific members of the group.

A specific area of research in group behaviour is the dynamics of teams. Team effectiveness refers to the system of getting people in a company or institution to work together effectively.

The idea behind team effectiveness is that a group of people working together can achieve much more than if the individuals of the team were working on their own.

ORGANIZATIONAL CHANGE/DEVELOPMENT

A separate but related discipline, occupational health psychology (OHP) is a relatively new field that combines elements of industrial-organizational psychology, health psychology, and occupational health. Unlike I-O psychology, the primary emphasis in OHP is on the physical and mental health and psychological well-being of the person.

TRAINING AND OUTLOOK

Graduate programs

A comprehensive list of US and Canadian master's and doctoral programs can be found at the web site of the Society for Industrial and Organizational Psychology (SIOP).

Some helpful ways to learn about graduate programs include visiting the web sites on the SIOP list and speaking to I-O faculty at the institutions listed. Admission into I-O psychology Ph.D. programs is highly competitive given that many programs accept a small number of applicants every year.

There are graduate degree programs in I-O psychology outside of the US and Canada. The SIOP web site also provides a comprehensive list of I-O programs in many other countries.

Job outlook

According to the Bureau of Labour Statistics (2007), the job outlook for industrial-organizational psychologists is promising. Businesses enlist the services of these psychologists in order to retain employees and maintain a good work ethic. I-O psychologists specializing in research often conduct studies within companies to aid in marketing research.

In 2006, the median annual salary for industrial-organizational psychologists was $86,420(US).

INDUSTRIAL RESTRUCTURING AND INFORMAL WORK

There are a number of studies on the impact of the closure of the textile industry on the lives of the workers. This industry had played an important role in the growth and development of two major cities in Western India, Mumbai and Ahmedabad.

The closure of this industry has resulted in a large section of workers in the formal sector being forced to take up low paying, insecure jobs in the informal sector. It is noticed that there was a rapid decline in Mumbai's textile industry after the long strike of 1981-82 led by the fire-brand trade union leader, Dr. Datta Samant. Many blame him and his union for the subsequent closure of the mills. However, how does one explain the rapid decline of the textile industry in Ahmedabad? There were no strikes there. When work stopped in Mumbai, the industry in Ahmedabad should have boomed because of the shortage of cloth due to the strike. Instead it too started to fall. Hence it would be too simplistic to blame the workers or irresponsible trade unionism for the catastrophe.

Darryl D'Monte book, *Ripping the Fabric,* on the decline of the textile industry is an important study on Mumbai. The book is really a history of the decline of Mumbai's textile mills. He analyses the situation and the actors involved, namely, the government and its policies, the representative union, Rashtriya Mill Mazdur Sangh, the exploitative mill owners who were looking for an opportunity to close their operations as the mill lands were more lucrative if sold for housing the affluent and, the underworld which was introduced to the scene by these actors. He notes that the decline of the textile industry occurred due to a host of reasons but none of these were attributed to labour. The problem of disposing of mill lands is discussed in an earlier paper.

Bhowmik and More (2001) examine the socio-economic adjustments of families that have undergone decline in living standards within a brief period of time. This study covers the lives of workers who lost their jobs during and after the long drawn strike of 1981-82. Over 100,000 of the 250,000 mill workers lost their jobs. Even after the mills re-opened after the strike the conditions of the workers were no better because most mills shut down soon after.

By 1991 the total workforce had shrunk to 85,000 and at present it is around 30,000. The mill workers who had for decades enjoyed secure and respectable jobs were now forced to seek employment in the informal sector and they have joined the ranks of the urban poor.

The study tries to examine the social institutions through which they can survive. The condition of workers in Ahmedabad has attracted more studies. Supriya Roychowdhury (1996) studied the impact of industrial restructuring in the textile industry in Ahmedabad. The decline in the textile industry took place in the decade 1984-94. She found that sections of organised labour were being pushed out of the formal sector in the process of industrial restructuring. The representative trade union (Textile Labour Association, started by Mahatma Gandhi) did nothing to help. Most of these workers were forced to eke out their existence by working in the informal sector. Jan Breman (2001) too comes to the same conclusion. He found that over 100,000 jobs were lost resulting in the informalisation of a vast majority of the sacked workers. He asserts that Gujarat can thus be understood as an experiment for trying out what will happen to state and society under a policy regime that does not attempt to harness the most brutal consequences of a market-led mode of capitalist protection.

Another study of the textile industry in Ahmedabad was conducted by S. S. Mehta and Dinesh Harode (1998). They state that closure of industrial units in developing economies may lead to serious consequences since their limited investable resources and relatively limited alternative employment opportunities cannot easily absorb resultant loss of jobs, production and revenue. Moreover the present legal and institutional framework to deal with the problem of industrial sickness in India has been found inadequate, particularly in protecting the interests of the workers. The textile crisis in Gujarat makes the inadequacies of the present framework quite glaring.

Organising the Unorganised

We can see from the above discussion that the labour in the informal sector is heterogeneous and also has certain specific features that distinguish t from labour in the formal sector. The labour in this sector is poorly paid and they have insecure jobs. Both factors make it difficult to organise them into collective organisations like trade unions. However, collectivisation is perhaps the only way these workers can fight for their rights. How do they organise themselves is the main problem. There have been some studies on organising the unorganised workers. The National Labour Institute (now known as V. V. Giri National Labour Institute) has been conducting camps in different parts of the country to raise the consciousness of workers in the informal sector. Vidyut Joshi (1990) has done an evaluative study of these attempts. The study helps in understanding the problems encountered in organising the informal sector workers. It also suggests feasible organisational strategies.

Rajeshwari Deshpande's (1999) study of the Hamal Panchayat in Pune is another case of organising the unorganised. The Hamal Panchayat is a successful attempt at mobilising the labourers in the informal sector. It has been attempting to create a broad-based political alliance of unorganised workers and the urban poor forcing both state and civil society to recognise their specific identities and acknowledge their contribution to the economy and society.

The different experiences and the strategies in organising labour in the informal sector are discussed in a book edited by Ruddar Dutt (1997). The papers presented cover theoretical issues as well as case studies of organising these workers through unions, credit societies and co-operatives.. Another such book is edited by Sarath Davala (1994). The papers published are mainly by activists who share their experiences. There are also papers on different strategies for organising. Both volumes are important contributions towards understanding the problems faced by labour in the informal sector and the likely solutions.

Social Security

One of the ways of providing some relief to labour in the informal sector is through social security. In India, social security and retirement benefits are much sought after. These are provided to labour in the formal sector. Hence the eagerness to get jobs in this sector. In case social security, that would include educational facilities for children and health facilities for all, was provided to all citizens would there be such a clamour for jobs in the formal sector? For the poorly paid worker in the informal sector who has neither security of employment nor resources to cover major illnesses, life is one endless struggle against poverty. However, is it possible to support a social security financially?

The withdrawal of the Welfare State in India has accentuated the problems of workers in the informal sector. Noronah and Sharma (1999) raise this and related issues in their paper on displaced workers. The welfare state had protected common citizens by providing them free medical aid and education. It also provided work at the time when work was not available and food grains at cheap rates when there were food shortages or when prices rose abnormally. The withering away of this state has caused great burden on the people. To make matters worse this withdrawal took place at a time when industries, especially the older ones, were closing down, rendering thousands jobless.

The state of Kerala has been successful in promoting social security through welfare boards. Each board represents a trade and workers in that trade are members of the board. The board provides for a number of facilities for its members based on the funds it has. Funds for the board are collected through contributions of the workers and the employers. In some cases a levy is imposed on the trade/industry concerned. S. Mohanan Pillai (1996) has conducted a study on the welfare boards in Kerala. The paper also examines the functioning of the oldest board, namely the Kerala Headloader's Welfare Scheme.

R. C. Datta (1998) finds that the neglect of social opportunities due to lack of adequate progress and social security has been detrimental to economic and social development. He further states that in order to remedy this situation public action must play a central role in ensuring expansion and monitoring social security. He focuses on the Mathadi (head load) labour markets in Mumbai. He finds that the Mathadi Boards are a case of public action enabling these manual workers in the informal sector to achieve protective social security benefits. Renana Jhabvala's (1998) states that in the context of the changed world economy and the decline of the welfare state there is considerable debate on the need to provide social security to the informal sector. Her study looks at the possible mechanisms for social; security provisions, insurance, security funds and state supported childcare. This theme is further explored in an edited volume by Jhabvala and Subramanian (2000). The papers in this collection deal with the various social security schemes and the experiences of mass organisations in evolving and implementing some of these schemes.

Women and Work

We shall try and assess the studies relating to gender. It is interesting to see that the major work in this category was undertaken by sociologists in the 1990s. We do not find much work in the late 1980s but as we progress to the 1990s, the volume increases. This perhaps indicates that though the subject of women and work in the urban-industrial sector was not given its due importance in the earlier phase, its importance is increasing.

There are however serious gaps in research in this section. For example a large section of the research is concentrated in the informal sector. Undoubtedly, women workers for a third of this sector and hence it is natural that it should attract interest of researchers. However, a similar interest in the formal sector would be interesting.

We have little information on how women in these industries fare, except for the fact that their numbers are dwindling. The Information and Communication Technology sector has attracted a large number of female workers. In most cities where this type of outsourcing is done, females predominate in the labour force.

These may be better paid and skilled jobs, but given the fact that the jobs are insecure, the workers hardly have any rights at their workplace and no post-retirement benefits, these holders of such jobs are actually in the informal sector. These is need to study this growing phenomena. There have been some studies on this sector but they are just the minimal. Perhaps there will be greater promise of studies in the near future. A question being discussed since the 1970s is how women's employment affects their domestic activities. The issue of women working the 'double shift' is often raised in developing countries. The first shift is in their place of work, where they work for a wage. The second shift starts at home, where women have to continue doing household work. ISA Baud, a Dutch sociologist, has tried to explore this problem in her study of gender aspects of industrialisation in India and Mexico (Baud 1991). The study takes into account the petty production units employing mainly casual female labour. There are descriptions and discussions of women's employment in the textile and shrimp processing industries in India and the shoe industry in Mexico. Alongside the author examines the differential position of women in the household in all three cases. She goes on to discuss the factors which determine the differential bargaining position of women in the household situation in relation to the different forms of production.

Baud (1992) has examined the effects of industrialisation on women workers in developing countries. Her paper is concerned with the changes occurring in women's employment during the current industrialisation process. More specifically the study deals with how women's employment varies within large, small scale and artisanal forms of production and the implications this has for women's bargaining power within the household. Hilary Standing (1991) explores a similar theme. Her study on women's employment and family in Calcutta (Kolkata) focuses on the impact of their intra-household relations and familial ideologies. Standing uses a mixed methodology combining a sample survey of women workers along with detailed structured and unstructured interviews with several members of the household of each of the employed women.

Uma Kalpagam (1994) explores different aspects of labour and gender in her collection of papers. The different papers deal with diverse issues but there is a thematic unity in the sense that most of the studies deal with patriarchy and gender. Examples from the garment industry, electronics and service and processing sectors show that women get 'crowded' in unskilled, low-wage jobs. Kalpagam finds that the patriarchical role of the state reinforces cultural norms where women are constructed as dependent.

This provides the rationale for women's subservience to males in the family, household, property ownership and other facets of their lives. This further justifies the treatment of women as the labour reserve to be employed at lower wages. Finally, her analyses shows that it is only where women have organised themselves to articulate their demands that one finds a ray of hope and, of course, the only option for getting rid of the overall oppressive system.

Joseph and Prasad (1995) discuss the reality of gender at work. The book focuses on women and their facets of work in the marine food processing units, construction workers, operating of an NGO among rural women and study of labour administration and labour law enforcement in Maharashtra. The authors discuss the role of a trade union that became productive with the active participation of women. However, women within it are marginalized. The book also talks about the NGO Disha which works on the 'gender and development" approach where women are seen as resources and as full-fledged participants in development. The labour administration system in Maharashtra is critiqued as it highlights the biased recruitment process. It also exposes limited employment for women, the problems they encounter while balancing home with their work.

Another interesting study on women in fish processing industry (besides the ones by Baud and Joseph *op. cit.*) is by Warrier (2001). The author has based her findings on an in-depth survey of 60 workers from Kerala and a broader sample of 250 from the different production centres. The paper discusses the nature of the fish processing industry in India at a general level and focuses on issues concerning the migrant women workforce. This industry is situated in various parts of the country and its labour force is almost exclusively of migrant women. A preponderant majority are from Kerala but of late women from Tamil Nadu, Andhra Pradesh and Karnataka have also joined. The migrants are recruited by agents who not only provide them work but also maintain control over their work and life. Leela Fernandes' (1997) monograph on women in the jute mills in Kolkata focuses on the political processes through which categories are constructed. She highlights the tension in India between a 'national' level discourse of a unitary 'working class' and the political fragmentation of workers and trade unionists in the local context. She moves beyond the narrow confines of unionised politics to examine the negotiation of power in the everyday life of the family, neighbourhood, shop floor and other areas.

The book contributes towards a better understanding of workers' politics and trade union practice and the marginalisation of women workers in the organised (formal) sector. It also brings out women's resistance to the ideology of domesticity and the devaluation of their work roles, the restricted scope for independent collective action and generational transmission of hierarchies among them. An interesting but important study on women and work under patriarchy is by Nirmala Banerjee (1999). In this essay she dissents from the most prevalent interpretation of women's secondary position and pay which argue generally that greater employment opportunities can give women more independence. She is critical of the hard-core Marxist approach of Maria Mies who explain that capitalism relies on 'housewifisation'. Banerjee points out that in East and South East Asia, capitalism has in fact drawn women into the labour market rather than binding them down as housewives. Banerjee points out that a major cause for women's marginalisation was due to a trade union movement that did not specifically take up gender issues. The trade union movement undoubtedly had an enormous impact on the lives of the working people. However the same organisation was used to protect only male workers and in effect it turned against women workers. Banerjee does not clarify whether the trade union movement is inherently anti-female as it progresses or is it because its orientation is changed by vested interests. Moreover she does not suggest any solutions. Would she recommend scrapping of the trade union movement or would she want separate trade unions for women?

Banerjee and Mitter (1998) have conducted a study on Indian workingwomen's response to technical changes in a globalising world. The authors examine several instances of women from diverse backgrounds who interact with changing technologies at their work. The analyses show that inspite of the many difficulties the reasons why women have been the greater losers (compared to men) are surprisingly similar.

The increase in the employment of women in the informal sector is discussed in a few studies. Unni (2001) provides evidence of the growing informalisation of the female labour force in South Asian countries. There are two broad components of the informal economy, i.e., non-wage and wage employment. The share of the first component has been rising in the 1980s and 1990s. Within non-wage employment, certain invisible groups such as home-based workers and street vendors are vulnerable to changes in the global and local economy. The increasing casualisation of the workforce is evidence of an increase in the second broad component. Within wage employment, home-workers or outworkers and informal workers in the formal enterprises are vulnerable. The low quality of employment available to women in the informal economy is brought out by evidence on the wages and incomes received and differentials in earning.

While discussing the same phenomenon, V. Vanamala (2001) notes that state-sponsored incentive schemes and exemptions to the small-scale sector have encouraged the increase of the informal industrial sector. These concessions are on capital investment but the state has not taken any step to that industry provide the statutory welfare benefits and proper working conditions for its workers. Her study of an engineering unit shows that there is not only growing casualisation of labour with recruitment on contractual basis, but also an increase in feminisation of the workforce as women are engaged to operate most production processes. This case is somewhat unusual because most studies on small-scale industrial units show that there is little feminisation of the workforce. Hence Vanmala's case study could be more of an exception than a rule.

Kuntala Lahiri-Dutt (2001) discusses the marginalisation of women workers in the coal mining industry. The mines employed women in coal mines in various stages of production. These women belonged to tribal or lower caste communities. Their role continued to be significant as long as technology remained labour-intensive and collieries were small and surface-bound. The expansion of the industry and increasing mechanisation saw a decline in women's participation. Lahiri-Datt's research is based in the Ranigunj coal belt in Eastern India. She describes how the work of resource extraction becomes gendered, the growing marginalisation of women and their alienation from access to environmental resources and their transformation into illegitimate and invisible beings. While on the subject of marginalisation on women in the mining industry it is necessary to note that this happened with the ban on women working underground before the Second World War. The ILO has a convention to this effect. Such a ban has meant that women can work only on the surface. The only jobs available are those involving labour-intensive and poorly paid activities while the better-paid jobs were below the surface. Hence it is not technology but a ban that led to marginalisation of women workers in the mines.

While on the subject of job losses of women in the formal sector it should be noted that their marginalisation came from certain protective legislation such as ban on underground work in mines and a ban on night work in factories. Another important legislation was on maternity benefit. Amrita Chhachi (1998) has discussed this issue in her analysis of the Maternity Benefit Bill of 1929. Her study focuses on the Bombay Legislative Assembly debates over the bill. She brings to light the various issues raised in these debates. However her main focus is on the main issue the bill brought to the fore, namely, who should bear the cost of reproduction of labour: the state, capital (employer) or the husband? Though her study is on the Bill passed in 1929, the issues raised are very contemporary.

CHANGING ROLE OF TRADE UNIONS IN THE FORMAL SECTOR

The trade union movement had a remarkable impact on the character of Mumbai. Stephen Sherlock, an Australian researcher, notes that the power of organised labour in Mumbai was due to the support it got from a sympathetic government. However after the reforms of 1991 the attitude of the government changed. As a result the trade union movement has started loosing much of its capacity to influence class formation at the level of consciousness and struggle. Past successes were the result of determination and sacrifice of the pioneers in the field. The fruits of this struggle were canalised into organisations which depended on an environment created by the state. The changed circumstances should have prompted the trade union movement to change its tactics. Unfortunately this has not happened as there appears to be some reluctance on the part of the trade unions to recognise the limitations of past achievements and to relate to the new working class.

The veteran sociologist N. R. Sheth (1993) takes a critical look at the trade union movement. The point he stresses is that there are three parties in the industrial relations scenario, namely, employer, workers and trade unions. He notes that while conventional trade unions are supposed to organise workers against employers, the employers have begun to see methods of participative management as a means to combine with workers against unions. He further contends that unions and employers too collude against the workers. This is mainly because of the political links of the unions. If the political party supports certain policies that are anti-worker, the trade union too would follow that policy.

Though there are several hard truths in Sheth's paper there are some problems too. For example, his impression that workers' participation in management is a tool for the management to turn workers against unions is not correct. In most cases in the public sector, elections to the participative bodies are usually contested on the basis of trade union affiliation. In other words, trade unions strengthen their base through these bodies. Moreover, trade unions can use these participative bodies to further their objectives of making employers transparent in their dealings. In fact in the present crises of trade unions, it is recommended that workers' participation in management could be a means of reviving trade unionism.

The other point made by Sheth, that trade unions may not represent the interests of workers because of political reasons may be correct. He has given the example of the CITU in West Bengal which will never organise any protest if it is against the interests of the state government. For example CITU protests strongly against privatisation of the public sector in India but its West Bengal unit is silent when the state government privatises state government undertakings or has joint partnerships with the private sector. The same could be said of INTUC under Congress regime and BMS under the UPA regime. The INTUC did not protest against the reforms of 1991 though every other union did so. Similarly BMS was much muted in its criticism of certain anti-labour policies of the UPA government.

For a long time, the absence of a database on employment and trade union formation in organised industry has posed major difficulties for researchers and policy makers, and perhaps to activists. In order to overcome this void the Friedrich Ebert Stiftung, a German labour research organisation, commissioned studies in eight industries to determine the extent of trade unionism and casualisation (Davala 1992) in them. These included, Tea, Jute, Coal, Ports and Docks, Engineering, Power and, Chemical and Pharmaceutical. The researchers collected the data by personally visiting the chosen industries, enterprises and trade unions. A census was taken on the concerned enterprise rather than a sample. This has provided the total data on the subject. The studies in the book are important for the study of industry, trade unions and casualisation. Some of the industries covered—Ports and Docks, Coal and Power—were in the public sector while others were in the private sector. One of the major findings is that casual and contract labour is replacing permanent labour in all these industries.

The state's influence on trade unions has been discussed by some social scientists and by trade unions themselves. The earlier works tried to explain that the government after independence was pro-labour and it had passed laws to protect the working class. This may be to some extent correct if we compare labour policy during the colonial period when the government was hostile to labour and to trade unions. E. A. Ramaswamy in his earlier work *Power and Justice* had pointed out that the state's prolonged interest in protecting labour was actually harming the movement. Instead of challenging the employers, trade unions had become more interested in getting state support for their demands. Bhowmik's (1996, 1998) articles on trade unions and the state brings out similar findings. He finds that multi-unionism, regarded as the main problem of the labour movement, is caused to a large extent by the laws granting protection to labour. The Trade Unions Act of 1926 has remained unchanged till the present. It allows seven workers to come together to form a union. However the Act only provides guidelines for registration of trade unions, it does not provide for recognition. Recognition is left to the employer's discretion. Hence even a union representing a fraction of the total workers can get recognised as the representative union by management. Similarly, the Industrial Disputes Act allows disputes to be raised by unions or individual workers.

An assessment of the trade union movement after liberalisation has been done by Ratnam et al. al. (1994) and by Sawant (1994). Both books have included papers that represent different views on the subject. The publication also has papers representing the employers' point of view as well as that of labour. In general, studies on labour after 1991 try to show the declining conditions of labour.

Worker Co-operatives

Worker co-operatives are organisations that are owned and controlled by workers. Though they are not uncommon in the developed countries and they have been in existence for several decades (in fact since the late eighteenth century) they hardly exist in developing countries. As compared to the developed countries, worker co-operatives in India started fairly late. The first such co-operative was started in the tea industry with workers of a tea plantation in West Bengal taking over the control of the plantation. In Tripura too the state government encouraged workers of sick or closed plantations to take over and manage these. A few such plantations are still functioning.

Soon after liberalisation the Sick Industries (Special Provisions) Act was amended. The Board of Industrial and Financial Restructuring was set up under the Act and its main purpose was to examine sick or closed industries in the private sector and suggest how they could be improved or if needed, wound up. One of the provisions in the Act stated that the BIFR could hand over management of the company to its employees if they formed a co-operative and expressed willingness to take charge. Kamani Tubes was the first company that was converted to a worker co-operative under the Act. B. Srinivas (1993) has conducted a full-fledged study of this experiment.

He also describes the problems the workers and their families faced after Kamani Tubes closed. Some workers sold their houses, some withdrew their children from school, other delayed their daughters' marriages and some migrated to their villages in search of work.

Three workers committed suicide. The study examines whether worker takeover of a factory can be a possible means of reviving a sick industry by making workers masters of their own destiny. Srinivas has provided detailed analysis of the formation of the co-operative and workers' participation in its functioning.

Unfortunately, Kamani Tubes has failed. E. A. Ramaswamy studied this demise. He found that the failure was mainly because the leaders had not continued the democratic processes of decision-making. The financial problems were also there but failure of participation made workers wary of the leaders. The old divide between workers and managers was re-created; the main difference was that the workers now regarded the leaders as the management. As a result, productivity fell and so did the profits. The worker shareholders too lost interest in the functioning of the company.

Kamani Tubes was a sensational case that had attracted attention of the media throughout the country. At the same time there are other cases, that were not as high profile as Kamani but they still continue to function, though not with high profits. Bhowmik (Ibid) has analysed the case of such co-operatives in the tea industry, one case in West Bengal and three in Tripura. He found that the trade union played a major role in motivating the workers (this is also true of Kamani Tubes).

The specific factors for the tea industry were that workers were isolated in the plantations, their belonging to tribal groups also was important as this added to social solidarity. Besides this, the role of the state is also important. The plantations in Tripura have succeeded because the state is favourable but the plantation in West Bengal was not successful, not because the co-operative failed, but because the state government opposed it.

Bhowmik and Sarker (2002) conducted a study on worker co-operatives in Kolkata. These co-operatives were also formed out of closed factories in the 1980s. Some of them are still in existence. The reasons for the continued existence of some were due to the backing of their unions, high rate of participation in decision-making and the initial backing of the state government.

Labour in Plantations

The plantation industry is the largest employer in the formal sector, after the Railways. The total number of permanent workers in the tea plantation industry is over one million with another 500,000 temporary workers. Though these workers are in the formal sector in the sense that they get legal protection in their work, their wages are very low and their problems are not widely known because they lie isolated in the plantations away from the public gaze. Bhowmik, Xaxa and Kalam (1996) studied the working class in tea plantations of West Bengal, Assam and Tamil Nadu respectively. The conditions of the workers in the south (Tamil Nadu and Kerala) were much better than that of Assam and West Bengal, though the bulk of the labour force (75%) is employed in the two latter states. The southern states not only paid better wages, they also adhered to the provisions laid down by the Plantation Labour Act with regard to housing, education, sanitation and water supply. The plantations in the northern part were woefully lacking in these amenities.

Sarker (1994) highlights the changing patterns of life of tribal workers in tea plantations of North Bengal. He finds that some of the roles of the unions directly influence the life of the workers while others do it indirectly. Collective bargaining has a direct bearing on their working life whereas trade unions have an indirect bearing on their cultural, religious and political institutions. In another study, Bhowmik (1993) found that nearly all the tea plantation workers in North Bengal are unionised, though this has had little effect in increasing their wages or living conditions. The workers know that if there were no unions their conditions would be even worse.

Women play a major role in tea production. In fact tea is the only industry where women workers form over half the workforce. However they are marginalized in their work as well as in the trade unions. Shobhita Jain (1987) has studied the role of female labour in a plantation in Assam. This is an important and in-depth study on the subject. She concludes that there is greater equality among the sexes in the plantations because of the ethnic background of the workers. They are from tribal communities in Chota Nagpur region and there has been a tradition among the impoverished of granting more freedom to women than in the caste Hindu communities.

Sarker and Bhowmik (1998) explore the reasons. They find that though tribal societies have lesser degree of gender discrimination, it is there none the less. The plantation workers in the tea plantations of Jalpaiguri district and of Assam are mostly tribals from the Chota Nagpur region. Work in the plantation is also very gender specific and women are rarely promoted to the ranks of supervisors or gang leaders. These posts are invariably occupied by men. The trade unions too reflect the same structure, with office bearers being mainly males. Moreover, the engagement of women in household work keeps them away from union activities. The trade unions leadership (who are mainly drawn from the Bengali middle classes) have not tried to intervene and change the situation.

Plantations all over the world engage migrant labour. Ravindra K. Jain (1993) has dealt with the continuities and discontinuities between recruitment of labour within Tamil Nadu for export to other countries, especially Malayasia. These workers were engaged in the rubber plantations. He looks at the process of labour control in both the 'enclaves' (the plantations) and the 'hinterland'. He discusses briefly on the Articulation Theory and the Deproletarianisation Theory to explain the process of labour migration and control between Tamil Nadu and Malayasia. His paper includes an interesting postscript on the ethnography of colonialism.

Studies on Voluntary Retirement

Many of the large companies have resorted to down sizing in order to reduce labour costs. The concerned workers are forcibly made to 'voluntarily' retire. The methods were earlier subtle but crude. The targeted group of workers could be frequently harassed by the management, they could be transferred to other plants or offices of the company in other areas etc. All these were done with a view that the workers would not be able to bear this harassment and they would seek a compromise. After the reforms of 1991, the employers' organisations all demanded that government should frame an 'exit policy' that would enable any industry to close down. This was fiercely opposed by trade unions and government decided against such a policy. At the same time, it allowed companies to reduce their work force through a process known as the Voluntary Retirement Scheme. The companies could offer voluntary retirement to their workers by giving them a better retirement package than what they would have got under the law. This would lure workers to accept these terms and quit. In reality what happened was that companies did offer the VRS but if the response was not as much as expected, they would use other tactics to 'convince' their workers. For example one of the commonest ones was of spreading the rumour that the concerned factory or office would close down within a short while and workers would be transferred to another plant far away. Hence if workers did not accept the time-bound offer of VRS, they would have to either move to the other factory or if they wanted to resign then, they would get only the compensation provided by law and nothing more. Hence, it was found that the first offer of VRS had lukewarm response but the second round (after these rumours were spread) had much better response.

Myrtle Barse (2001) has studied the impact of this scheme in some large companies in Mumbai. She finds that it has had a marked impact on the nature of employment and in changing the quality of life of the workers. The paper has case studies of workers who have taken VRS and how their lives changed. Most could not find alternative work and their compensation evaporated within a few years. Their living standards reduced drastically and some could find low paid work in the informal sector. She suggests that the government or other organisations such as their trade unions or NGOs should help workers who accept VRS in investing their money properly and also providing for health insurance.

Noronah (2001) studied the Bombay Dock Labour Board and how globalisation has changed its functioning. He notes that by setting up the BDLB a modicum of social security was provided for sudden economic crisis and at times of recession when work was not readily available. The advent of globalisation and containerisation has reduced the need for labour. The Board had to resort to VRS for the workers which turned out to be disastrous for them and for the Board too as it faced a funds crunch after paying the large sums as compensation. This is one case of when both employer and employee suffered because of VRS.

Ratan Khasnobis and Sudipti Banerjea (1996) come to similar conclusions while studying VRS in Durgapur in West Bengal. The study explores the mechanisms behind the workers' acceptance of VRS in the Durgapur Industrial Area of West Bengal. Though there is willingness on the part of workers to accept compensation in some cases, there is sizable number of instances of coercion from the management forcing the workers to accept the deal. Moreover, the amount is used for unproductive purposes. The worker thus has little left to start self-employment ventures.

JOB SATISFACTION AND COMMITMENT

Job satisfaction reflects an employee's overall assessment of their job particularly their emotions, behaviours, and attitudes about their work experience. It is one of the most heavily researched topics in industrial/organizational psychology with several thousand published studies. Job satisfaction has theoretical and practical utility for the field of psychology and has been linked to important job outcomes including attitudinal variables, absenteeism, employee turnover, and job performance. For instance, job satisfaction is strongly correlated with attitudinal variables such as job involvement, organizational commitment, job tensions, frustration, and feelings of anxiety. Job satisfaction also has a weak correlation with employee's absentee behaviours and turnover from an organization with employees more likely to miss work or find other jobs if they are not satisfied. Finally, research has found that although a positive relationship exists between job satisfaction and performance, it is moderated by the use of rewards at an organization and the strength of employee's attitudes about their job.

Productive behaviour

Productive behaviour is defined as employee behaviour that contributes positively to the goals and objectives of an organization. When an employee begins a new job, there is a transition period during which he or she is not contributing positively to the organization. To successfully transition from being an outsider to a full-fledged member of an organization, an employee typically needs job-related training as well as more general information about the culture of the organization. In financial terms, productive behaviour represents the point at which an organization begins to achieve some return on the investment it has made in a new employee. There are three common forms of productive behaviour in organizations: job performance, organizational citizenship behaviour (OCB), and innovation.

Job Performance

Job performance represents behaviours employees engage in while at work which contribute to organizational goals. These behaviours are formally evaluated by an organization as part of an employee's responsibilities. In order to understand and ultimately predict job performance, it is important to be precise when defining the term. Job performance is about behaviours that are within the control of the employee and not about results (effectiveness), the costs involved in achieving results (productivity), the results that can be achieved in a period of time (efficiency), or the value an organization places on a given level of performance, effectiveness, productivity, or efficiency (utility).

To model job performance, researchers have attempted to define a set of dimensions that are common to all jobs. Using a common set of dimensions provides a consistent basis for assessing performance and enables the comparison of performance across jobs. While there is disagreement about the exact dimensions of job performance, there is agreement on two major categories of job performance: in-role (technical aspects of a job) and extra-role (non-technical abilities such as communication skills and being a good team member).

To assess job performance, reliable and valid measures must be established. The most commonly used measures are ratings of employee performance on specific tasks and on overall job performance. While there are many sources of error with performance ratings, error can be reduced through rater training and through the use of behaviourally anchored ratings scales. Such scales can be used to clearly define the behaviours that constitute poor, average, and superior performance. Additional factors that complicate the measurement of job performance include the instability of job performance over time and the restriction of variation in individual performance by organizational forces. The determinants of job performance consist of factors having to do with the individual worker as well as environmental factors in the workplace. According to Campbell's Model of The Determinants of Job Performance., job performance is a result of the interaction between declarative knowledge (knowledge of facts or things), procedural knowledge (knowledge of what needs to be done and how to do it), and motivation (reflective of an employee's choices regarding whether to expend effort, the level of effort to expend, and whether to persist with the level of effort chosen). Regardless of the job, three determinants stand out as predictors of performance: (1) general mental ability (especially for jobs higher in complexity), (2) job experience (although there is a law of diminishing returns), and (3) the personality trait of conscientiousness (people who are dependable and achievement oriented, who plan well). These determinants appear to influence performance largely through the acquisition and usage of job knowledge and the motivation to do well.

ORGANIZATIONAL CITIZENSHIP BEHAVIOUR

Organizational citizenship behaviour (OCB) refers to productive behaviours that are not part of an employees' formal job description. There are five categories of organizational citizenship behaviours: (1) altruism, (2) courtesy, (3) sportsmanship, (4) conscientiousness, and (5) civic virtue..

There are three different explanations for why employees engage in organizational citizenship behaviour. The first has to do with positive affect, an overall positive mood increases the frequency of helping behaviour. The second explanation, which stems from the equity theory, is that employees reciprocate fair treatment that they have received from the organization. The third explanation is that some employees have personality traits that predispose them to participate in organizational citizenship behaviour. There are also employees who will perform organizational citizenship behaviour to influence how they are viewed within the organization. While these behaviours are not formally part of the job description, performing them can certainly influence performance appraisals.

Innovation

Innovation is a form of productive behaviour that employees exhibit when they come up with novel ideas that further the goals of the organization. Innovation at an individual level is dependent on task-relevant skills (general mental ability and job specific knowledge), creativity-relevant skills (ability to concentrate on a problem for long periods of time, to abandon unproductive searches, and to temporarily put aside stubborn problems), and task motivation (internal desire to perform task and level of enjoyment). There are things that organizations can do in order to breed innovation in the workplace. Some of these items include providing creativity training, having leaders encourage and model innovation, allowing employees to question current procedures and rules, seeing that the implementation of innovations had real consequences, documenting innovations in a professional manner, allowing employees to have autonomy and freedom in their job roles, reducing the number of obstacles that may be in the way of innovation, and giving employees access to resources (whether these are monetary, informational, or access to key people inside or outside of the organization).

Counterproductive behaviour

Counterproductive behaviour can be defined as employee behaviour that goes against the goals of an organization. These behaviours can be intentional or unintentional and result from a wide range of underlying causes and motivations. It has been proposed that a person-by-environment interaction can be utilized to explain a variety of counter-productive behaviours. For instance, an employee who steals from the company may do so because of lax supervision (environment) and underlying psychopathology (person) that work in concert to result in the counterproductive behaviour.

The forms of counterproductive behaviour with the most empirical examination are ineffective job performance, absenteeism, job turnover, and accidents. Less common but potentially more detrimental forms of counterproductive behaviour have also been investigated including theft, violence, substance use, and sexual harassment.

Leadership

Leadership is a process of influencing and supporting and motivating others to work enthusiastically or effectively towards achieving the objectives or goal. A leader acts as a catalyst, who identifies the potential of a worker and tries to put that into reality. A leader can be a positive leader or a negative leader.

A leader's influence within an organization or group has been said to stem from two primary sources, that person's personal characteristics and their position within the organization. Personal power, also made up of two factors called expert power and referent power, is derived from elements like an individual's personality, their knowledge base, their ability to effectively interact with others, and their demonstrated level of effort. Positional power, also often referred to as legitimate power, is derived from the leader's position within the organization, and the authority imbued in them either directly or indirectly by the organization's controlling parties to provide either rewards or sanctions for performance. The leader's role is to use this influence to encourage those within the organization to focus their actions toward the accomplishment of the organization's goals. Distinction should be noted between management v. leadership. Managers process administrative tasks that organize work environments. Leaders conduct those same tasks while also inspiring and motivating the workforce for which they oversee. Managers cope with complexity, leaders cope with change. Managers participate in stepwise tasks of planning and budgeting, organizing and staffing, and controlling and problem solving. In contrast, leaders approach these stages of business development through equivalent tasks of setting a direction or vision, aligning people or communication, and motivating and inspiring, respectively.

OPERATIONAL ORGANIZATIONS AND INFORMAL ORGANIZATIONS

The set organizational structure may not coincide with facts, evolving in operational action. Such divergence decreases performance, when growing. E.g. a wrong organizational structure may hamper cooperation and thus hinder the completion of orders in due time and within limits of resources and budgets. Organizational structures shall be adaptive to process requirements, aiming to optimize the ratio of effort and input to output.

An effective organizational structure shall facilitate working relationships between various entities in the organization and may improve the working efficiency within the organizational units. Organization shall retain a set order and control to enable monitoring the processes. Organization shall support command for coping with a mix of orders and a change of conditions while performing work. Organization shall allow for application of individual skills to enable high flexibility and apply creativity. When a business expands, the chain of command will lengthen and the spans of control will widen. When an organization comes to age, the flexibility will decrease and the creativity will fatigue. Therefore organizational structures shall be altered from time to time to enable recovery. If such alteration is prevented internally, the final escape is to turn down the organization to prepare for a re-launch in an entirely new set up.

Success Factors

Common success criteria for organizational structures are:

- Decentralized reporting
- Flat hierarchy
- High transient speed
- High transparency

- Low residual mass
- Permanent monitoring
- Rapid response
- Shared reliability
- Matrix hierarchy.

History

Organizational structures developed from the ancient times of hunters and collectors in tribal organizations through highly royal and clerical power structures to industrial structures and today's post-industrial structures.

INFRASTRUCTURE DEVELOPMENT

It is well known that no amount of subsidies or incentives can compensate for lack of infrastructure development in a particular area. The experience world over has amply proved that infrastructure development holds the key in promoting industrial development of an area. Government will give specific emphasis on infrastructure development, particularly in backward areas.

The State has already set up Gujarat Infrastructure Development Board under the chairmanship of Hon. Chief Minister to allow single point expeditious clearance of infrastructure development projects with private sector participation. The Board would also lay down guidelines and norms for identification of such projects and their clearances. Investment in specified infrastructure will be provided due weightage in determining the quantum of incentive under the new Incentive Policy.

Land Laws

Easy availability of the right type of land is a crucial factor in the location of an industrial unit. The present laws governing grant of land for industry are rather cumbersome. The State Government will introduce suitable amendments in the present land laws to make land available for setting up industry without protracted paper work and delay. Procedure for the grant of permissions under various land reform laws would be simplified and time-bound clearances assured.

At present, non-agriculturists cannot purchase agricultural land without the prior approval of the Government. This provision causes undue delay in acquiring land for industrial use. Amendments will be carried out in the Bombay Tenancy and Agricultural Lands Act so that bonafide entrepreneurs could purchase land for setting up industrial projects without any delay. Conversion of agricultural land for Non-Agricultural (NA) use for industrial purposes would also be simplified by the introduction of the concept of Deemed NA.

Government would stipulate precautionary conditions so that there is no misuse of these facilities and that lands acquired under these provisions are utilised for industrial use within a specified time period. To reduce delay in grant of permission for acquiring land for industrial use, Government will consider further delegation of powers to the Collectors. Government has identified Agro and Food Processing Industries as one of the Thrust Industries so that the farmers in the State could get better returns for their products in addition to generation of employment in rural areas. In order to ensure that Agrobased projects can be set up with necessary linkages to ensure easy availability of raw material and increase productivity of agriculture in local areas. Government has decided to make necessary arrangements including contractual marketing agreement with farmers.

Land Use Planning and Zoning

With rapid industrialisation and urbanisation of Gujarat, in order to ensure easy availability of land. Government intends to introduce the concept of land use planning to ensure optimum utilisation of land. Government will try to ensure that rich agricultural land is not diverted for the purpose of industry. To ensure this, it will identify specific sites in backward regions of the State which could be developed for the setting up of industrial estates/zones with necessary infrastructural facilities. One of the main objectives of zoning on the basis of land use planning would be the location of industries in clusters so that the environmental protection measures can be adopted through setting up of common effluent treatment plants, disposal of treated effluents etc. Government will try to prevent haphazard growth of industries which may make pollution control measures as well as optimum utilisation of land difficult.

Industrial Townships and Urban Development

Urbanisation is the concomitant to industrialisation process. Experience in the State, which is one of the most urbanised States in the country, shows that this is creating a severe burden on the existing urban infrastructure and services which in any case have been already stretched far beyond their designed capacity. In designing industrial growth centres and clusters, therefore, instead of adopting an estate development approach, therefore, instead of adopting an estate development approach, industrial township approach has become necessary. Creating industrial parks with all urban facilities added on, and also promoting new township to act as focal point in urbanisation are some of the aspects which the State would like to promote as a part of the new industrial policy. Development of such township would decelerate, to some extent, the haphazard growth being experienced by the cities and towns in the State.

The state would like to promote private sector initiatives in setting up industrial parks and the new townships which can attract investments from not only within the country but also from abroad. Establishing new ventures is not merely confined to setting up of factories and production facilities. When the State wants to reap the full advantage of flow of investment, it is necessary that facilities like Trade and Finance Centres, Corporate Headquarters, Exhibition Centres, Convention Centres and other facilities of international standard are created for smooth and rapid execution of trade and business dealings. The State is experiencing serious inadequacy in this regard. It is therefore, intended to take up projects for creating such complexes in and around metropolitan centres. The State would be seeking the cooperation and help from well-known designers, planners and developers in undertaking such ventures.

Power

Gujarat has been fortunate enough to be in a reasonably comfortable position as far as availability of power is concerned. Demand for power has been growing at a rate of 8% to 10% per annum. Apart from requirement of power in the industrial sector, consumption of energy has been growing at a rapid rate in domestic, commercial and agricultural sectors. The State Government has taken the initiatives of promoting new generating capacities with projects totalling 3000 MW in various stages of implementation. However, looking to the rapid rate of industrialisation and urbanisation in the State, it will be necessary to increase the power generating capacity from the present 6165 MW to over 15000 MW by 2000 AD. This will require massive investment for which the State Government has welcomed private sector participation. Major investments by the private sector in generation and distribution of power will require comprehensive review of the existing statutory provisions, policies and procedures relating to the power sector.

The role of Gujarat Electricity Board vis-a-vis the private sector entrants into power sector will also have to be set out in clear terms. Government will address these issues in its Power Policy which is on the anvil. The State Government will encourage modernisation in industrial units to adopt energy conservation and use of non-conventional sources of energy as well.

Road Development

This importance of road development for improving transportation and communication network cannot be over-emphasised. Economic viability of several major projects depends upon the existence of road linkages of the right king. Road privatization is getting more and more importance in developing countries. Gujarat has already initiated this process by making amendments in the Motor Vehicles Act. A list of roads with privatization potential has already been prepared. With the Gujarat Infrastructure Development Board laying down the guidelines governing private sector participation, the development of this important infrastructure will take off rapidly.

Port Development

Gujarat has over 1600 kms. of coastline and 40 minor and intermediate ports which could be the base for tremendous development. This potential can offer excellent locations for promoting hinterland industrialisation and globalization. To encourage port based industrialisation, linkages will be provided by setting up infrastructural facilities like tank terminals, warehouses, customs houses and social infrastructure. More potential sites would be identified and prioritised for development by Gujarat Maritime Board, Gujarat Industrial Investment Corporation for joint sector or for privatisation. These ports will be run on commercial basis and would generate own resources for maintenance and future growth. What is critical in this regard is to ensure optimum utilization of this inelastic resource. Systematic development of the coast has the potential of making Gujarat the window to the World, as well as the major entry point for investments flowing into the country. In this context, the State will declare new Port Policy.

Human Resources Development in Industrialisation

The rapid industrialisation of Gujarat has highlighted the need for human resources development which holds the key in all round improvement in technology, innovation and productivity. Human resource development will have to cover the entire gamut from basic education, vocational and technical education to professional qualification. Providing skill-specific vocational educational facilities to meet the requirement of industry in a specific area is the best way of generating employment opportunities in local areas.

For this purpose, industry will be involved to project the area-specific requirement of various skills, and also in finalising the curriculum in ITIs and Polytechnics so that the local youth could acquire the necessary skills to get absorbed in the industries coming up in the area. At the end of the spectrum of human resource development is the generation of manpower with professional qualifications. With the rapid industrial development and consequential faster growth in the service sectors, a large number of professionals would be required in Gujarat. The State has been fortunate enough to have national level institutes of ex-cellence such as Indian Institute of Management (IIM), National Institute of Design (NID) and Institute of Rural Management (IRMA). However, students from the State have not been able to take full advantage of the location of these institutes in the state. The State Government will initiate efforts to enable the students from Gujarat to successfully complete for admission into these institutes so that they are available to sustain the rapid growth of economy in the State. In addition, the State Government will promote, with the active participation of the private sector, setting up of various management, professional and engineering institutes in different parts of the State. The State Government will also pursue with Government of India the setting up of an Indian Institute of Technology (IIT) in Gujarat in order to provide suitable opportunities to the students in the State and the Region with regard to facilities of higher technical education to meet the requirement of the industries. The State Government will also consider setting up of separate University for technical education. Satellite education will also be encouraged.

Environmental Protection and Pollution Control

The requirement of sustainable development entails the need to tighten the pollution control measures and environmental safety in the State. The chemical and petrochemical industry alongwith dyes, dye intermediates and pharmaceuticals triggered the industrial transformation of the State in the 70s and the 80s. Since most of the laws relating to pollution control and environment safety came into force in the 80s, there has been some laxity in adhering to the stipulated parameters by the industrial units which had been set up prior to that.

In order to comply with the legal provisions as also the standards prescribed by Gujarat Pollution Control Board, the State has contemplated a number of measures like supporting the setting up of common effluent treatment plants in industrial clusters, facilities for collection and disposal of effluents and hazardous wastes in such clusters, tightening the implementation of the laws, strengthening the machinery of Gujarat Pollution Control Board and also supporting the industries in some ways.

Industrial development cannot be at the cost of the environment. Alongwith strictly implementing the pollution and environment protection measures, the State would be striving to set right the irregularities in this regard, which has taken place in some industrial clusters. The State would also like to confine the development of highly polluting industries to the zones and designated estates specifically set up for industries so that the pollution control measures can be managed economically and the standards in this regard can be met adequately.

Agro-based Industries

The State Government intends to put emphasis on the development of Agro and Food Processing Industries with the specific objective of ensuring better returns to the farmers for their products as well as creating employment opportunities in the rural areas. The strategy would be to promote industries based on specific farm products in particular areas with priority given to, items having export potential. Infrastructural facilities for this purpose in the form of chain of cold storage, post-harvest storage facilities, cargo complex and facility of air freighting of fresh fruits and vegetables and cut flowers at Ahmedabad airport, etc. Will be developed. Government will disseminate latest technologies in all land-based activities covering agriculture, horticulture, animal husbandry and aquaculture, so that the farmers in specific areas are able to provide the inputs to sustain agro-industry complexes. Private sector will be encouraged to set up such complexes with specific extension measures to compliment the Governments efforts at increasing agricultural yields.

Mineral-based Industries in Gujarat

Gujarat has several valuable minerals which if properly explored and exploited can go a long way not only in accelerating development of the industry, but also in correcting regional imbalances in the industrial development as many of these minerals are occuring in relatively backward areas of the State. A fine example of this is Lignite. Exploration carried out in the past one decade or so has resulted in identification of good deposits in Kutch and Saurashtra. Lignite based power projects are being set up in these areas. Large limestone deposits are helping in setting up of several cement plants in the State. Other minerals like Bauxite, Bentonite, Marble, Graphite, Granite, Flourspar, etc. Are attracting industrial ventures all over the State. The State intends to systematise the exploration and exploitation of the mineral resources and in doing so, value addition would be one of the basic considerations. Even application of latest satellite remote sensing technology will be encouraged for exploration of minerals. In order to organise the mineral based activities on scientific basis and also to simplify and streamline the present policies, it is intended to bring out a State Mineral Policy during the current year. In addition, setting up of mineral based industries will be encouraged.

3

Organisational Psychology in Industry and Workers

Recognising the role of MSE associations in policy formulation, advocacy, dissemination of information, steps will be taken to form such associations in places without such associations and strengthen their capacity of the existing ones. Recognising that workers' organisations in the MSE sector are few and need strengthening, it will be the endeavour of the Government to encourage formation of workers' organisations that will enhance their ability to secure basic conditions of work (e.g. toilets, drinking water, eating facilities), minimum wages, social protection, voice and representation, social mobilization/ awareness generation, skill training and access to housing.

The formation of Workers Facilitation Centres for such purposes as registration and servicing of social security will be encouraged. 8 Skill Development Recognising the enormous deficit in basic education and formally acquired skills by the working people, skill development will be recognized as an important component of active labour market policies of the government.

Matching Training with Demand

Labour market information systems will be set up adequately to annually assess the labour market requirements, identify labour-intensive high-growth sectors, so that skills development can be planned and delivered accordingly to meet the demands. The focus on skill training and development will fall on the informal or unorganised sector of the work force. Appropriate programmes and schemes will be developed (some are already underway, such as the Skills Development Initiative) and introduced throughout the country to meet the requirements of such workers.

Recognising the inadequacy of institutional capacity in the public sector in training of trainers, policies and programmes will be introduced for the participation of the private sector as well as the non-profit sector such as cooperatives, NGOs and philanthrophic institutions. To encourage acquisition of formal skill training by socially disadvantaged groups (e.g. SCs/STs) special packages will be introduced to provide scholarships, hostel facilities and tool kits.

Standards and Certification

The employability of trainees must be made the main focus of all future training efforts, including components such as curriculum development, training delivery, certification etc. A system of independent certification for candidates passing through skill training as well as trainers will be instituted with appropriate standards. This will be done at the national and state levels by designating competent institutions in public, private and non-profit sectors. A system of accreditation along the lines adopted by the University Grants Commission (in respect of institutions of higher education) will be introduced.

Greater involvement of industry in various initiatives mentioned above is crucial. To ensure greater involvement and interaction, existing and successful models will be assessed and their replication with appropriate adaptations will be taken up. Linkage with Education System and other programmes. From a long term point of view, skill training has to come through vocational education. Given the limited capacity of existing institutions, government will enhance the seating capacity (in public, private and non-profit sectors) by creating new institutions and offering vocational education as an option at the high school level of Class 9. Special focus will be given to rural areas and to youth from disadvantaged social groups.

Given the fact that a majority of the work force has an educational level of less than 5 years (including illiterates), functional literacy programmes will be strengthened and extended. This will be done on the basis of a review of the achievements of the National Literacy Mission as well as the literacy campaigns carried out by civil society organisations. Skill training and development will be made an important component of public programmes and schemes especially those focused on a large number of beneficiaries such as the National Rural Employment Guarantee Programme, National Rural Health Mission, Sarva Shiksha Abhiyan, ICDS and Mid-Day Meal Programme. This will give considerable advantage to women in rural areas as these activities are mostly, if not only, suited to them and predominantly spread over the villages in the country.

EMPLOYMENT POLICY

Employment

There are two main ways of looking at employment, either:

- the number of people with jobs, or;

- the number of jobs.

These two concepts represent different things as one person can have more than one job. People aged 16 or over are classed as in employment, if they have done at least one hour of work in return for wages, salary or for a benefit, or if they have a job that they are temporarily away from. People who do unpaid work in a family business and people on government-supported training (GST) and employment programmes are also included according to the International Labour Organisation (ILO) convention. A person is also considered to be employed if they have a job but are not working for the following reasons:

(1) temporary illness or disability;
(2) personal or family responsibilities;
(3) bad weather;
(4) labour dispute at the place of work;
(5) vacation; and
(6) other unspecified reasons i.e. if someone is on strike, no matter how long the strike lasts, that person is still considered employed.

Full-time employment refers to people who usually work thirty or more hours per week, except in the case of people who work less than thirty hours per week but consider themselves to be employed full-time. Part-time employment refers to people who usually work less than thirty hours each week. A voluntary part-time worker chooses to work fewer than thirty hours a week, either because he or she is a student, has personal or family responsibilities, or wants to spend their time in other pursuits. The reasons for voluntary part-time employment may not be known; some people may not need the income of a full-time job. The involuntary part-time worker prefers full-time work but can only find part-time employment. Permanent employment means any job which does not have a specific termination date. Short-term jobs are classified as temporary. Seasonal jobs, for example in the construction and fishing and farming sectors, are still considered permanent and often require The employment rate is the number of people in employment expressed as a percentage of the relevant population (usually the working age population).

Information on the number of jobs is mainly collected through postal employer surveys and gives the number of employee jobs. The total number of work force jobs is calculated by summing employee jobs, self-employment jobs from the APS, those in HM Forces and Government-supported trainees. Vacant jobs are not included. Self-employment is becoming more and more prevalent with people providing services on a contract basis, producing goods, and selling someone else's product as examples. Earnings is a measure of the money people receive in return for work done gross of tax. It includes salaries and bonuses but does not include non-monetary perks such as benefits in kind. This differs from income, which is the amount of money received from all sources. Income includes interest from building society and bank accounts, dividends from shares, benefit receipts, trust funds, etc.

ORIENTATIONS OF EMPLOYERS AND WORKERS

The diffusion of British conceptions of voluntarism helps to account for the decentralized system of industrial relations in Hong Kong. Since the law does not positively prescribe for the recognition of unions, collective bargaining or enterprise joint consultation, Hong Kong employers are free to negotiate with individual workers at their respective workplaces. Insofar as Hong Kong employers see 'labour as a commodity to be hired at the cheapest price and laid off or dismissed as the market dictates', this mirrors the British invention of labour as a fictitious commodity since the repudiation of paternalism in the pre-industrial era.

This 'loose' regulatory framework also enabled the emergence of diverse employment practices within the labour market. Given Hong Kong's open economy and the 'permissiveness' of the regulatory framework, employers of varied national origins became agents of diffusion of somewhat different institutional models of employment practices with respect, for example, to payment and training systems. Most employers, however, combined features of authoritarianism and benevolent paternalism in labour management and resisted sharing decision making about employment conditions with unions. The one exceptional case in the private sector of a collective agreement that covers substantive and procedural matters involves Cable and Wireless Limited, a public enterprise incorporated in the United Kingdom. In this case, it was the top management, then comprised of British expatriates who were familiar with formal labour relations from their home country experience, who not only encouraged local staff to form a union in 1970 but also initiated the proposal for having a collective agreement with the union. This exception illustrates that the critical factor was not the market that determined the outcome, but rather a foreign management's institutional conceptions of how relations should be structured.

The underdeveloped legal and institutional framework could not have been sustained without the acquiescence of the expanding industrial working class. A key issue in this respect concerns the nature of worker orientations to the employment relationship. One line of argument is that 'neo-Confucian' values, claimed to be reproduced through the family and educational institutions in the newly industrialized East Asian economies, predisposed workers, both male and female, to comply with managerial authority and avoid confrontation. Another cultural explanation, one tailored more specifically to Hong Kong, stresses the impact of the 'refugee mentality' on workers' industrial attitudes and behaviour. A substantial portion of the rapidly growing post-World War II population was comprised of refugees fleeing from the political turmoil and changes in China. As first generation migrants, their primary interest was in maximizing their short-term income. Encountering a laissez faire economy without a state-sponsored safety net, they also had to depend to a large extent on the familial group for economic survival.

Salaff (1981: 8) describes the Hong Kong Chinese family system as a centripetal type which 'gathers in its forces by demanding the primary loyalty of its members and mobilizing their labour power, political and psychological allegiances on behalf of kinsmen'. A consequence was an ethos of 'utilitarianistic familism' that gave precedence to familial interests over societal or other group interests and produced a relatively low level of social involvement with co-workers and neighbours. The primacy of family loyalties, short time-horizons and social detachment from co-workers militated against social investment in organizational efforts aimed at changing the rules of the labour market. A low level of 'social capital', regarded as a key factor underpinning political apathy, can also account for the low level of unionization and collective action among workers. This type of orientation prompted workers to seek alternative opportunities for improving their economic status in the dynamic postwar economy. If employers did not meet their substantive expectations, they could exercise the exit option individually by changing jobs. The effectiveness of this option was enhanced as establishments proliferated in the growing sectors of manufacturing such as garments, electronics and plastics. High labour mobility in manufacturing thus became an alternative to collective organization and negotiation for improving their economic status.

The colonial system also dampened the development of working-class interest in a more formal representational and participatory role for labour. The absence of a democratic ideology or democratic political institutions meant there was no model on which to base the demand for an extension of democratic practices to industrial relations. An apolitical orientation was also fostered through the educational system. In line with practices in Britain and in its colonies, the postwar Hong Kong colonial educational system was geared to maintaining an apolitical image of the school curriculum. Concerned about the growing influence of pro-communist educational efforts in the colony, the colonial government established a Special Bureau within the Education Department in 1949 to counter those efforts. Other forms of control were also imposed on textbooks, syllabuses and the registration of schools to prevent communist infiltration and the politicization of education. Civic education, created as a school subject in 1953, emphasized proper conduct and the responsibilities of a good citizen rather than civic rights, participation and democracy. Moreover, opportunities for students to participate in school governance were minimal. As a result, Hong Kong's postwar younger generation was socialized through schooling into a culture of political alienation. This was hardly conducive to the development of conceptions of industrial democracy.

The impact of the Chinese family, the refugee mentality and the colonial educational system in limiting the potential for collective challenges to managerial authority should not be exaggerated, however. Strong anti-colonial and anti-foreign sentiments were present among a sizable minority during the postwar years. These sentiments sustained political unionism and, on occasion, could be activated to challenge employers' and even the state's authority. Nevertheless, the combination of the legal and regulatory institutions of voluntarism and a cultural aversion to collective action, derived from the influence of background institutions of family and the education system, fostered the dominance of individualist and instrumental labour market strategies. The political character of the main union movement during most of the postwar period further reinforced the use of these strategies. This type of unionism was not regarded as useful by most workers, who preferred either to avoid involvement with politically oriented associations or else were strongly alienated from the pro-communist unions in particular. It is necessary, therefore, to turn to this institutional construction of political unionism.

Union Orientations

The colonial state's permissive and non-interventionist approach to labour relations has both reinforced, and been reinforced by, the orientation and character of the Hong Kong trade-union movement. During the early post-World War Two period 'a pattern of British-style collective bargaining seemed to lie ahead' as major unions presented the larger firms with concerted wage demands. It is the subsequent retreat of trade unions from collective bargaining that needs to be explained.

The main reason why collective bargaining never became a major objective of Hong Kong trade unions can be traced to the institutional environment in which they first emerged. Hong Kong trade unions shared with their Chinese counterparts the same indigenous sources of institutional models: triad societies, craft guilds and political parties. The influence of these traditional organizational forms and practices on modern labour organizations in China and Hong Kong had two repercussions. First, it contributed to the fragmentation of the labour movement. Second, guild origins imbued Hong Kong's trade unions with a primary emphasis on mutual aid functions.

In addition to their welfare orientation, the unions' involvement as principal agents in the political rivalry between the Kuomintang and Chinese Communist Party also deflected their resources and commitments away from developing a strong workplace presence or from seeking formal relationships with employers. This cannot be explained in terms of market processes and economic incentives and disincentives. While the economic approach predicts that weak unions will turn to politics in order to reshape industrial relations governance structures, the type of political activities in which Hong Kong's trade unions engaged did not historically conform at all to this outcome.

The peculiar nature of the political orientation of Hong Kong's trade-union movement can be traced to the institutional environment during its formative period in the first two decades of this century. While the link between the guild origin of Hong Kong trade unions can be described as mimetic, the impact of Chinese political parties on unions can be viewed as a variant of coercive isomorphism.

The political environment when unions emerged in China in the early decades of the twentieth century was replete with revolutionary and nationalistic movements. Within this environment, the dominant goals and objectives of nascent secondary associations became infused with nationalism. Whatever their other pursuits, the promotion of China's national interest became the universal principle legitimizing their existence. Trade unions were no exception. Nationalism soon came to be identified with support for one of the two dominant political parties in China. Influenced by both the guild model and the Chinese political parties, the basic structure and orientation of Hong Kong's labour movement took shape by the 1920s: '... a multiplicity of associations in the crafts and traditional industries of the Colony each heavily influenced by guild traditions of exclusiveness combined with mutual aid for members; and in addition a group of large unions organized on an industrial basis-notably amongst seamen, dockers, tramway workers and printers-motivated by political ideals of nationalism and anti-imperialism.'

As the civil war in China intensified after the Second World War, this basic structure of trade unionism was more or less reproduced intact in Hong Kong.

This politicized model of organizational development has impeded the union movement's effectiveness in advancing workers' employment interests. The political character of the unions also gave both the government and the employers grounds for resisting formal bargaining relations with the unions. The other 'pillar' of voluntarism in Hong Kong has thus been the indifference of the FTU and the TUC towards formal collective bargaining and the absence of sustained and coordinated pressures by the trade-union movement on the colonial state for legislative changes and political reforms beneficial to labour.

Only by taking into consideration the influence of the institutional environment during the formative period of the Hong Kong union movement can we make sense of its peculiar political orientation.

We have sought to demonstrate and assess the relevance of economic, political and sociological approaches to the origins of economic governance structures for explaining why the organization of Hong Kong's industrial relations did not develop the degree of formalization or centralization found in other industrialized market economies. The economic perspective would explain this outcome in terms of the smooth operation of the largely unregulated competitive labour market and workers' ability to capitalize on the market to maximize their individual welfare in the context of an expanding economy. This perspective takes for granted, however, what needs to be explained, namely why the labour market operates in such a competitive manner. It also fails to explain why collective bargaining did not develop, even in circumstances that elsewhere are considered favourable.

The political explanation would account for the emergence of an unregulated labour market by focusing on how, within an authoritarian political system that excluded representation of labour, the interests of the colonial state and the dominant financial-commercial business elite meshed to support the British voluntarist tradition as a policy and strategy for the governance of Hong Kong's industrial relations. However, this perspective is unable to account for the trade-union movement's failure to pursue working class interests by attempting to influence public policies through extra-political channels. A political approach would also predict that the state (as well as employers) would exercise much tighter control over industrial relations, including suppression of trade-union activities, than it actually did.

In our view, neo-institutional sociology is best able to solve these puzzles generated by the application of the economic and political perspectives. The diffusion of British conceptions and institutional models for the governance of industrial relations explains the 'positive non-interventionism' or 'permissiveness' characteristic of the Hong Kong colonial government's approach to industrial relations. This approach was premised on the belief that workers and employers, as autonomous individuals, should be left to solve their problems individually or collectively as they preferred, and normally without interference by the state, while at the same time the state had a duty to protect the more vulnerable employees from threats to their health and safety at the workplace and from excessive exploitation. The permissiveness of this governance framework created space for the emergence of somewhat diverse employment practices at the enterprise level.

The absence of state regulation of wages and protection against unfair dismissal, as well as the lack of unemployment benefits, helps to explain why workers became highly sensitive to labour market incentives and developed individual strategies for taking advantage of market opportunities. Furthermore, within the voluntarist framework and buttressed by the influence of the family and educational systems, employees adopted an individualist and instrumental orientation to work and the labour market, while employers have sought to maximize their control of the labour process and maintain flexibility. The sociological neo-institutional perspective can also explain why the Hong Kong union movement did not act in ways that might be expected from the rational choice approach to the study of trade unionism (Crouch 1982). The effects of the institutional environment at the time that modern unions emerged left an enduring imprint on their objectives and strategies that diverted them from seeking more formalized and centralized rule-making arrangements. This fits with the argument that an organization's character is initially shaped by the historical conditions at the time of its founding, and that, once formed, this character is likely to continue to exert a profound influence on subsequent behaviour.

The institutional environment thus constituted the overarching framework within which the distinctive nature of Hong Kong's industrial relations system developed. Our analysis testifies to the impact of the colonial political economy on Hong Kong's labour relations, but also that politics and economics have operated within the broader, earlier established institutional framework.

Sometimes, they were inconsistent with the institutionalized rules and occasionally that led to modifications of the framework governing industrial relations. In other instances, political power and economic interests reinforced the existing institutional framework. For example, the power structure and political imperatives under British colonialism were consistent with a largely arms-length approach to economic and social affairs. Laissez.faire was a rational strategy of rule given Hong Kong's governing coalition and power structure. However, the 'crisis of legitimacy' facing colonial rule in the late 1960s led to a departure from the voluntarist tradition as the colonial state expanded legal protection and improved labour standards and benefits for workers. Hong Kong's pattern of industrial development also generated an industrial and enterprise structure that proved inimical to unionization and collective bargaining. While the practice of collective bargaining has not been institutionalized, Hong Kong's decentralized and competitive labour market is entirely consistent with the formal structure of employment relations which embodied the 'institutional myth' of freedom of contract and the view of labour as a commodity.

In this respect, the three perspectives on the explanation of governance structures are not mutually exclusive, but contribute to our understanding of the Hong Kong case at a distinct level of analysis. The sociological neoinstitutional perspective highlights the social constitution of actors and their interests and the dominant policy framework. The political perspective then pitches its explanation at the intermediate level by showing how political struggles link the different actors and the broader policy framework to specific institutional outcomes. The economic perspective examines actions and calculations at the proximate level, i.e., how certain forms of transactions become 'rational' and 'efficient' given the political and institutional contexts.

Due to the postwar continuity of British colonial rule over Hong Kong, coupled with the union movement's acceptance of the industrial relations governance framework, Hong Kong's industrial relations were not restructured in ways comparable to that of other post-colonial states in the region, such as those in Malaysia, Singapore and South Korea, which outlawed left-wing unions, imposed stricter controls over union activities and finances, or sought to politically demobilize labour by restructuring the union movement. The divergence between Hong Kong and Singapore in the organization of their industrial relations is especially striking given the similarities in terms of the legacy of British colonial rule and the Chinese ethnicity of the majority of their populations. The People's Action Party (PAP), on taking power in Singapore in 1959, amended the existing trade-union law to prevent the development of splinter unions and multi-unionism, supported a pro-government union federation while refusing to register an oppositional federation, passed new legislation in 1960 and again in the late 1960s that restricted unions' freedom to bargain collectively, and, in 1982, amended the trade-union law once again by redefining unions as having objectives of consensus and productivity improvement instead of the 'confrontational objectives of the original ordinance'. The union movement was thus gradually depoliticized through state action, and unions became 'absorbed into promoting national goals'. The contrast between the re-organization of industrial relations in post-colonial Singapore with the continuity of the framework governing industrial relations in Hong Kong suggests that political arguments may apply best during a period of major political transformation, when there are significant shifts in the power structure. Under such conditions, the pre-existing institutional assumptions may be called into question and the intensification of conflicts among political actors may then allow new models of industrial relations to gain ascendancy.

This raises the question of what will happen to the governance of industrial relations following the end of British colonial rule and Hong Kong's return to Chinese sovereignty on 1 July 1997. The severing of Hong Kong's colonial link to Britain may result in a new process of institutional isomorphism. China's modelling of industrial relations has been more paternalistic than the British approach and relies less on the institutional myth of voluntarism and freedom of contract. The Chinese government also has a much lower level of tolerance for an autonomous and militant union movement. A possible scenario is that the organization of industrial relations will gradually become more centrally and formally regulated from the top down after 1997 in ways that will bring the governance of Hong Kong's industrial relations closer to that of other post-colonial societies in the region.

WOMEN WORKERS AND THEIR SPECIAL CONCERNS

The National Employment Policy recognises the severe constraints faced by women workers in terms of (a) lack of recognition of their contribution in many economic activities that are not adequately measured, (b) discrimination specially heightened by social disadvantages and (c) wide gap in opportunities, wages and security as compared to men workers (d) lack of supportive structures to facilitate their employment..

Gender Sensitive Macro Policies

Gender sensitive employment policies that take into account the special circumstances and problems of women will therefore enunciated from time to time. Such policies will aim at shifting women from invisible to visible work, from low productive employment, especially in agriculture, to high productive employment, and from low wage and no social security to higher wage with social security work conditions. Complimentary policies such as credit policies result in male bias. This will be corrected by taking special measures to access credit and such other facilities for women entrepreneurs and home based workers.

Technology policies often lead to more displacement of women than men workers. Promotion and innovation of gender sensitive technology will be undertaken in aiding women workers and enhancing their participation.

Formal credit as well as employment and development institutions will be guided, and if necessary mandated, to link with the SHGs to provide a range of services. The models that are currently working in some states will have to be studied and adapted to the conditions of other states. For this the central government will encourage state governments with appropriate technical and financial assistance to initiate suitable policies and programmes. Women as a percentage of work force in SEZs is very high and their participation in unorganised sector within EPZs almost double that in organized work.. There needs to be special focus on the women's participation in trade related employment, and the nature of such employment.

Identifying Sectors

Sectors where women's participation is significant will be identified for specific focus as, for example, in agriculture, food processing, fishing, plantations, forestry, horticulture, export intensive manufacturing, tourism and care services with a view to introduce technology that are drudgery reducing and/or labour augmenting thereby creating conditions for employment generation, a decent work and higher productivity. Policies and programmes for skill training and development for women will have a specific component of entrepreneurship development for women-headed micro and small enterprises.

Facilitating Structures

Special institutional mechanisms will be created to cater to women's employment, such as information centres and organisational structures. to promote decent employment in emerging sectors and activities. Special facilities (in the form of committees) will be established in clusters and large enterprises to ensure that basic conditions of work with dignity are provided for women workers and that no discriminatory practices are allowed. These relate to (i) sanitary, drinking water, eating and child care facilities, (ii) ensure the payment of minimum wages wherever applicable, (iii) enforcement of safety standards and (iv) representation of women in collective bodies of workers.

A specific area in which women have responded in large numbers arising out of economic compulsions is their high level of participation in the National Rural Employment Guarantee Programme (NREGP).

It will also be the endeavour of the government to ensure that wage payments are carried out in a timely and transparent manner and create such systems (like Post Office or Bank Savings Accounts) that will both ensure timely and full payment and empower them in the long run in dealing with modern financial institutions. Special attention will be given to the educational and skill training requirements of women workers thereby addressing, inter alia, the perceived bias against women workers in the labour market

Organisation and Empowerment

Given the greater deficit in organisation and representation of women workers, especially in the informal economy, special programmes and enabling conditions will be created for organizing informal women workers and strengthening their collective capacity. The Self Help Groups of women have emerged as an innovative form of organisation for accessing credit, marketing as well as other services.

While encouraging the spread of this organisational form to areas where it is currently either absent or low presence, policies will be put in place to ensure that micro credit graduates from consumption smoothening to livelihood credit that will have a focus on the creation of productive employment with backward-forward linkages.

VULNERABLE WORKERS

In an economy where an overwhelming proportion of workers are in the informal sector whose defining characteristics are low productivity, small size of enterprises and absence of job and/or social security to workers, vulnerability should be reckoned as all pervasive. However, there are specific segments of workers who are at a distinct disadvantage arising out of their helpless ness in terms of local distress, distress induced migrants, working children, workers with physical challenges or those in bondage like conditions.

Migrant Workers

Effective enforcement of the Inter-State Migrants Act of 19xx will be ensured to regulate the recruitment as well as terms and conditions of work. The state governments will ensure that migrant workers have access to basic amenities such as shelter, drinking water and sanitation, health care and access to schooling for the children. In addition, it will also ensure, through appropriate legislation that the social security scheme for workers in the unorganised sector are also made available to the migrant workers.

Child Labour

Tackling child labour (which is declining) calls for policies and programmes to improve the livelihood security of poor families to which they belong. Provision of gainful employment especially during lean seasons, better enforcement of minimum wages of adult workers, provision of basic social security and contingent social security will be strengthened. In addition, child-centred programmes such as ICDS and Mid-Day Meals in schools will be extended to cover the whole country and steps taken to enhance their effectiveness. An area requiring special focus is to strengthen access to schooling especially in rural areas. The augmented programme of Sarva Shiksha Abhiyan is expected to ensure universal enrolment of children in schools. Special schemes will be introduced to states that account for an overwhelming proportion of children out of school. State governments and local self governments will be encouraged and incentivised to ensure provision of quality education. The family-centric and convergence-based child labour approach will be promoted through policy and schemes, particularly at the district levels. Special schemes will be introduced for states that account for an overwhelming proportion of children out of school. Regionally focused policies and programmes will therefore get special attention.

Bonded Labour

There exist various interpretations of the term bonded labour. Operational definitions will need to be adopted. Policies and schemes aimed at preventive aspects will be strengthened to reduce the incidence of bonded labour that largely, if not only, arises from debt-bondage. Special schemes for rural, poor households from such socially disadvantaged groups as Scheduled Castes and Tribes, who constitute the majority of bonded labour, will be introduced in areas of origin. With the aim of tackling the reasons for bondage or bondage-like situations.

FLEXIBLE EMPLOYMENT RELATIONSHIPS

All of these mechanisms are used for providing public services without using public employees, and in many cases through other funding sources besides appropriated funds. Yet even in those cases where public services continue to be provided by public employees working in public agencies funded by appropriations, massive changes have occurred in employment practices.

Chief among these are increased use of temporary, part-time, and-seasonal employment; and increased hiring of exempt employees (those outside the classified civil service) through employment contracts. These two devices, along with the increased use of outside contractors, have markedly changed the face of the public work force.

Increasingly, employers reduce costs and enhance flexibility by meeting minimal staffing requirements through "permanent" employees, and by hiring "contingent" (temporary, part-time or seasonal) workers to meet peak workload demands. These positions usually offer lower salaries and benefits than career positions.

And employees can be hired and fired "at will" (without reference to due process entitlements of civil service employees, or collective bargaining agreements). Skill requirement of these jobs are reduced by job-redesign or work simplification. Where commitment and high skills are required on a temporary basis, employers may seek to save money or maintain flexibility by using contract or leased employees to positions exempt from civil service protections.

Exempt positions are classified, in that positions must be created and funded before they can be filled. But they are not classified within civil service systems, so their incumbents are not "permanent" (at least, not in the sense of having a property interest in their positions).

Instead, the terms and conditions of these positions are specified through performance contracts specifying pay and benefits, and limiting the term of employment. While contracts may be routinely renewed with the approval of the employee and the employer, employees may also be discharged "at will" in the event of a personality conflict, a change in managerial objectives, or a budget shortfall.

Frequently, once employees become exempt, they lose their "bumping rights" back into a classified position in the event of a reduction in force (RIF). Increasingly, managerial and technical employees are hired into these types of contracts. They increase the salary and benefits that can be offered to highly qualified employees, and they enhance managerial flexibility to trim personnel costs quickly, should this be necessary, without having to resort to the bureaucratic chaos precipitated by the exercise of "bumping rights" during an RIF situation.

The impact of these two devices is accelerated by retirement "buyouts," which offer employees close to retirement age an incentive to retire early within a limited period of eligibility ("window").

In a typical example, employees with 17-20 years of service (in a jurisdiction with a 20-year eligibility requirement for retirement) may be offered, for a limited time period of two months, the opportunity to resign and receive retirement benefits equal to those they would have received with three additional years' service.

And the employer may even "sweeten the pot" by offering to pay its share of the cost of employee and family health benefits during the early retirement period (before the employee is eligible for Medicare). If the plan is designed properly so that enough employees retire to save substantially, but enough stay to provide for organizational continuity and skills, both employer and employee benefit. The employee gets an option to retire early at close to current salary; the employer gets to fill the vacant position with an entry-level employee at a much lower salary. The major drawback for the municipality is unexpectedly large lump-sum payments for accrued annual leave or sick leave.

EMPLOYEE TRAINING

Empirical research supports common sense—leadership matters to an organization's effectiveness. Leadership skills can be learned; although learning on the job is too haphazard a way to ensure an organization's viability. A leadership development programme (LDP) requires nine overlapping tasks, which should be managed by HR professionals.

Each task answers a basic question:

- What kind of candidates is the organization looking for?
- What does it take to be a good leader in the organization?
- How does one become a programme participant?
- How does the participant stack up as a leader right now?
- What specific actions should the participant take to become a better leader?
- In what ways is the LDP reinforced by other HR systems?

- How can the participant's work group be part of the developmental process?
- Is there a leadership succession plan?
- Is the LDP giving a satisfactory return on investment?

It is axiomatic that superior organizations have superior leaders. Yet, broadly skilled leaders are in short supply. The time-honoured way of learning one's technical specialty, and then somehow transitioning into supervision is not a reliable method for producing adequately trained staff.

Most organizations need a vigorous and deliberate way to improve the skills of supervisors, managers, and executives. They need a leadership development programme (LDP). Although costly, an LDP is a wise investment for a compelling reason— well-led organizations tend to attract quality applicants, produce satisfied employees, incur less unwanted turnover, engender loyal customers, and yield impressive financial returns.

However, it is fair to raise a basic policy question in deciding how to ensure the organization is leadership ready: buy or build. Under the "buy" approach, the organization relies upon recruiting and selecting talented leaders from outside. This is a fast way to get skilled personnel with fresh ideas and obviates the need for erecting an expensive internal development programme.

The major disadvantages of not developing from within are a likely decrease in morale for those bypassed and temporary dips in productivity while new leaders "learn the ropes." In addition, unionized organizations may encounter additional resistance.

The prime advantage of building leadership talent, besides eliminating the disadvantages of going outside, is twofold. First, the organization gets to groom the next generation in line with its culture and strategic agenda. Second, the organization has greater control over the supply of leaders with the requisite skills, making strategic implementation faster.

The need for talented leaders exists, and on balance, it appears the benefits outweigh the costs of creating an LDP within the organization. The following plan provides an overview and detailed outline of the nine essential tasks for creating a leadership development programme to help current and future leaders reach their potential in the service of organizational goals.

Core Programme Premises

Two premises, based on ample evidence, are at the program's foundation. First, leadership matters to an organization's performance. Hence, an organization should concentrate resources on securing, developing, and keeping good leaders. Second, it is possible to develop leaders. Leaders may be born, but they are also made.

Several other premises guide this plan:

- LDP develops the whole person, not only one's skills at work. Many people can benefit from some aspects of the programme. (In this respect, leadership development can be viewed as an organization-wide initiative, "operationalized" through the widespread use of individual development plans.)
- Most organizational members have opportunities to lead at work. Many people can benefit from some aspects of an LDP.
- Leadership is fundamentally a relationship between leaders and followers; the context in which the leader resides must be considered in creating developmental activities.
- Valid assessment and measurement of progress are necessary.
- Growth entails motivation, substantial effort, challenge, and a willingness to accept risk and setbacks.
- People learn best in a nurturing environment.
- Certain traits—enduring personality characteristics—correlate with leadership effectiveness. Careful selection improves the odds of developing the most promising candidates. Selection, versus open enrollment, should be part of the programme.
- Developing leaders requires considerable effort and expense. Measuring overall success allows us to make the programme more effective and efficient. We must evaluate the programme, and to do this we must have clear goals.

Each premise suggests a value. Build these values into the programme if they agree with the current or ideal culture of your organization. If not, adjust the programme accordingly. Little is more dispiriting to participants than for the organization to create an unrealistic "cultural island," only to thrust graduates back into an environment that does not support, and may even punish, different ways of leading. In this respect, leadership development is a product and a shaper of the organization's culture.

Employee Training and Management Development

Training is defined as the systematic development of the knowledge, skills and attitudes required by an individual to perform a given task or job successfully. Training aims at improving the organisation's performance through the enhanced performance of its employees. While training helps employees do their current jobs, development prepares individuals to handle future responsibilities.

The major purposes of training are improving employee performance, updating employee skills, avoiding managerial obsolescence, preparing for promotion and managerial succession, and satisfying personal growth needs.

Training needs are determined based on the organisation's and the employee's needs.

Organisations provide training to employees in the areas of company policies and procedures, specific skills, human relations, and managerial skills. Some organisations also provide apprentice training. There are two types of training methods - on-the-job and off-the-job. In on-the-job training methods, an employee is given training in the actual work situation, where he learns by doing and through direct experience.

Some of the on-the-job methods of training are job instruction training, apprenticeship and coaching, job rotation, and committee assignments. Off-the-job training refers to the training given to an employee away from the immediate work area. Here the employee focuses his attention upon learning from the trainer's lectures or through simulated exercises.

Off-the-job training methods include classroom lectures; various simulation exercises like case exercises, experiential exercises, computer modeling, vestibule training and role playing; and programmed instruction. Systematic evaluation of training activities helps in evaluating the success of the training programme.

Training increases productivity, reduces the level of supervision required, reduces accidents related to work and increases organisational stability. Apart from training, an organisation should also concentrate on management development. Management development is a systematic process of growth and development by which employees develop their skills and abilities to manage.

It is future oriented and is concerned with education of the employees. Management development improves a manager's ability to understand problems and arrive at solutions. It helps the manager in effective handling of his different work roles like planning, monitoring performance, communication and development.

Management development programmes are designed to meet specific objectives, which contribute to both employee and organisational effectiveness.

There are several steps in the process of management development. These include reviewing organisational objectives, evaluating the organisation's current management resources, determining individual development needs, designing and implementing development programmes, and finally, evaluating the effectiveness of these programmes.

The two categories of development methods are on-the-job development, and off-the-job development. Some of the widely used on-the-job development methods are: coaching, job rotation, under study assignments and multiple management. Off-the-job development methods include simulation exercises, sensitivity training, transactional analysis, conferences and lectures. To ensure the success of the management development programmes, they have to be evaluated from time to time.

Typical Reasons for Employee Training and Development

Training and development can be initiated for a variety of reasons for an employee or group of employees, e.g.,:

- When a performance appraisal indicates performance improvement is needed
- To "benchmark" the status of improvement so far in a performance improvement effort
- As part of an overall professional development programme
- As part of succession planning to help an employee be eligible for a planned change in role in the organisation
- To "pilot", or test, the operation of a new performance management system
- To train about a specific topic

Typical Topics of Employee Training

1. Communications: The increasing diversity of today's workforce brings a wide variety of languages and customs.
2. Computer skills: Computer skills are becoming a necessity for conducting administrative and office tasks.
3. Customer service: Increased competition in today's global marketplace makes it critical that employees understand and meet the needs of customers.
4. Diversity: Diversity training usually includes explanation about how people have different perspectives and views, and includes techniques to value diversity.
5. Ethics: Today's society has increasing expectations about corporate social responsibility. Also, today's diverse workforce brings a wide variety of values and morals to the workplace.
6. Human relations: The increased stresses of today's workplace can include misunderstandings and conflict. Training can people to get along in the workplace.
7. Quality initiatives: Initiatives such as Total Quality Management, Quality Circles, benchmarking, etc., require basic training about quality concepts, guidelines and standards for quality, etc.
8. Safety: Safety training is critical where working with heavy equipment, hazardous chemicals, repetitive activities, etc., but can also be useful with practical advice for avoiding assaults, etc.

9. Sexual harassment: Sexual harassment training usually includes careful description of the organisation's policies about sexual harassment, especially about what are inappropriate behaviours.

General Benefits from Employee Training and Development

There are numerous sources of online information about training and development.

Several of these sites (they're listed later on in this library) suggest reasons for supervisors to conduct training among employees. These reasons include:

- Increased job satisfaction and morale among employees;
- Increased employee motivation;
- Increased efficiencies in processes, resulting in financial gain;
- Increased capacity to adopt new technologies and methods;
- Increased innovation in strategies and products;
- Reduced employee turnover;
- Enhanced company image, e.g., conducting ethics training (not a good reason for ethics training!);
- Risk management, e.g., training about sexual harassment, diversity training.

Cross-training (Business)

Cross-training in business operations involves training employees to engage in quality control measures. Employees are trained in tangent job functions to increase oversight in ways that are impossible through management interactions with workers alone.

Advantages

- Helps patrons/customers/clients in the long run, as employees are empowered to answer questions about the entire organisation.
- Requires staff to re-evaluate the reasons and methods for accomplishing their work; inefficient methods, outdated techniques and bureaucratic drift are challenged, if not eliminated.
- Raises an awareness of what other departments do.
- Routine scheduling is enhanced with the ability to move staff about the "Operation".
- Better coverage, increased flexibility and ability to cope with unexpected absences, emergencies, illness, etc.
- Can increase the "employability" of staff who have the opportunity to train in areas they were not originally hired for.

Other advantages include:

- Increased flexibility and versatility,

- Appreciated "intellectual capital"
- Improved individual efficiency,
- Increased standardization of jobs,
- Heightened Morale.

EMPLOYEE GRIEVANCES AND DISCIPLINE

The logic of empowering work teams to control production leads to the extension that the employees themselves would be just as knowledgeable, or more knowledgeable than supervisors about who would be best for the job, or how individual employees are performing. It should be noted that just because a team has control over work processes, it does not necessarily follow that the team must also have control over personnel issues.

However, for the concept of team self-direction and empowerment to be meaningful, a strong, compelling argument can be made for the team to have control over personnel issues. Some authors have raised the concern that team members would not be objective in their evaluations of employees; either they would treat the person as a friend and not be willing to confront the employee if there were problems, or, possibly, they would want to drive an employee out who did not conform to the group's non-work related norms. However, the same criticism can be made regarding the objectivity of the supervisor.

Comparative research is lacking to indicate whether personnel decisions made by a supervisor are better or worse than those made by a team. As was noted earlier, there is a dearth of any empirical studies regarding the conduct of discipline by a team. Although one can argue that teams can make as objective personnel decisions as supervisors, two conditions need to be present in order for the system to properly function. First, the team must have developed good interactive skills, have worked as a cohesive team, and have mastered controlling work processes.

Team self-direction is a developmental process. In making the transition to a work team, employees need to learn how to function as a group and begin working on production processes with which they have a high degree of familiarity. The success or failure of the team to be able to modify work processes is an indicator as to whether the team is able to be empowered with the personnel decision process.

If a team has been judged mature enough to handle personnel decisions, then the team must receive extensive training in the personnel process as the second condition. (This poses an interesting problem. Who determines if the team is mature enough? Management, the team itself, other teams automatic if certain conditions are present). Training in the personnel process is another one of the components of training in which quality management mandates.

The team has already received task and work improvement training, e.g., statistics, quality control methodology, and training in group processes. Training in personnel procedures requires that the team understand the basic requirements of equal employment law.

Selection requires that the team understands the process both from an organizational and legal perspective. Discipline also requires training. This training component would cover the interpersonal aspects of confrontation, problem definition, and clarification, progressive discipline, employee legal rights, and the concept of just cause, or whatever the organization uses as the basis for discipline.

In summary, personnel decision making is a logical extension of the team empowerment process. For the team to function, it must be experienced and mature in group processes and it must receive training in both the legal aspects of personnel selection as well as the organizational policies which govern personnel.

Discipline Process Models for Teams

Although there are many variations on organizational structures for disciplinary processing, there would appear to be three major models that can be constructed around the degree of autonomy that the organization will allow. The first model is the team as recommender.

The team makes what it feels are appropriate recommendations for discipline to management and then management may accept, modify or reflect the recommendations as necessary.

This model safeguards the organization from legal or technical problems that might arise in a disciplinary hearing. If the organization was serious about optimizing empowerment, this model could provide a developmental step in the process of full team self-direction.

The second model is at the opposite end of the spectrum. In this model the team is completely autonomous in making personnel decisions. Team members are completely responsible for selection and disciplinary decisions. This model can only be implemented when the team has developed sufficient maturity and has been trained in personnel procedures. Barkman has suggested that one of the team members might receive advance human resources training and serve as a resource to the team.

The third model falls between the extremes of the first two models. The team proposes the disciplinary plan, but instead of being reviewed by management, the plan is reviewed by members of other work teams who may make modifications accordingly. This model allows for peer review, which should prevent any inappropriate extreme action from occurring.

It is important to note that any of the above three models or their variations are considered to be the last, extreme step. For all three models, quality theorists posit that an important preliminary step must occur: there must be informal intervention by team members to work with an employee who is having problems. Every effort has to be made to counsel and assist an employee. If additional training is necessary, it must be provided. The employee must receive every opportunity to improve before any formal mechanism of discipline is implemented.

The human resources department could serve as an expert to the team as the team develops its disciplinary plan and could assist the team to avoid any legal problems. Although the above would suggest that with maturity and training, a team should be able to be empowered to handle discipline, there are some serious issues and problems that need to be addressed before empowerment in this area can be fully implemented.

Issues and Problems

The disciplinary process, more than the selection process, is a minefield of procedural dictates. In the public sector the employee's employment has been viewed by the courts as a property right. As a consequence, the courts have developed procedural safeguards to ensure that the employee's due process rights are not violated. The safeguards have been developed based on the experience of the traditional hierarchical organizations and would require some adaptation in a system that utilized empowered teams for discipline.

Another question in the public sector is that the law often reserves the authority for personnel actions to the agency head or manager responsible for the jurisdiction, e.g. the appointing authority; or, it reserves the right to the governing board, e.g. Board of Education. If a team has been empowered, then the personnel authority would have to act as ratifiers and should not change the recommendation. Whether courts would allow the appointing authority or governing board to abrogate their responsibility in this area is questionable unless the basic authorizing statutes were revised. This problem reinforces the need for management and the governing body to be committed to the tenants of quality management and the consequences of empowerment. At the present time some managers or boards will overrule recommendations for discipline, not because of flaws in the disciplinary procedure, but for political reasons. It is unlikely that the political pressures will disappear just because a jurisdiction has implemented quality management.

INDUSTRIAL RELATIONS AND EMPLOYMENT RELATIONSHIP

Industrial relations refers to processes and outcomes involving employment relationships. Frequently the term is used in a narrower sense, for employment relationships involving collective representation of employees in the form of a labour union or employee association, especially in the United States. At the other extreme, industrial relations has been defined by Thomas A. Kochan, in his book *Collective Bargaining and Industrial Relations,* as "all aspects of people at work," but there are clearly some aspects of people at work that entail highly technical subjects (e.g., industrial hygiene, ergonomics) which are not normally regarded as falling within the mainstream of industrial relations study.

As an academic subject area, industrial relations is often defined as an interdisciplinary field of applied study. This conception recognizes that employment relationships entail practical problems and other phenomena that transcend any one traditional discipline (e.g., economics). To fully appreciate the multifaceted nature of many industrial relations issues, one must draw from a variety of perspectives, including economics, psychology, sociology, political science, and law, among others. For example, employee compensation issues may be usefully addressed in terms of economic theory, but psychological theories offer useful insights on employee attitudes toward and reactions to compensation matters. Whether the nature of industrial relations issues is sufficiently unique to justify considering industrial relations a" true discipline" has been controversial, but most scholars appear to favor the interdisciplinary subject view. Nevertheless, John Dunlop, a key figure in industrial relations theory, continues to argue (in a 1998 article in *Advances in Industrial and Labour Relations)* for the advantages of "industrial relations systems theory" over other theoretical disciplines (e.g., economics), and contends that industrial relations is a genuine discipline.

In The *Origins and Evolution of the Field of Industrial Relations in the United States,* Bruce E. Kaufman attributed the popularization of the term "industrial relations" to a Commission on Industrial Relations created by the federal government in 1912. That commission was created to investigate and report on conditions in "industry" that gave rise to labour problems, including conflict between employers and employees (and their organizations) that often erupted in violence and strikes. Thus the term "industrial relations" referred to "relations" between employers and employees in "industry." Better industrial relations were seen as the solution to labour problems.

Although the term "industry" or "industrial" (as in "industrial relations") connotes for many "heavy" industry (e.g., steel mills, auto assembly plants), this connotation is much narrower than the field's conception of industrial relations. At least to most industrial relations scholars, the term "industrial" is used broadly, as in distinguishing industrialized societies from agrarian societies. As noted by Dunlop (in *Industrial Relations Systems)* and his colleagues, industrialization gives rise to employment relationships as we know them today, in which large numbers of people work for and in large part follow the direction of others in exchange for wages or salaries and other compensation. This is in contrast to agrarian societies where the farmer is typically self-employed, directing his or her own labour and obtaining his or her livelihood as the difference between revenues and expenses. Thus industrial relations refers to relations between employers and employees not only in heavy industry but also in retailing, government, financial services, education, and recreational services, for example. In fact, even agricultural production, when organized in a form where an employer relies extensively on the services of hired workers, as is increasingly the case, can be said to fall within the purview of industrial relations.

Similarly, industrial relations is not limited to formal employment relationships, but rather to what one might call "functional employment relationships." There are many instances where workers are technically classified as self-employed" independent contractors," and yet for practical purposes these workers are essentially employees. The construction industry provides many examples of this. Many laws governing employment are limited to formal employment relationships, and independent contractor status is often used by firms as a means of cutting labour costs, possibly by avoiding or evading legal obligations to employees. Related to this, temporary employment services whereby firms contract for workers with another firm (which technically employs the workers, paying their wages and possibly benefits such as health insurance), have grown dramatically in recent years. Many firms have found this a cost-effective alternative to traditional employment arrangements. These two types of arrangements are part of a larger and growing work phenomenon that many refer to in terms of the "contingent workforce." This phenomenon contrasts with traditional employment relationships in which one is employed by the firm that controls the work site as a matter of law as well as in a practical sense, and in which the work relationship is generally assumed to be relatively permanent. Some would include many part-time workers as well as many independent contractors and temporary employees in a definition of the contingent workforce. In any case, conceptions of industrial relations as the study of "all aspects of people at work" clearly do not limit the field to formal or legal definitions of employment.

As noted earlier, in the United States especially, the term industrial relations is sometimes viewed more narrowly as referring solely to relations between employers and employee representation organizations, i.e., labour unions, and related phenomena such as union organizing, collective bargaining (negotiations between employers and unions over work matters), and the effects of unions on employment terms and society. In this view, the importance of industrial relations in the United States has fallen apace with the decline of unions over the past four decades. Since the mid-1950s, when unions represented roughly one-third of employees, U.S. union representation has declined so that today unions represent about one-seventh of employees (13.9 percent in 1998). (This overall unionization rate conceals considerable variation across industries. To illustrate, the unionization rate, according to the U.S. Department of Labour's Bureau of Labour Statistics, is about 10 percent in private sector employment, but close to 38 percent in public sector employment.)

The terms "human resources" and "human resources management" have emerged as preferred labels referring to employment issues in the absence of unions, although these terms are not always sharply distinguished from industrial relations. For some, industrial relations is a field within human resources while for others human resources is a field within industrial relations. Clearly, however, the human resources terms have become more popular and the industrial relations term has become less popular as unions have declined. It would be a mistake to regard these changes as merely semantic. Perhaps at the heart of the substantive matter, in simplified form, is the question of whether employment matters will be determined unilaterally by management (the human resources view) or jointly by employers and employees through negotiations with employee representation organizations. Unilateral management determinations tend to be viewed as the norm in setting employment terms or at least specifying the conditions and limitations of employee influence under the human resources view, and collective bargaining tends to be seen as exceptional and often stemming from management's failure to manage properly its human resources (i.e., unions are seen as a result of management's mistakes). In contrast, industrial relations specialists tend to view collective bargaining (and other forms of joint determination) as a normal and legitimate process, or even a preferable process, for determining the bulk of employment matters. Legislation, such as minimum wage laws or bans on child labour, is also seen as a means to remedy labour problems. Of course, markets, laws, technology, worker attitudes, and social norms present constraints on determining employment matters in any case.

CURRENT STATUS OF THE FIELD

At this time industrial relations remains the preferred term for describing the field among scholars. One indicator of this is that the major professional association among scholars, which also includes many practitioner members, is the Industrial Relations Research Association. Many industrial relations scholars are also active in the Academy of Management's Human Resources Division, in discipline-based professional associations such as the American Economics Association or the American Psychological Association, or in more specialized professional associations (e.g., for dispute resolution specialists).

There has, however, been controversy concerning whether the field has become too closely associated with the narrower conception of industrial relations, i.e., union-management relations, and there have been calls for name changes with the intent of better conveying the broad sense of the field (e.g., "employment relations") or to signal that the field recognizes and wishes to keep in step with trends toward a greater predominance of nonunion employment settings. In the 1980s and 1990s especially, many firms and academic programs tended to play down or even eliminate reference to industrial relations terms, and instead tended to elevate or adopt human resources terms in their job titles, department names, etc. In *The New Look in Wage Policy and Employee Relations,* Audrey Freedman documented many changes in managerial approaches to industrial relations in leading U.S. firms during the late 1970s and early 1980s.

Apart from this trend, the industrial relations field, like many, has associated with it a large number of alternative or closely related terms, including labour relations, collective bargaining, employee relations, and union-management relations. The collective bargaining term may be particularly significant. As noted earlier, collective bargaining, whereby employers negotiate with unions representing employees to establish contracts specifying terms and conditions of employment, holds a central and legitimate place in the view of most industrial relations specialists. In broad conceptions of industrial relations, it is merely one of a number of alternative mechanisms for establishing terms and conditions of employment. Yet to many, collective bargaining is or at least has traditionally been the "heart" of industrial relations in the United States. Thus it is not unusual to find introductory courses and texts in industrial relations referencing collective bargaining in their titles. In a sense, the view this terminology suggests is that union formation, labour law, and certain other matters are essentially preludes to collective bargaining, whereas contract administration (especially grievance procedures and grievance arbitration whereby employee complaints of contract violations are resolved through union-management negotiations or a neutral party's decision in the event negotiations fail), union effects on employment matters, and so on, are consequences of collective bargaining. Yet in much of the world, and increasingly over recent decades in the United States, collective bargaining per se occupies a less central place in industrial relations. In addition, the disciplinary areas that contribute to industrial relations often have their own terms that refer to industrial relations but which also may include additional related subjects within the discipline. These include labour economics, industrial psychology, industrial sociology, labour law, and labour history. Similarly, management scholars often regard human resources management as a field within management that includes industrial relations or labour relations as one of its more specialized areas.

Whether one defines industrial relations broadly or narrowly of course influences which topics one would consider specializations within industrial relations. Under a narrower definition of industrial relations, specialized subjects could include industrial relations theory; labour organizations (unions and employee associations); management of industrial relations; labour and management history; labour and business law; collective bargaining and negotiations; industrial conflict (especially strikes); grievance procedures, arbitration and mediation, and other dispute resolution techniques; worker participation or industrial democracy; the effects of unions on employment terms and on society more broadly; and "comparative" or internationally oriented perspectives on industrial relations. A broader definition of industrial relations would include not only these but also topics that fields such as human resources tend to see as their domain, including training and development, workforce diversity, compensation, selection and staffing, and other employment legislation (laws and regulations directly affecting employment terms, such as laws on pensions, safety, and minimum wages, as opposed to "labour law," which mainly governs relations between employee organizations and employers).

As an academic subject, industrial relations tends to be taught either as a subject within management (what one might call "the business school model") or as a separate subject within an institute or school devoted primarily to industrial relations or industrial relations and human resources. After World War II, when unions were still in ascension and had already established themselves as a major power in the U.S. political economy, many of the more industrialized states established or expanded specialized institutes or schools for industrial relations at their major universities. Typically, a major force for this movement was the state's organized labour movement (unions and employee associations), arguing that just as business schools at public universities served the needs of industry, schools were needed to serve the needs of workers. The political compromises struck in state legislatures generally produced a more neutral institution with an emphasis on studying how to maintain and promote industrial peace as well as training students in industrial relations to be employed by industry, government, and labour organizations. In addition to research and more traditional academic degree programs, these institutions often included a "labour education" or "labour studies" component aimed clearly at the needs of organized workers and their organizations. Examples of these institutions include the Institute of Labour and Industrial Relations at the University of Illinois, the School of Labour and Industrial Relations at Michigan State University, the Industrial Relations Research Institute at the University of Wisconsin, and the New York State School of Industrial and Labour Relations at Cornell University. Similar programs were established or expanded in many other states in the Great Lakes region, the Northeast, and on the West Coast. These programs tend to stress graduate and professional level education, although some offer undergraduate courses and degrees.

With the decline of unions in recent decades and the tremendous expansion of business schools at many universities and colleges, at least two important changes in the research and teaching of industrial relations have occurred. First, the specialized industrial relations institutions have tended to follow industry's call for more emphasis on human resources management and less on union-management relations. Second, business schools have become major centres of industrial relations research and teaching, but more as a result of their sheer size and number than as a result of its emphasis within the business school curriculum. In fact, due to its distinctive values and assumptions industrial relations has often been something of an awkward fit within business schools, which have found human resources management a more comfortable fit. In any case, currently both business schools and specialized schools or institutes in industrial relations are major centres for research and teaching of industrial relations. In addition, some traditional discipline programs (e.g., economics, psychology) are major centres for research and teaching on some aspects of industrial relations.

TRADES UNIONS AND SOCIALISM

The modern proletarian movement has two kinds of antagonists: one, the straightforward but brutal antagonists, propose to suppress and to crush it by force. This kind has already experienced so many defeats, its method has proved itself to be so abortive, that it is losing today, with the thinking and discerning capitalists themselves – at least for the time being – ever more of its credit. All the better does the other kind prosper that says: "Divide and rule," which, since forcible means do not avail, seeks to weaken the proletarian movement by splitting it. These opponents to the rule of the proletariat pose as its friends; they are not brutal but "ethical," and for this reason they are all the more dangerous. They artfully try to represent different proletarian organizations as being antagonistic; they appear as advocates of sections of the proletarian movement, in order to propagate distrust and even hatred against the entire movement. Some of these precious friends of labour avail themselves of national distinctions to incite workingmen against workingmen, others turn religious distinctions to the same account. However, the most intelligent and eminent among their number try to create discord between the trades union and the Social Democratic movement. These people always have in mind the example afforded by England. While on the continent of Europe the Social Democracy pushes ahead irresistibly and victoriously, in spite of special arbitrary legislation and of proscriptions, in spite of June butcheries and of bloody May weeks, the Chartist movement in England came to naught about the time when the trades unions were recovering ground, and so it happened that nowhere does the capitalist class wield today the political power more supreme than in England, the country possessing the most efficient, the most numerous the best organized, as well as the freest and most independent working class in the trades union movement. No wonder that this example should excite the envy of all wide-awake capitalist politicians and national economists on the continent of Europe and that their ardent efforts should be directed towards filling the reigning classes as well as the proletarians with enthusiasm for that English pattern.

It stands to reason that one nation can and should learn from others, as it can thereby save a great deal of costly experience. However, to learn from somebody does not mean simply to initiate that person slavishly, hut to profit by his experience and knowledge so as to make a sensible and free use of them. If there is a trades union to be organized effectively, it is indispensable to consult the English pattern. Of this nobody was earlier convinced than Marx who already in 1847 called attention to the English pattern of trades unions; and if the trades union movement in Germany and in Austria has developed so quickly, this is true, above all, to the "International" and to the Social Democracy, both of them influenced most powerfully by Marx's teachings.

But if we have to determine the relation between trades unionism and Social Democracy, between trade and class organization, between economic and political struggles, in that case we can learn from the English nation only how that relation should *not* be.

Never has this become more evident than just at present, when in consequence of the collapse of the liberal party even the pretence of a political influence on the part of the English working class has disappeared and when English trades unionism is anxiously striving to promote the formation of a new independent workingmen's party, in which endeavour it finds itself, however, most hampered by the instincts it itself has fostered, the instincts of trade egotism and of disregard of all efforts towards a more remote and higher aim. The present stage of the English trades union movement is the least suitable one to make its previously existing relation to politics appear in an ideal light.

It has often been remarked that the trades union movement, where it does not go hand in hand with an independent political movement, i.e., where it is not saturated with socialist thought, acquires somewhat the character of the bygone guilds.

It has also frequently been pointed out that this guild-like character shows itself first of all in that the workingmen organized in trades unions form and constitute, similar to the old-time Journeymen organized in guilds, an aristocracy of labour, which isolates itself from the unorganized workingmen, which raises itself above them, which pushes them down the deeper into the social mire, the quicker it elevates itself. Where, however, the trades union movement is at work in the closest intellectual contact with the political movement of an independent labour party, there the trades unionists come to be the chosen champions of the entire proletariat, there they improve, along with their own condition, that of their class. The increase of duties, resulting herefrom, is compensated by having the economic and political basis of their achievements rendered more solid than that of the achievements of a labour aristocracy.

The more such an aristocracy of labour leaves the unskilled, unprotected, unorganized parts of the proletariat to shift economically for themselves, the more these come to be the breeding centres of scabs who stab organized labour in the back on every occasion and thus paralyse every decided action. On the other hand the workingmen organized in trades unions cannot constitute for themselves alone a political party, but always only one part, and indeed often a powerful one, of such a party. If they leave the unorganized workingmen to their own political resources instead of uniting with them in one political party, then the former must become the tail of a capitalist party that pretends to be friendly to the workingmen, hut which, no matter how it tries to protect the interests of its proletarian voters, can never muster the necessary courage in face of capitalism and is doomed to fail the sooner, the more the proletarian character of its followers clashes with its own capitalist notions – just as is manifested to us by the fate of the Liberal party in England.

Then again, of course, England also shows us how much the success of the Social Democracy stands in need of the foundation afforded by a powerful trades union movement. Though, as the writer of this book has been assured by people that have been Chartists themselves, there was a closer connection between Chartism and trades unionism than modern historians of trades unionism suppose, it is a fact that the time when Chartism flourished was one of depression for trades unions; Chartism had no strong and steady economic organizations to fall back upon, and that explains much of the unsteadiness and precariousness of its development.

Modern English socialism, however, placed itself in its beginnings in pretty strong opposition to the trades union movement; a stand that may be easily explained, considering the former conservative character of the trades unions; but which, nevertheless, was wrong and of no advantage to the English Social Democracy. But in the course of time the trades unionists have lost more and more their antipathies to socialism, and, vice versa, the socialists have ever more been losing their antipathies to trades unionism, so we find at an ever-increasing rate the same people at work in both camps, and therefore we may expect that slowly but surely a relation between the two movements will be established similar to the one that has always existed with us in the labour movement of Austria and Germany.

In view of all this we have not the slightest reason to look for outside patterns regarding the relation between trades injurious effect of splitting and weakening the latter, but it also curtails its chances of development.

We have compared the isolated trades unions to the journeymen's organizations of old, – the guilds. What has become of the latter? They have disappeared along with the system of guilds without the least share on their part in surmounting this system. Their prosperity was linked most intimately with that of the masters of the guilds; the downfall of the latter meant that of the former. The same fate is menacing the isolated trade union; it can only prosper if the capitalist system of production at home continues to progress. Its progress is very closely bound with constant and swift enlargement of the capitalist sphere of power and exploitation. As soon as the industrial capital of a country has once reached the limit of its ability to expand briskly, then the time of decline sets in for the isolated trades unions. Such a decline manifests itself the same as with the journeymen's associations of by-gone times, not in the decrease of their membership, but in that of their ability and desire to struggle. Instead of at the expense of their exploiters they rather try in partnership with them to sustain and to improve their economic condition by monopolistic isolation of their trade and by increased fleecing of the people at large.

Particularly in England, the industrial capital of which has already in many lines reached the limit of rapid expansion; we see signs of such reactionary tendencies, e.g., with its textile workers who not only frequently vote for the conservatives, but who are also reactionary in an economic sense, who rave about bi-metallism and child labour, etc.

In the most striking manner, however, the reactionary tendency of some isolated trades unions of England discloses itself in the trade alliances, which since 1890 have appeared now in one and then in another trade. These alliances are based upon agreements between a trades union and a combine of manufacturers, whereby the manufacturers agree to only employ members of the trade unions and these on their part pledge themselves to only work for the manufacturers belonging to the combine, i.e., only for those manufacturers that sell their products at the higher prices decided upon by the combine. In this way all competition against the combine will be rendered impossible. These trade alliances, which are praised by our bourgeois friends of labour as the commencement of harmony between capital and labour, propose therefore nothing less than to induce the workingmen to share in the scheme of the combines to raise prices and to exploit the public. They are expected to assist the manufacturers in fleecing the community and to receive in return a part of the booty. In this manner it is not any more the capitalist but the community that would become the enemy of the workingman, or rather of the aristocracy of labour, which has turned from an exploited person into an exploiter.

However, the innate incongruities between capital and labour are so great that we know of no trade alliance of any duration. These incongruities are frequently so great as to nip the endeavors towards the realization of a trade alliance in the bud. This is very fortunate for social development, for, could the trade alliances exist and grow, they would inflict incalculable harm. Consider, for example, the consequences, should the scheme to start a trade alliance in the coal-mining industry, as has been attempted, succeed and should the coal miners be turned into accomplices of the policy of the combine, into promoters of a coal famine – a maneuver particularly tempting under the sliding scale of wages. The entire balance of the workingmen would be compelled to declare war not only against the coal barons but as well against the coal miners! And what a prospect, if other orders of workingmen in important lines of industry followed suit; if in place of the struggle between capital and labour, we should witness the struggle between different monopolies in which workingmen in the pay of their organized masters would enter the field against their fellow workingmen!

Any independent labour movement would be impossible, and the labour aristocracy organized in trades unions would be chained most tightly to the capitalist class and forced on by its own interest to help the advancement of capitalist politics at home and abroad.

Of course we will not come to that pass, for the reason already stated, that, where the combines are the strongest there the antagonism against the workingmen is also the greatest; and also for the reason that the bourgeois friends of labour will never succeed in isolating the trades unions from the rest of the proletarian movement, or to keep up such isolation where it now exists. But, in consideration of the present raving about trade alliances, it is not amiss to picture a state in which they should prevail.

Entirely different from these reactionary and futile attempts on the part of isolated unions to improve the economic condition of their members in countries already approaching stagnation of capitalist production, must be the endeavors of such trades unions as go hand in hand with a strong and class-conscious Social Democracy. The more the development of capitalist commodity-production stagnates or free competition is crowded out by combines and trusts, the more a class-conscious labour movement will try not to impart by reactionary experiments a new artificial life to some lines of production; but it will endeavour to further economic development by replacing capitalist production for sale by socialist production for use. When, for instance, the coal miners, where they exclusively rely upon their trades union organization, place their hope upon a trade alliance with the coal barons, they will there, where they support the Social Democracy, strive for an increase of political power of the proletariat for its effective use for workingmen's protective laws, and finally for the expropriation of the mines.

Today already production for the commonwealth in the shape of production for state and community becomes a factor of steadily growing economic importance. Today it is no longer the textile industry but the iron industry upon which the entire economic prosperity of a nation depends. If the latter prospers, new life pulsates through the entire social body; if it stagnates we have general depression. The iron industry, however, is again to a large extent dependent upon state and communal politics; state and street railroads, canalizations, army and navy orders, etc., exert a perceptible influence upon economic conditions. Modern states certainly exert this influence largely in idly wasting the means at hand, especially for militarism; they develop production, they employ the productive powers, but at the same time they permit civilization to be stunted; yes, in some countries like Italy, Russia and Austria militarism leads not only to a waste of products, but also of productive powers, and consequently to a shrinkage of production.

The more capitalism passes over from free competition to monopoly, the greater the number of its industrial branches that have become unable to develop adequately, the more the influence of state and community on the character and extent of production increases, the more necessary it will be for every class to gain influence on state and community, the more fatal will be the isolation of trade unions that prevents the proletariat from depending and promoting its interests effectively, the more indispensable it will be that the trades unionists are inspired with socialist discernment and socialist enthusiasm the more necessary, on the other hand, that the Social Democracy should be able to rely upon a numerous army of organized trades unionists, on which rest the deepest and firmest roots of its power.

The trades unions will not disappear along with the capitalist mode of production like the journeymen's organizations vanished with the guilds. On the contrary, they will constitute the most energetic factors in surmounting the present mode of production and they will be the pillars on which the edifice of the socialist commonwealth will be erected.

THE EMPLOYMENT RELATIONSHIP AND WORKERS' PROTECTION

Context of the Lack of Protection

It has been mentioned above that the Meeting of Experts was held in May 2000. The Meeting highlighted the lack of protection of workers in certain situation in which the legal scope of the employment relationship did not accord with the realities of working relationship. The context in which this lack of protection has arisen varies considerably from one region to another and from one country to another, but in all cases it is linked to significant changes in the structure of employment. Some of these changes are associated with globalization, technological change and transformations in the organisation and functioning of enterprises, often combined with restructuring in a highly competitive environment. In the words of the World Commission on the Social Dimension of Globalization.globalization has set in motion a process of far-reaching change that is affecting everyone. In terms of the degree to which they benefit countries, industries and enterprises, the impact of these changes is very uneven.

Changes in workers. status and mass redundancies, especially in developing countries or those in transition, are frequently related to major financial crises, external debt, structural adjustment programmes and privatization. These realities have been reflected in a drastic reduction in countries. financial capacity and a deterioration in conditions of employment and work. Especially significant has been the growth of the informal economy and undeclared employment in this context.

Associated with these developments, changes in the structure of the workforce have been accentuated by migration from one country to another or from one sector of the economy to another. Other factors include a strong shift to services, greater participation of women, higher skill levels of young people in certain countries and deskilling of workers in others. Changing lifestyles, education levels and expectations also lead to workers demanding more flexibility. The attitudes or workers' and the way in which they cope with finding and keeping a job.

Many enterprises, for their part, have organised their activities so as to utilize labour in increasingly diversified and selective ways, including various kinds of contracts, the decentralization of activities to subcontractors or self-employed workers, or the use of temporary employment agencies. These arrangements are encouraged by rapid developments in technology and new management systems in response to the growing demands of competition. This kind of flexibility has frequently been preceded or accompanied by legislative and institutional reforms to enhance the supply and demand for labour or to promote self-employment with the aim of stimulating job creation.

Repercussions of the Lack of Protection

It goes without saying that the lack of labour protection adversely affects workers and their families. At the same time, however, the absence of workers. rights or guarantees can be counterproductive to the interests of the enterprise itself and have a negative impact on society generally. Moreover, there is some evidence indicating that these changes affect women more than men. Workers in these situations not only lose their rights under labour law, but also have difficulty securing the protection of the competent inspection services or seeking redress through the labour courts. Many countries exclude them from or on the fringe of social security protection. They, compared with those workers recognised as employees, receive less favourable benefits.

Besides employees, employers can also be affected by the lack of labour. It may affect them to the extent that it undermines productivity and distorts competition between enterprises, both at national and sectoral or international level, often to the detriment of those who comply with the law. The lack of legal certainty can also result in judicial decisions reclassifying.self-employed. workers as employees, with considerable unforeseen economic consequences for enterprises. At the same time, the reality of work without any prospect of stability or promotion can ultimately make workers lose their commitment to the enterprise and contribute to an increasing and costly labour turnover.

The lack of training, including training for work in environments where there are inherent risks are another dimension of the lack of labour protection. Enterprises can be reluctant to invest in training workers who will probably not be with them for long. The user enterprise is unlikely to train the workers supplied by another firm, except for very specific purposes. Untrained workers are more vulnerable to accidents in the workplace and can hamper the competitiveness of the enterprise. Furthermore, a lack of investment in training can undermine national competitiveness. In addition, in some sectors which have large numbers of unprotected workers, the negative image can create serious problems of recruitment and retention of workers. We can cite the construction industry as one example.

If there is the lack of labour protection, it has impact on the health and safety of third parties and society in general. Some accidents, such as those caused by heavy vehicles or major accidents in industrial plants, have caused damage to the environment, as well as injuries and fatalities to third parties. Situations of extensive use of subcontracting has shown the link between accident risks and the lack of workers' protection.

The issue is not subcontracting itself but its improper use, which can create or aggravate risks. Lack of protection can also have a considerable financial impact, in terms of unpaid social security contributions and taxes. For example, in the United States, according to Treasury Department estimates, misclassification of dependent workers (employees) as independent workers results in a loss of some US$2.6 billion each year in unpaid contributions to social security, the healthcare system (Medicare) and the federal unemployment insurance scheme, as well as US$1.6 billion in income tax. In brief, protection is necessary. Protection is important not only for the sake of workers and enterprises, but also because there are public goods at stake.

Uncertainty with Regard to the Law

The frequency of disputes about legal nature of a relationship for the provision of labour is increasing. The employment relationship may be objectively ambiguous or disguised. Both situations create uncertainty as to the scope of the law and can nullify its protection.

Workers who are involved in triangular employment relationships face many problems. These problems pose different legal questions. These are workers employed by an enterprise (the provider) who perform work for a third party (the user) to whom their employer provides labour or services. For these employees, their employment status is not in doubt, but they frequently face difficulties in establishing who their employer is, what their rights are and who is responsible for them.

Changes in the legal status of workers, whether real or apparent, seem to be a sign of the times and are commonly observed not only in traditional sectors such as transport (truck drivers, taxi drivers), construction and clothing, but in new areas as well, such as sales staff in department stores, or certain jobs in wholesale distribution or in private security agencies, although there are considerable differences from one country to another and from region to region.

Objectively Ambiguous Employment Relationships

So far a standard employment relationship is concerned, the situation of the workers' is not normally open to doubt. In some cases, however, a worker may have a wide margin of autonomy and this factor alone may give rise to doubt as to his or her employment status. There are situations where the main factors that characterize the employment relationship are not apparent. It is not a case of a deliberate attempt to disguise it, but rather one of genuine doubt as to the existence of an employment relationship. This may occur as a result of the specific, complex form of the relationship between workers and the persons to whom they provide their labour, or the evolution of that relationship over time. Persons who are normally self-employed may find themselves in such situations. Such self-employed persons include electricians, plumbers and computer programmers. These situations may also occur to persons who gradually enter into a permanent arrangement with a single client.

In other cases, especially in work environments affected by major changes, it is possible and sometimes necessary to resort to a range of flexible and dynamic employment arrangements which can be difficult to fit into the traditional framework of the employment relationship. A person may be recruited and work at a distance without fixed hours or days of work, with special payment arrangements and full autonomy as to how to organise the work. Some workers may never even have set foot in the enterprise if, for example, they have been recruited and work via the Internet and are paid through a bank. However, perhaps because they use equipment supplied by the enterprise, follow its instructions and are subject to subtle but firm control, it may be that the enterprise quite naturally considers them as employees. There is still another phenomenon which is challenging the traditional employment framework. This phenomenon is the emergence of e-lancers or electronically connected freelancers.

There are, between the employment relationship and self-employment, economically dependent workers who are formally self-employed but depend on one or a few clients for their income They are not easy to describe, let alone quantify, because of the heterogeneous nature of the situations involved and the lack of a definition or statistical tool.

In cases where the contract is clearly intended to procure the services of a self-employed worker, it is in employers' interest to make sure that they have not misclassified the worker, as they can be held financially liable if the authorities find that the worker is in fact an employee.

Disguised Employment Relationships

There is a kind of employment relationship which is lent an appearance that is different fro the underlying reality, with the intention of nullifying or attenuating the protection afforded by the law or evading tax and social security obligations. Such kind of employment relationship can be regarded as disguised one. It is thus an attempt to conceal or distort the employment relationship, either by cloaking it in another legal guise or by giving it another form. Disguised employment relationships may also involve masking the identity of the employer, when the person designated as an employer is an intermediary, with the intention of releasing the real employer from any involvement in the employment relationship and above all from any responsibility to the workers.

The employment relationship ca most radically be disguised by giving it the appearance of a relationship of a different legal nature, whether civil, commercial, cooperative, family-related or other. Some of the contractual arrangements most frequently used to disguise the employment relationship include a wide variety of civil and commercial contracts which give it the semblance of self-employment.

The employment relationship can be disguised in still another way. This is done through the form in which it is established. While the existence of an employment relationship is not in question, the nature of the employment relationship is intentionally misrepresented so as to deny certain workers. rights and benefits. For the purposes of this report, such contract manipulation amounts to another type of disguised employment relationship, resulting in a lack of protection for the workers concerned. This is the case, for example, of contracts concluded for a fixed term, or for a specific task, but which are then repeatedly renewed, with or without a break. The worker does not acquire the rights and obtain the benefits provided to employees by labour legislation or collective bargaining. This is the most visible effect of this type of contract manipulation.

The trend towards replacing the employment contract with other types of contract in order to evade the protection provided under the Termination of Employment Convention, 1982 (No. 158), was noted by the ILO Committee of Experts on the Application of Conventions and Recommendations in 1995.

"Triangular" Employment Relationships

It is when employees of a provider work for another person (the user) that triangular employment relationships occur. It has also been mentioned above. A wide variety of contracts can be used to formalize an agreement for the provision of work. Such contracts can have beneficial effects for the provider's employees in terms of employment opportunities, experience and professional challenges. From a legal standpoint, however, such contracts may present a technical difficulty as the employees concerned may find themselves interacting with two (or more) interlocutors, each of whom assumes certain functions of a traditional employer.

It goes without saying that there are cases also of objectively ambiguous or disguised 'triangular' employment relationships. A triangular employment relationship normally presupposes a civil or commercial contract between a user and a provider. It is possible, however, that no such contract exists and that the provider is not a proper enterprise, but an intermediary of the supposed user, intended to conceal the user's identity as the real employer.

Though the phenomenon of triangular employment relationships is obviously now on the increase, it has always been there. The national studies identified a growing tendency among enterprises in many countries to operate through other enterprises or with their collaboration. In these situations, workers provided by different enterprises can be found working on the user's own premises or outside, even in a different country. There may be various forms of triangular employment relationships. The best known is the use of contractors and private employment agencies. Another very common arrangement is franchising. In this case, an enterprise allows another enterprise or a person to use its trademark or product, in principle on an independent basis. However, the franchisee has financial obligations towards the franchiser, which normally exercises control over the franchised business, including its staff.

In an employment relationship where workers deal with just one person, there is usually no doubt about the identity of the employer. This person is the one who hires the worker or who performs the normal functions of an employer: assigning tasks, providing the means to perform them, giving instructions and supervising their performance, paying wages, assuming risks, making profits and terminating the employment relationship. The situation may be different, however, in a triangular employment relationship, when these roles are assumed separately or jointly by more than one person and any one or a number of them may be perceived as the employer, in which case the employee may reasonably wonder: who is in fact my employer?

For example, the workers may not have the knowledge of the exact authority from whom they can claim payment of remuneration or compensation for and accident at work, and whether they can file a claim again the user when the direct employer disappears or becomes insolvent. Doubt as to the identity of the employer, or the involvement of the user in the employment relationship, leads to the following key questions in the case of triangular relationships: what are the worker's rights are they the rights agreed by the employee with his or her employer (the provider), or those of the employees employed by the user, or a combination of the two? It is often the case that workers are unaware of whose being responsible for their rights. The logical answer, which is normally consistent with the law, is that employers are primarily responsible for the rights of their employees, whether they are a contractor, an employment agency, a cooperative or any other employing enterprise or entity. However, the role of the user can be crucial with respect to ensuring respect of these rights (such as limits on working hours, rest breaks, paid leave, etc.). There are laws which in some circumstances also assign a measure of responsibility to the user, as the person who benefits directly from the labour of the worker and who often appears to be an employer or someone similar to an employer.

Depending on the circumstances and national law, the employer (or provider) and the user may bear joint and several liability, so that the worker can claim against both or either of them without distinction. In other circumstances, the user bears subsidiary liability, in the sense that a claim may only be brought against the user in the event of non-compliance by the provider. This subject is also dealt with by a number of ILO instruments.

Difficult legal issues arise when determining the identity of the employer and other possible parties to triangular employment relationships, of the workers' right and of the persons responsible for ensuring those rights. However, the major challenge lies in ensuring that employees in such a relationship enjoy the same level of protection traditionally provided by the law for employees in a bilateral employment relationship, without impeding legitimate private and public business initiatives. It can summarily be said that employees, in cases of triangular employment relationships, are frequently confronted with various interlocutors. In such circumstances, it is essential that such employees know who the employer is, what their rights are and who is responsible for them. It is equally important to determine the position of the user with respect to the employees of the provider enterprise. A balanced and constructive approach to the question should take into account the legal difficulties involved, and the legitimate interests concerned.

It is necessary to take measures to close this gap or growing divergence between the law and the reality of the employment relationship. The objective should be to update and clarify the law governing the employment relationship so as to facilitate recognition of the existence of an employment relationship, and deter attempts to disguise it. Given the proliferation of objectively ambiguous and disguised situations and the growth of triangular relationships, member States, with the involvement of the social partners, could examine their legislation so as to identify any deficits in the light of their own specific problems and comparative law. This would enable them to determine the nature and extent of the measures needed. Enabling the laws on the employment relationship to be regularly updated as part of an ongoing and dynamic process is the outcome of this exercise.

The legal origins hypothesis and its application to labour law

The legal origins theory, which was initially advanced by Rafael La Porta, Florencio Lopez-de-Silanes, Andrei Shleifer and Robert Vishny (henceforth "LLSV"), maintains that the common or civil law origin of a given country's legal system is a major factor in its approach to regulating the economy.

As Juan Botero *et al.* put it, "countries in different legal traditions utilize different institutional technologies for social control of business... common law countries tend to rely more on markets and contracts, and civil law (and socialist) countries on regulation (and state ownership)". Since most countries in the world inherited their legal systems from one of a small number of parent countries by virtue of colonization, military conquest or some other mode of legal transplantation, legal origin operates as an exogenous factor, to some degree independently of the political and economic context of each system.

Its influence shows in the tendency of systems to adopt rules of a particular type and, eventually, in economic outcomes. Complementarity across legal and economic institutions ensures that systems remain on separate paths: at national level, "path dependence in the legal and regulatory styles emerges as an efficient adaptation to the previously transplanted legal infrastructure".

The empirical basis for the legal origins claim is a series of studies based on the construction of multi-country data sets which provide a measure of the degree of regulation in particular areas of economic activity. These studies suggest that common law systems provide superior protection to shareholder and creditor rights than do civil law systems.

These different levels of regulation are linked, in turn, to differences in the size of financial markets (shareholder protection) and in the share of private credit in the economy (creditor protection). In addition, common law systems are shown to impose fewer barriers to entry into product markets, to rely on less "formalized" dispute-resolution procedures, and to rely to a greater degree on private contract and litigation as mechanisms of enforcement, than their civil law counterparts.

Botero *et al.* extend this approach to labour law. They analyse labour regulation in three areas: employment protection law, the law governing employee representation and industrial action, and the law of social security. The method adopted is to code legal rules, for the most part, with values in a range from 0 to 1, with 0 indicating no protection and 1, maximum protection for the interests of the employee.

Altogether over 100 variables are contained in their index, with the social security index accounting for somewhat more than a third of these. The analysis broadly confirms the findings of the earlier LLSV studies on shareholder rights and creditor rights: legal origin matters, in the sense that common law countries, as a whole, regulate the employment relationship less than civil law countries.

A similar result is found for the industrial relations law index, though the effect of legal origin is not as strong here. Nordic-origin and French-origin systems of social security are found to be more generous than those of the common law, but this is not the case with German-origin systems. In terms of outcomes, Botero *et al.* find that a higher level of regulation on their index correlates with higher levels of youth unemployment, lower rates of male labour force participation, and a larger informal economy. However, these effects are confined to systems with above average per capita incomes. This finding is interpreted as evidence that the more strongly labour laws are enforced, the more inefficiencies they produce.

Explanations for the legal origins effect: The authors of the principal legal origins papers have presented their findings as empirical discoveries, without attempting to offer a wider theoretical framework into which they could be fitted. It was left to other authors, most notably Thorsten Beck and Ross Levine, to offer, in a series of papers, two broad sets of explanations. The first of these, known as the "adaptability channel", holds that the common law, being mostly the product of case law, evolves incrementally to meet the needs of the economy as they change over time. The civil law, it is argued, is more "rigid" as change can only occur in the event of a fundamental revision of the codes and other statutory texts which constitute the principal sources of the law; in civil law jurisdictions, case law does not constitute a formal source of legal rules as it does in the common law.

The second explanation is based on the so-called "political channel", which holds that common law systems are more effective than their civil law counterparts in reducing opportunities for wasteful rent-seeking. As legislation plays a more important role in the civil law than in the common law, regulatory capture is less likely in civil law systems.

A variant of this argument claims that the tradition of judicial independence in the English common law has given rise to rules which protect individual property rights against expropriation by the State. The two sets of claims can be seen as complementary, as in the work of F.A. Hayek. The problem with these explanations is not that adaptability (or efficiency) and politics do not matter - they clearly do. The issue is with the particular assumptions made about their links to legal origin.

The supposed links depend on questionable stylized facts about the common law and civil law. They certainly go against the grain of recent comparative legal scholarship, which has arrived at a more nuanced understanding of the differences between systems than that of the works of René David and other comparatists of the 1960s, who popularized the idea of legal families.

Ugo Mattei, for example, has argued that the idea that common law judges have discretion to adapt rules to changing economic circumstances, while civil law judges are bound to apply, through rigid deductive logic, the strict legal text of the code, is "dramatically misleading, being based on a superficial and outdated image of the differences between the common law and the civil law".

The drafters of the French civil code certainly sought to limit doctrine of judicial precedent, but "neither before nor after the French codification could any of the civil law systems be fairly characterized as the one described by the French post-revolutionary scholars". Arguments about whether judicial decisions are a formal "source" of law in civilian systems aside, Basil Markesinis's work has established beyond doubt the prominent role of judicial decision-making in the civil law world.

Gunther Teubner and Katharina Pistor have highlighted the extent to which doctrines that are regarded as being at the core of the distinctive civil law approach to economic regulation, such as the application of the concept of good faith to commercial contracts, were in fact judicial innovations.

If we look beyond the stylized facts used by legal origins adherents, it is immediately apparent that the vast majority of rules in the areas of company law and labour law are statutory in origin in the common law and civil law alike.

The growth of companies legislation in the common law world since the middle decades of the twentieth century - a trend which, far from abating, shows recent signs of intensifying with the adoption of the huge Companies Act, 2006, in the United Kingdom - has led commentators such as Paul Davies to argue that common law judges now have less discretion to develop the law than their civil law counterparts.

Whereas common law judges have limited room for manoeuvre in interpreting statutes, civil law judges have inherent powers to develop the law using "general clauses", such as good faith, which mitigate the apparent rigidity of the codes.

This is not to deny that there are significant differences in regulatory style between the common law and civil law. There is a case for saying that civil law systems today give greater scope to mandatory rules in the area of economic regulation than does the common law.

Even in the area of commercial contract law, governing relations between economic entities where no issues of consumer or employee protection arise, judges in France and Germany retain the power to control unfair or "abusive" contract terms, contrary to the formal emphasis on freedom of contract in such relationships in the English and American common law.

From a common law point of view, the civil law approach constitutes a formal constraint on the contractual autonomy of the parties. From the civil law perspective, however, the mandatory rules of law which give expression to good faith and related notions in commercial dealings are viewed as one of the foundations of the contractual relationship, which cannot operate in isolation from these principles.

Similarly, the concept of "capacity", which, in the common law, is seen as explaining a few isolated cases where the power to make binding agreements is denied (to the young, for example, or to the very ill), is seen, in civil law systems, as concerned with establishing the legal preconditions for the right to enter into enforceable contracts. Under civil law, the contract is not a relationship regulated by law, but one constituted by it.

It is an open question how far such differences of "legal culture", expressed at the level of juridical discourse, result in substantively different rules across legal systems. A prominent view in contemporary comparative legal scholarship, expressed by Konrad Zweigert and Hein Kotz, is that "different legal systems give the same or very similar solutions, even as to detail, to the same problems of life, despite the great differences in their historical development, conceptual structure, and style of operation".

As a result, they suggest, "we find that as a general rule developed nations answer the needs of legal business in the same or in a very similar way". The concept of "functional equivalents", which they developed to explain how formal diversity of legal rules masks a deeper functional continuity, is an indispensable tool of comparative legal analysis, and arguably of comparative analysis more generally.

But functional continuity need not imply that rules are precisely equivalent in their effects. One illustration of this relates to a basic feature of contemporary labour law systems, namely definition of the scope of the "employment relationship" as the object of mandatory and other rules of labour legislation.

The common law approach has long been to stress that the existence of the employment relationship is a matter for the contracting parties, who are free to contract on whatever terms they wish; only if the agreement they make qualifies as an employment contract will they be subject to the compulsory provisions of legislation. In 1988, an English Court of Appeal judge commented that a person "is without question free under the law of contract to carry out certain work for another without entering into a contract of service. Public policy has nothing to say either way".

This view can be contrasted with that of the Labour Chamber of the French Court of Cassation which, in 2000, enunciated this somewhat different statement of principle: "the existence of an employment relationship does not depend on the will of the parties however they have expressed it, nor on the label which they give their agreement, but on the factual matrix within which the relevant labour services are carried out".

The Criminal Chamber of the Court had previously ruled in 1985, in a case concerning workers who had been given the title of "artisans" by their employer under agreements purporting to be "sub-contracts", that the will of the parties "is insufficient to remove from workers the social status that necessarily attaches to them by virtue of the manner in which they carry out their tasks".

In Germany, the Bundesarbeitsgericht, in a decision of 1967, took a similar view, arguing that as "German labour law is mandatory" so is the application of employee status, so that "only in borderline cases can account be taken of how the parties have labelled a particular contract".

None of these statements can be taken completely at face value, and the three systems are closer together than might be supposed when considering these decisions in isolation: in Britain, courts will disregard a "label" or description of the contract which does not accord with the practice of employment, while French and German courts will take into account the view of the parties in borderline cases.

But it is also true that the common law approach has led to the use of standard contract terms to avoid the terms of protective statutes, to a far greater extent than is possible in France and Germany, where the legal definition of the employment relationship is subject to stricter rules.

It is possible to identify here the role of deeply ingrained assumptions about the role of the law in regulating economic relationships which have the potential to shape the interpretation and, in the final analysis, the social and economic effects of substantive rules of law.

If important differences between common law and civil law approaches exist both in terms of the law-making process, and at the more intangible level of regulatory culture and "legal style", they could potentially hamper the flow of ideas from one system to another. Conversely, they could facilitate the exchange of legal models within the main legal families, as in the case of judicial borrowings, which are well known in the common law world, or of cross-national legal commissions such as those that have long operated in the Nordic systems. To that extent, a legal origins effect could be expected to arise from the division of systems into different legal families. However, the strength of such an effect would differ from one context to another, in particular when set against opposing tendencies for the convergence of rules deriving from the forces of cross-national harmonization, regulatory competition and the activities of transnational legal services and accounting firms.

Account must also be taken of the extent to which legal rules, their foreign origin notwithstanding, are "endogenized" by local economic and political contexts. This is a theme common both to the modern comparative legal doctrine of functional analysis and to the varieties-of-capitalism approach of the contemporary political science literature.

The latter identifies a voluntaristic approach to labour law regulation in "liberal market" systems, which is complementary to institutions' support of dispersed share ownership and the prioritization of financial interests in corporate governance. By contrast, the integration of worker interests into the structure of the firm through co-determination, in its various forms, can be seen to be complementary to patterns of concentrated share ownership and a "stakeholder" orientation of company law in "coordinated market" systems.

Differences in regulatory style have played a role in institutionalizing these lock-in effects, making them more difficult or costly to shift at national level, and creating the conditions for the persistence of diversity.

According to this argument, a critical issue is the timing of the major legal innovations induced by nineteenth century industrialization - especially the adoption of private law codes on the mainland of Europe and equivalent moves towards legal modernization in Britain. Britain's early industrialization meant that the modern business enterprise began to emerge before the legal transition from late-medieval or early-modern forms of regulation had been completed. In France and most of the rest of Western Europe, by contrast, private law codes were introduced decades before largescale industrialization. This had profound implications for both legal and economic development. In Britain, the characteristic legal forms of the business enterprise - the contract of employment, in labour law, and the company limited by share capital, in company law - had not fully developed, outside certain areas of the economy, when industrialization got under way.

On the Continent, they were already in place and able to support the emergence of large-scale industrial enterprise. One consequence of Britain's early industrialization was the persistence into the final decades of the nineteenth century of the quasipenal master-servant model, which not only delayed the appearance of the contract of employment as a juridical concept, but indeed helped institutionalize the conception of the enterprise as the employer's unencumbered property.

On the Continent, penal legislation governing work relations gave way more quickly to the concept of juridical equality between worker and employer which had been embodied in the codes. In French labour law, the employer's powers of control were subsequently mediated by the development of mandatory social legislation {ordre public social), while in Germany a similar mediating role was played by mutual contractual duties of trust and loyalty.

The timing and nature of industrialization in different systems are arguably much more powerful forces shaping present-day diversity than legal origin, though the latter may be one of the "carriers of history" preserving and perpetuating diversity across systems. Historical contingency, rather than economic efficiency, played a major role in determining which legal models were transplanted and to what effect. Through colonization, developing countries received legal forms from the relevant parent systems.

Legal origins theorists assume that common law systems received from Britain an approach to lawmaking and legislative drafting, and a particular view of the importance of the autonomy of the contracting parties, which differed from the inheritance of systems influenced by the traditions of continental Europe. This view is assumed, rather than demonstrated, in the legal origins literature.

There is, however, a substantial body of evidence concerning the diffusion of a particular legal model of work relations associated with British colonization. What British colonies received in the area of work relations was a modified form of the master-servant model. The persistence of the master-servant model in Britain into the late nineteenth century - itself the contingent result of Britain's early industrialization - led to its early adoption in British colonies in North America, the West Indies, Africa, India and Australia.

In some cases master-servant laws were still being enacted as late as the 1930s. Only at this late stage did the Colonial Office in London begin to ameliorate the effects of the laws - a move often resisted by local employers. Prosecution rates were high and penal sanctions were widely relied on, with their use increasing in the course of the nineteenth century. In Britain, master-servant laws were used to stabilize labour supply, reduce the bargaining power of workers and shore up managerial prerogative in the mainly small-scale manufacturing enterprises characteristic of its industrial structure; in the colonies, the same laws were used to assist in the dispossession and separation from the land of indigenous populations and to maintain the supply of cheap labour which was essential to plantation and mining-based economies.

The influence of this form of regulation only waned with the growing influence of ILO Conventions, decolonization and democratization in the course of the twentieth century. What this historical-institutional approach suggests is that legal origin works through an "institutional channel" which tends to preserve certain cross national differences.

The common law is no more disposed to the production of efficient rules than the civil law; rather, legal rules in each jurisdiction are more or less adaptive to local economic conditions, but without adaptativeness implying optimality. The force of legal origin in the face of pressures for convergence - such as regulatory competition or harmonization through standard setting - depends on context.

This is a "weak" legal origins effect, in contrast to the strongly functionalist one identified by the predominant theories of the "adaptability" and "political" channels. The degree to which such an effect has actually operated to influence the path of economic development across systems cannot be assumed a priori but is a matter for empirical analysis, which needs to focus on particular cases if the mechanisms of diffusion are to be properly understood.

We now take a closer look at the empirical foundations of the legal origins approach.

4

Value in Organizational Psychology

INTRODUCTION

Organizational Psychology is a subject which applies the principles of psychology into one of the most important areas of people's life-work. Specifically, we work with the human aspects of the workplace and aim at improving people's efficiency, and hence organizational effectiveness, through our knowledge about human functioning. There exist a group of professionals who share a similar aim and are working closely with us, the human resource professionals. Despite the close relationship with HR professionals, Organizational Psychologists are distinctive professionals. Unfortunately, there is always some confusion among the general public that people just cannot tell who is who. More importantly, even some HR professionals do not know what we are doing and what can we offer them.

When we tell them we are Psychologists, a frequent reply is "but we don't have any mental problems"! As Organizational Psychologists, we work with a wide range of domains that are related to people's everyday work life. We design work activities, schedules and workplaces; we design reward principles that are based on human motivation theories; we develop training principles and train the trainers; we develop selection procedures and tools; we formulate performance appraisal systems; and we advise on organizational development issues as well as career development decisions. As you may recognise, our work reaches every working individual on the planet and our working field is very closely related with the work of HR professionals.

VALUE OF PSYCHOLOGY OF MANAGEMENT

Third, we must consider the value of the study of the psychology of management. This question, like the one that precedes it, is answered by

Scientific Management. It has demonstrated that the emphasis in successful management lies on the *man*, not on the *work*; that efficiency is best secured by placing the emphasis on the man, and modifying the equipment, materials and methods to make the most of the man. It has, further, recognized that the man's mind is a controlling factor in his efficiency, and has, by teaching, enabled the man to make the most of his powers. In order to understand this teaching element that is such a large part of management, a knowledge of psychology is imperative; and this study of psychology, as it applies to the work of the manager or the managed, is exactly what the "psychology of management" is.

Five Indications of This Value

In order to realize the importance of the psychology of management it is necessary to consider the following five points:—

1. Management is a life study of every man who works with other men. He must either manage, or be managed, or both; in any case, he can never work to best advantage until he understands both the psychological and managerial laws by which he governs or is governed.
2. A knowledge of the underlying laws of management is the most important asset that one can carry with him into his life work, even though he will never manage any but himself. It is useful, practical, commercially valuable.
3. This knowledge is to be had *now*. The men who have it are ready and glad to impart it to all who are interested and who will pass it on. The text books are at hand now. The opportunities for practical experience in Scientific Management will meet all demands as fast as they are made.
4. The psychology of, that is, the mind's place in management is only one part, element or variable of management; one of numerous, almost numberless, variables.
5. It is a division well fitted to occupy the attention of the beginner, as well as the more experienced, because it is a most excellent place to start the study of management. A careful study of the relations of psychology to management should develop in the student a method of attack in learning his selected life work that should help him to grasp quickly the orderly array of facts that the other variables, as treated by the great managers, bring to him.

Purpose of This Book

It is scarcely necessary to mention that this book can hope to do little more than arouse an interest in the subject and point the way to the detailed books where such an interest can be more deeply aroused and more fully satisfied.

It is not the purpose of this book to give an exhaustive treatment of psychology. Neither is it possible in this book to attempt to give a detailed account of management in general, or of the Taylor plan of "Scientific Management" so-called, in particular.

All of the literature on the subject has been carefully studied and reviewed for the purpose of writing this book, — not only what is in print, but considerable that is as yet in manuscript. No statement has been made that is not along the line of the accepted thought and standardized practice of the authorities. The foot notes have been prepared with great care. By reading the references there given one can verify statements in the text, and can also, if he desires, inform himself at length on any branch of the subject that especially interests him.

This book aims not so much to instruct as to arouse an interest in its subject, and to point the way whence instruction comes. If it can serve as an introduction to psychology and to management, can suggest the relation of these two fields of inquiries and can ultimately enrol its readers as investigators in a resultant great field of inquiry, it will have accomplished its aim.

DEFINITION OF MANAGEMENT

To discuss this subject more in detail —

First: What is "Management"?

"Management," as defined by the Century Dictionary, is "the art of managing by direction or regulation."

Successful management of the old type was an art based on no measurement. Scientific Management is an art based upon a science, — upon laws deducted from measurement. Management continues to be what it has always been, — the *art* of directing activity.

Change in the Accepted Meaning

"Management," until recent years, and the emphasis placed on Scientific Management was undoubtedly associated, in the average mind, with the *managing* part of the organization only, neglecting that vital part — the best interests of the managed, almost entirely. Since we have come to realize that management signifies the relationship between the managing and the managed in doing work, a new realization of its importance has come about. Inadequacy of the Terms Used

It is unfortunate that the English language is so poor in synonyms in this field that the same word must have two such different and conflicting meanings, for, though the new definition of management be accepted, the "Fringe" of associations that belong to the old are apt to remain. The thoughts of "knack, aptitude, tact, adroitness," — not to speak of the less desirable "Brute Force," "shrewdness, subtlety, cunning, artifice, deceit, duplicity," of the older idea of management remain in the background of the mind and make it difficult, even when one is convinced that management is a science, to think and act as if it were.

It must be noticed and constantly remembered that one of the greatest difficulties to overcome in studying management and its development is the meaning of the terms used. It is most unfortunate that the new ideas have been forced to content themselves with old forms as best they may.

Psychological Interest of the Terms

Psychology could ask no more interesting subject than a study of the mental processes that lie back of many of these terms. It is most unfortunate for the obtaining of clearness, that new terms were not invented for the new ideas. There is, however, an excellent reason for using the old terms. By their use it is emphasized that the new thought is a logical outgrowth of the old, and experience has proved that this close relationship to established ideas is a powerful argument for the new science; but such terms as "task," "foreman," "speed boss," "piece-rate" and "bonus," as used in the science of management, suffer from misunderstanding caused by old and now false associations. Furthermore, in order to compare old and new interpretations of the ideas of management, the older terms of management should have their traditional meanings only. The two sets of meanings are a source of endless confusion, unwarranted prejudice, and worse. This is well recognized by the authorities on Management.

CLASSICAL ORGANIZATION THEORY

Classical organization theory evolved during the first half of this century. It represents the merger of scientific management, bureaucratic theory, and administrative theory. Frederick Taylor (1917) developed scientific management theory (often called "Taylorism") at the beginning of this century. His theory had four basic principles: 1) find the one "best way" to perform each task, 2) carefully match each worker to each task, 3) closely supervise workers, and use reward and punishment as motivators, and 4) the task of management is planning and control.

Initially, Taylor was very successful at improving production. His methods involved getting the best equipment and people, and then carefully scrutinizing each component of the production process. By analyzing each task individually, Taylor was able to find the right combinations of factors that yielded large increases in production.

While Taylor's *scientific management theory* proved successful in the simple industrialized companies at the turn of the century, it has not faired well in modern companies. The philosophy of "production first, people second" has left a legacy of declining production and quality, dissatisfaction with work, loss of pride in workmanship, and a near complete loss of organizational pride.

Max Weber (1947) expanded on Taylor's theories, and stressed the need to reduce diversity and ambiguity in organizations. The focus was on establishing clear lines of authority and control. Weber's *bureaucratic theory* emphasized the need for a hierarchical structure of power. It recognized the importance of division of labor and specialization. A formal set of rules was bound into the hierarchy structure to insure stability and uniformity. Weber also put forth the notion that organizational behaviour is a network of human interactions, where all behaviour could be understood by looking at cause and effect.

Administrative theory (i.e., principles of management) was formalized in the 1930's by Mooney and Reiley (1931). The emphasis was on establishing a universal set of management principles that could be applied to all organizations.

Classical management theory was rigid and mechanistic. The shortcomings of classical organization theory quickly became apparent. Its major deficiency was that it attempted to explain peoples' motivation to work strictly as a function of economic reward.

Neoclassical Organization Theory

The human relations movement evolved as a reaction to the tough, authoritarian structure of classical theory. It addressed many of the problems inherent in classical theory. The most serious objections to classical theory are that it created overconformity and rigidity, thus squelching creativity, individual growth, and motivation. Neoclassical theory displayed genuine concern for human needs.

One of the first experiments that challenged the classical view was conducted by Mayo and Roethlisberger in the late 1920's at the Western Electric plant in Hawthorne, Illinois (Mayo, 1933). While manipulating conditions in the work environment (e.g., intensity of lighting), they found that any change had a positive impact on productivity. The act of paying attention to employees in a friendly and nonthreatening way was sufficient by itself to increase output. Uris (1986) referred to this as the "wart" theory of productivity. Nearly any treatment can make a wart go away—nearly anything will improve productivity. "The implication is plain: intelligent action often delivers results".

The Hawthorne experiment is quite disturbing because it cast doubts on our ability to evaluate the efficacy of new management theories. An organization might continually involve itself in the latest management fads to produce a continuous string of Hawthorne effects. "The result is usually a lot of wheel spinning and cynicism". Pascale believes that the Hawthorne effect is often misinterpreted. It is a "parable about researchers (and managers) manipulating and 'playing tricks' on employees." Erroneous conclusions are drawn because it represents a controlling and manipulative attitude toward workers.

Writing in 1939, Barnard (1968) proposed one of the first modern theories of organization by defining organization as a system of consciously coordinated activities. He stressed in role of the executive in creating an atmosphere where there is coherence of values and purpose. Organizational success was linked to the ability of a leader to create a cohesive environment. He proposed that a manager's authority is derived from subordinates' acceptance, instead of the hierarchical power structure of the organization. Barnard's theory contains elements of both classical and neoclassical approaches. Since there is no consensus among scholars, it might be most appropriate to think of Barnard as a transition theorist.

Simon (1945) made an important contribution to the study of organizations when he proposed a model of "limited rationality" to explain the Hawthorne experiments. The theory stated that workers could respond unpredictably to managerial attention.

The most important aspect of Simon's work was the rigorous application of the scientific method. Reductionism, quantification, and deductive logic were legitimized as the methods of studying organizations.

Taylor, Weber, Barnard, Mayo, Roethlisberger, and Simon shared the belief that the goal of management was to maintain equilibrium. The emphasis was on being able to control and manipulate workers and their environment.

Contingency Theory

Classical and neoclassical theorists viewed conflict as something to be avoided because it interfered with equilibrium. Contingency theorists view conflict as inescapable, but manageable.

Chandler (1962) studied four large United States corporations and proposed that an organization would naturally evolve to meet the needs of its strategy — that form follows function. Implicit in Chandler's ideas was that organizations would act in a rational, sequential, and linear manner to adapt to changes in the environment. Effectiveness was a function of management's ability to adapt to environmental changes.

Lawrence and Lorsch (1969) also studied how organizations adjusted to fit their environment. In highly volatile industries, they noted the importance of giving managers at all levels the authority to make decisions over their domain. Managers would be free to make decisions contingent on the current situation.

Systems Theory

Systems theory was originally proposed by Hungarian biologist Ludwig von Bertalanffy in 1928, although it has not been applied to organizations until recently. The foundation of systems theory is that all the components of an organization are interrelated, and that changing one variable might impact many others. Organizations are viewed as open systems, continually interacting with their environment. They are in a state of dynamic equilibrium as they adapt to environmental changes. Senge (1990) describes systems thinking as: understanding how our actions shape our reality. If I believe that my current state was created by somebody else, or by forces outside my control, why should I hold a vision? The central premise behind holding a vision is that somehow I can shape my future, Systems thinking helps us see how our own actions have shaped our current reality, thereby giving us confidence that we can create a different reality in the future.

A central theme of systems theory is that nonlinear relationships might exist between variables. Small changes in one variable can cause huge changes in another, and large changes in a variable might have only a nominal effect on another. The concept of nonlinearity adds enormous complexity to our understanding of organizations. In fact, one of the most salient argument against systems theory is that the complexity introduced by nonlinearity makes it difficult or impossible to fully understand the relationships between variables.

Organizational Structure

Until recently, nearly all organizations followed Weber's concept of bureaucratic structures. The increased complexity of multinational organizations created the necessity of a new structure that Drucker called (1974) "federal decentralization". In federal decentralization, a company is organized so that there are a number of independent units operating simultaneously. "Each unit has its own management which, in effect, runs its own autonomous business." This structure has resulted in large conglomerates which have diversified into many different fields in order to minimize risk.

The project management organizational structure has been used effectively in highly dynamic and technological environments. The project manager becomes the focal point for information and activities related to a specific project. The goal is to provide effective integration of an organization's resources towards the completion of a specific project. Impementing a project management approach often involves dramatic changes in the relationships of authority and responsibility.

The matrix organizational structure evolved from the project management form (Kolodny, 1979). It represents a compromise between the traditional bureuacratic approach and the autonomous project management approach. A matrix organization has permanently established departments that provide integration for project management. The matrix form is superimposed on the hierarchical structure, resulting in dual authority and responsibilities. Permanent functionality departments allocate resources to be shared among departments and managers.

Systems theory views organizational structure as the "established pattern of relationships among the parts of the organization". Of particular importance are the patterns in relationships and duties. These include themes of 1) integration (the way activities are coordinated), 2) differentiation (the way tasks are divided), 3) the structure of the hierarchical relationships (authority systems), and 4) the formalized policies, procedures, and controls that guide the organization (administrative systems).

The relationship between the environment and organizational structure is especially important. Organizations are open systems and depend on their environment for support. Generally, more complex environments lead to greater differentiation. The trend in organizations is currently away from stable (mechanistic) structures to more adaptive (organic) structures. The advantage is that organizations become more dynamic and flexible. The disadvantage is that integration and coordination of activities require more time and effort.

The relationship between an organization and its environment is characterized by a two-way flow of information and energy. Most organizations attempt to influence their environment. Advertising campaigns and lobbying efforts are two examples. Some theorists believe that "... environments are largely invented by organizations themselves. Organizations select their environments from ranges of alternatives, then they subjectively perceive the environments they inhabit". Strategic decisions regarding product lines and distribution channels contribute to the selection of the organizational structure and the environment.

It is a commonly held tenant that people are less satisfied with their work in highly structured organizations. Many research studies have been conducted to examine the relationship between organizational structure and employee behaviour (e.g., satisfaction, performance, and turnover). However, the results of these studies are contradictory. Structural deficiencies can result in low motivation and morale, decisions lacking in timeliness or quality, lack of coordination and conflict, inefficient use of resources, and an inability to respond effectively to changes in the environment.

One enduring and controversial debate about organizational structure is whether or not there is a maximum desirable size for an organization, after which there will be declining effectiveness. Does an organization become increasingly dysfunctional as it exceeds its "ideal" size? Several researchers have hypothesized that organizational growth is beneficial only up to a point.

Most researchers support a curvilinear growth theory. Pfeffer and Salancik (1978) found that profitability increases with size and then tapers off. Warwick (1975) reported that the growth in the U.S. State Department resulted in decreased flexibility and responsiveness, even though specific steps had been taken to abate these problems. There are several theories to explain these findings. The most common explanation is based on the fact that an organization's size is usually positively correlated with age. Older (i.e., larger) organizations have become more rigid in their ways and they are less able to adapt to change. Another popular theory is that in larger organizations, workers' jobs become more specialized. The lack of variety creates a less motivating environment. Other theories have proposed that excessive size creates crippling coordination problems.

Organizational Birth and Growth

Clearly, one of the most dominant themes in the literature has been to define organizations from the perspective of their position on a growth curve. Cameron and Whetten (1983) reviewed thirty life-cycle models from the organizational development literature. They summarized the studies into an aggregate model containing four stages. The first stage is "entrepreneurial", characterized by early innovation, niche formation and high creativity. This is followed by a stage of "collectivity", where there is high cohesion and commitment among the members. The next stage is one of "formalization and control", where the goals are stability and institutionalization. The last stage is one of "elaboration", characterized by domain expansion and decentralization. The striking feature of these life-cycle models is that they did not include any notion of organizational decline. They covered birth, growth, and maturity, but none included decline or death. The classic S-curve typifies these life-cycle models. Whetten (1987) points out that these theories are a reflection of the 1960s and 1970s, two highly growth oriented decades.

Land and Jarman (1992) have attempted to redefine the traditional S-curve that defines birth, growth, and maturity. The first phase in organizational growth is the entrepreneurial stage. The entrepreneur is convinced that their idea for a product or service is needed and wanted in the marketplace. The common characteristic of all entrepreneurs and new businesses is the desire to find a pattern of operation that will survive in the marketplace. Nearly all new businesses fail within the first five years. Land and Jarman (1992) argue that this is "natural", and that even in nature, cell mutations do not usually survive. This phase is the beginning of the S-curve.

The second phase in organizational growth is characterized by a complete reversal in strategy. Where the entrepreneurial stage involves a series of trial and error endeavours, the next stage is the standardization of rules that define how the organizational system operates and interacts with the environment. The chaotic methods of the entrepreneur are replaced with structured patterns of operation. Internal processes are regulated and uniformity is sought. During this phase, growth actually occurs by limiting diversity. "Management procedures, processes, and controls are geared to maintain order and predictability". This phase is the rapid rise on the S-curve.

Organizational growth does not continue indefinitely. An upper asymptopic limit can be imposed by a number of factors. Land and Jarman (1992, p. 258) identify the most common reasons why organizations reach upper growth limits:

- Rapidly increasing internal and market place complexity in such areas a product proliferation and market divisions
- Internal competition for resources
- Increasing cost of manufacturing and sales
- Diminishing returns
- Declining share of the market
- Decreasing productivity gains
- Growing external pressures from regulators and influence groups
- Increasing impact of new technologies
- New and unexpected competitors.

The transition to the third phase involves another radical change in an organization. Most organizations are not able to make these changes, and they do not survive. "The organization must open up to permit what was never allowed in to become a part of the system, not only by doing things differently, but by *doing different things*". The organization needs to continue its core business, while at the same time engaging in inventing new business. This bifurcation is necessary because the entrepreneurial environment (of inventing business) is incompatible with the controlling environment of the core business.

The goal is a continuing integration of the new inventions into the mainstream business, where a re-created organization emerges. The core business is changed by the inventions it assimilates, and the organization takes on a new form. Land and Jarman (1992) believe that the greatest challenge facing today's organizations is the transition from phase two to phase three. "Organizations defeat their best intentions by continuing to operate with essential beliefs that automatically perpetuate the second phase." There are several factors that contribute to organizational growth. The most obvious is that growth is a by-product of another successful strategy. A second factor is that growth is deliberately sought because it facilitates management goals. For example, it provides increased potential for promotion, greater challenge, prestige, and earning potential. A third factor is that growth makes an organization less vulnerable to environmental consequences. Larger organizations tend to be more stable and less likely to go out of business. Increased resources make diversification feasible, thereby adding to the security of the organization.

Child and Kieser (1981) suggest four distinct operational models for organizational growth. 1) Growth can occur within an organization's existing domain. This is often manifest as a striving for dominance within its field. 2) Growth can occur through diversification into new domains. Diversification is a common strategy for lowering overall risk, and new domains often provide fertile new markets. 3) Technological advancements can stimulate growth by providing more effective methods of production. 4) Improved managerial techniques can facilitate an atmosphere that promotes growth. However, as Whetten (1987) points out, it is difficult to establish cause and effect in these models. Do technological advancements stimulate growth, or does growth stimulate the development of technological breakthroughs? With the lack of controlled experiments, it is difficult to choose between the chicken and the egg.

Organizational Decline

Until recently, most theories about organization development viewed decline as a symptom of ineffective performance. Well-managed organizations were expected to grow year after year. Implicit in these theories was the idea that organizational growth is synonymous with expansion. These theories reflected what scholars observed in the business world. Organizational growth was an indicator of successful management. Kenneth Boulding (1950) proposed a biological model of economics, characterized by birth, maturation, decline, and death. He argued that in all organisms, there is an "inexorable and irreversible movement towards the equilibrium of death." Many organizational theorists took strong exception to Boulding's biological determinism theory. They maintained that organizations are not constrained by a defined life cycle, and there is no indication that all organizations need to die.

The 1980's ushered in a new era where organizational decline was apparent everywhere. Management strategies involved reducing employees, salary freezes and reductions, cutting administrative overhead, and consolidating operations. It became clear that the traditional S-curve model was incomplete and did not address the issues of declining organizations.

One of the problems in the literature is that it is difficult to agree on a precise definition of organizational decline. Is a company in decline when it cuts back the number of employees in order to become more profitable? A common definition of decline is a decrease in profit or budget. Most theorists agree that decline negatively impacts individuals and the organization as a whole. Cameron, Whetten, and Kim (1987) argue that decline results in decreased morale, innovativeness, participation, leader influence, and long-term planning. They associate decline with, conflict, secrecy, rigidity, centralization, formalization, scapegoating, and conservatism.

Nystrom and Starbuck (1984) attribute organizational decline to over-confidence. According to this theory, a successful past can lure an organization to become over-confident in its ability to prosper. This leads to a lackadaisical attitude towards new innovations, quality, and customer satisfaction. Another theory is that large size promotes rigidity, which makes it cumbersome for an organization to respond to environmental changes. In applying the biological life-cycle model to organizations, Wilson (1980) identified two different types of organizational decline: "k" and """r" extinction. When an organization has reached the upper asymptopic limit defined by carrying capacity of its niche, it declines because of k-extinction. The organization has exhausted its environmental resources, or other organizations have begun competing for limited resources. When an organization falls short of its upper asymptopic limit, and begins declining without reaching its maximum potential, it is called r-extinction. Bad management or a failure to remain competitive are the most common reasons for r-extinction.

Bibeault (1982) proposed a four-stage model to describe the process of turning around an organization in decline. The key to the process was to replace the top personnel. Bibeault argued that only way to reverse a decline is to 1) change the management, the rationale being that "problem causers have little credibility as problem solvers". Chaffee (1984) also stressed the symbolic value of changing administrative personnel. Change in management is followed by 2) an evaluation stage, 3) implementing emergency actions and stabilization procedures, and finally, 4) a return to growth.

A different approach for describing organizational turnaround was proposed by Zammuto and Cameron (1985). Their model was based on the idea that turnaround could be accomplished by addressing five process domains. 1) The defence domain involves strategies for protecting the organization from a hostile environment. An example would be an organization that forms a common-purpose coalition with other organizations. 2) The offence domain involves expanding on the activities that the organization already does well. 3) Creating new domains consists of diversification activities. 4) The consolidation domain involves reducing the scope of activities by cutting back to core products and services. 5) The substitution domain involves replacing one set of activities with another.

In contrast to these theories, Harrigan (1980, 1981, 1982) and Porter (1980) have looked at how organizations respond to decline as a result of environmental limitations (i.e., k-extinction). Organizational activities often involve attempts to focus on a specific market niche in which the organization might have a competitive advantage. Another approach is to rapidly liquidate the organization, and extract as much remaining value as possible, although Harrigan (1982) notes that there are often financial, legal, structural, and emotional obstacles to this strategy. The most common response to organizational decline is retrenchment. Whetten (1987) identifies three sequential stages involved in the process. The first is one of identification. Management must be sensitive to problems when they first appear, and be able to meet the problems head on. The second is one of communication. Management must communicate a clear message of the organization's situation and instill confidence in its ability to meet the crisis. The third stage involves the implementation of a downsizing program. Sutton (1983) surveyed managers to examine their beliefs regarding how employees would react to an organizational closing. It was found that managers had several inaccurate perceptions. For example, managers' incorrectly believed that productivity and quality would plummet, employee sabotage and theft would increase, and there would be increases in conflict. On the other hand, Sutton's study did offer evidence that rumors were abundant, the best employees sought different employment, and that employee's had trouble accepting the closing.

The Learning Organization

Peter Senge (1990) defines learning as enhancing ones capacity to take action. "So learning organizations are organizations that are continually enhancing their capacity to create." Senge believes that organizations are evolving from controlling to predominantly learning.

Senge (1990) discusses learning disabilities in companies. One of the most serious disabilities is when people form a strong identification with their position. What they do becomes a function of their position. They see themselves in specific roles, and are unable to view their jobs as part of a larger system. This often leads to animosity towards others in the organization, especially when things go wrong. Another disability is that we are slow to recognize gradual changes and threats.

Senge (1990) refers to several other learning disabilities as "myths". He discusses the "myth of proactiveness", where "proactiveness is really reactiveness with the gauge turned up to 500%." Another myth is that we "learn from experience". Senge maintains that we actually only learn when the experience is followed by immediate feedback. Another myth is that management teams can provide creative and beneficial solutions. Senge maintains that the result of management teams is "skilled incompetence, where groups are highly skilled at protecting themselves from threat, and consequently keeping themselves from learning." Senge (1990) believes that new organizations can be built by adopting a set of disciplines, where a discipline is defined as a "particular theory, translated into a set of practices, which one spends one's life mastering." Thus, mastering a discipline becomes a life-long learning process.

According to Senge, there are five disciplines important to the learning organization. The first discipline is "building a shared vision". "Building" involves an ongoing process, and "shared" implies that the vision is held in common by individuals. A second discipline of "personal mastery" demonstrates a commitment to the vision. A third discipline involves the idea of mental models, where we construct internal representations of reality. An important element of using mental models is the need to balance inquiry and advocacy. A fourth discipline in that only shared mental models are important for organizational learning. The fifth discipline is a commitment to a systems approach.

Community

Gozdz (1992) believes that learning organizations are centred around the concept of community. "An organization acting as a community is a collective lifelong learner, responsive to change, receptive to challenge, and conscious of an increasingly complex array of alternatives." Communities provide safe havens for its members and foster an environment conducive to growth. Gozdz describes the community as group of people who have a strong commitment to "ever-deepening levels of communication."

M. Scott Peck (1987) describes the process of building a community in *The Different Drum*. An organization goes through a four-stage process. The first stage is one of denial. Group members ignore differences in power, and pretend that they are a community. Decision-making processes go unchallenged. The next stage occurs when differences between members become apparent. Attempts are made to restore the situation to what has worked in the past by eliminating differences. An organization enters the third stage when members realize that their efforts to control differences have failed. They begin communicating and true collaborative efforts emerge. In the final stage, there is the true spirit of community. Differences are embraced. Decisions are made collectively. Learning and innovation comes from the group as a whole Many organization experience brief periods of community, but they are not able to sustain those periods. Gozdz (1992) describes this failure as a lack of discipline and commitment.

There is an illusion that once a sense of community occurs within an organization it will remain constant. This is not the case. The sense of community or flow state is repeatedly lost. It can be deliberately regained at ever greater levels of organizational maturity, but only when sustaining community is seen and accepted as a path to developing mastery. This path is community as a discipline. According to Gozdz (1992), the job of the leaders in the process of community building is to keep peoples' attention focused on the process. The four stages of community development are repeated over and over again. New situations and contingencies arise that initiate new cycles in the growth process.

ORGANIZATIONAL PSYCHOLOGISTS AND HR PROFESSIONALS

The discrepancy between the knowledgebase of Organizational Psychologists and HR professionals has been documented in academic journals.

For example Sally Carless and colleagues pointed out that although there are important advancements in HR-related research, the everyday HR practice have benefited from it to a minimum level. They found that this is due to the lack of knowledge among HR professionals, especially when the training of the HR professionals emphasizes on general skill and knowledge in favour of science. In contrast, the training of Organizational Psychologists is built upon the scientist-practitioner model which emphasizes on both research and practical skills and stipulates that practice must be supported by scientific evidence.

Another reason may lie in the Continuous Professional Development (CPD) requirement. As Organizational Psychologists, CPD is a statutory condition for registration and this helps them to keep updated with the latest developments in the field. However there is no such requirement for HR professionals. Carless's study confirmed that Organizational Psychologists are experts in the field, especially in the area of selection and the authors articulated that "scientific integrity is a key differentiating feature of I/O (Organizational) psychologists." Having closely related working areas, our work is actually complementary to each other. Without Organizational Psychologists in the design and development work of various HR processes and tools, the HR professional would not be enjoying these scientific and highly effective products.

On the other hand, without the help of HR professionals we could never apply our work to such a broad range of people. Moreover, our relationship is much more complex and interactive than one might be aware of. Besides the above mentioned supplier-user relationship, HR professionals are also partners, advisors and sometimes suppliers for Organizational Psychologists.

HR professionals are our partners in projects where we provide them with the technical skills and knowledge while they take care of the operational part. Furthermore, HR professionals are experts of their company; therefore we work side by side during consulting jobs where we need them to assist us with internal matters as well as providing us with an insider view.

More importantly, as HR professionals are frequent users of our services and products, we rely a lot on their opinions and requests in developing our products and services. They are also providers of valuable data and participants for us to carry out scientific studies (e.g. validation of assessment tools). All in all, we are inter-dependent parties with entwined relationships rather than independent parties or competitors.

Being Organizational Psychologists, what can we offer to HR professionals? A lot. With the expertise in assessing human characteristics and knowledge about human performance, we are experts in selection.

Based on the understanding about the requirements of the job as well as the characteristics needed for any particular position, we can come up with an ideal person profile that the organization is looking for. Then we can design, or choose among proper tools that accurately measure the required characteristics, knowledge and skills.

According to research these procedures enable us to create the best selection system which predicts future performance of the employed staff. One should not be surprised that the best selection tools like psychometric tests, assessment centres, and structured interviews as well as standardized selection procedures are all designed and developed by Organizational Psychologists.

Organizational Psychology Profession and HR Field

Another contribution of the organizational psychology profession to the HR field is in training. A brief look at the training market reveals that it is flooded with many training courses and providers.

Obviously their quality varies and some of them do not even know what they are talking about! Our own company has undertaken work for clients who have come to us after being dissatisfied with trainers who appear to have simply taken some information from the internet to put together a training session without any real understanding of the subject matter!

As Organizational Psychologists we are working hard to turn around this situation. We are experts in training design; some understand how people learn and how people learn the best! In designing and delivering training courses, scientific human learning theories and training principles are followed, but not just by gut feelings or experience only. Factors like transfer of learning, specific needs of the organization and maintenance of learning are all fully considered.

Besides selection and training, Organizational Psychologists also offer various consultancy and advisory services to HR professionals. The range of work can be as small as reviewing a performance appraisal check list or an assessment centre exercise to as big as designing a tailored selection system. On top of that, we can also go into the organization to diagnose the roots of problems and solve them accordingly, using our scientific approach and advanced knowledge about mechanisms and dynamics within the workplace. However, as mentioned at the beginning of this article, one big obstacle we face is the lack of knowledge about our profession within the HR profession (particularly in Asia), as well as the public in general.

The implication is that we often face questions like "what is organizational psychology?", "what is the difference between Organizational Psychologists and HR consultants?" and even "why do I need to employ scientific tools and procedures?" It can be hard work explaining all this to prospective clients! Another related problem is people always think we are very expensive!

But the fact is all the products and services we offer are based on scientific research which means they have undergone lengthy and sophisticated processes of development and the cost of all these are huge. By employing our scientific tools and principles the benefit is long lasting and continuously contributing to the performance of the organization, and these are all documented in the scientific literature. Another hidden obstacle for us in Asia is caused by the organizational hierarchy. Very often, the first contact point between our clients and ourselves are assistants of HR professionals who have minimal understanding of what we are talking about. When they do not understand they just cannot relay our message precisely to their manager.

The result is obviously that the management level does not receive our message and the name of Organizational Psychology just remains unheard no matter how hard we try!

As Organizational Psychologists, we see a real need to educate the public, and more importantly, HR professionals about the subject of Organizational Psychology so that the fruit of science can be returned to them.

There are major overlapping work areas between Organizational Psychologists and HR professionals such as selection, training, career development and performance management, but we work on different levels and perspectives thus our relationship is actually collaborative rather than competitive.

Organizational Psychologists can offer help to HR professionals in various areas such as training design, development of selection systems, supervising performance management processes and many more. Nevertheless Organizational Psychologists in Asia face obstacles as the subject is relatively unheard of among HR professionals and communication is often blocked by organizational hierarchy.

Therefore one very important task for us as Organizational Psychologist is to promote this subject so that people know what we can offer and make use of our expertise! We are sure that with the growing popularity of the subject,

HR professionals, and other related professionals like career counsellors and coaches, will benefit highly from Organizational Psychology.

ORGANIZATIONAL BEHAVIOUR

Organizational behaviour is a misnomer. It is not the study of how organizations behave, but rather the study of individual behaviour in an organizational setting. This includes the study of how individuals behave alone, as well as how individuals behave in groups.

The purpose of organizational behaviour is to gain a greater understanding of those factors that influence individual and group dynamics in an organizational setting so that individuals and the groups and organizations to which they belong may become more efficient and effective.

The field also includes the analysis of organizational factors that may have an influence upon individual and group behaviour. Much of organizational behaviour research is ultimately aimed at providing human resource management professionals with the information and tools they need to select, train, and retain employees in a fashion that yields maximum benefit for the individual employee as well as for the organization.

Organizational behaviour is a relatively new, interdisciplinary field of study. Although it draws most heavily from the psychological and sociological sciences, it also looks to other scientific fields of study for insights. One of the main reasons for this interdisciplinary approach is because the field of organizational behaviour involves multiple levels of analysis, which are necessary to understand behaviour within organizations because people do not act in isolation. That is, workers influence their environment and are also influenced by their environment.

Individual Level of Analysis

At the individual level of analysis, organizational behaviour involves the study of learning, perception, creativity, motivation, personality, turnover, task performance, cooperative behaviour, deviant behaviour, ethics, and cognition. At this level of analysis, organizational behaviour draws heavily upon psychology, engineering, and medicine.

Group Level of Analysis

At the group level of analysis, organizational behaviour involves the study of group dynamics, intra- and intergroup conflict and cohesion, leadership, power, norms, interpersonal communication, networks, and roles. At this level of analysis, organizational behaviour draws upon the sociological and socio-psychological sciences.

Organization Level of Analysis

At the organization level of analysis, organizational behaviour involves the study of topics such as organizational culture, organizational structure, cultural diversity, inter-organizational cooperation and conflict, change, technology, and external environmental forces. At this level of analysis, organizational behaviour draws upon anthropology and political science.

Other fields of study that are of interest to organizational behaviour are ergonomics, statistics, and psychometrics. A number of important trends in the study of organizational behaviour are the focus of research efforts. First, a variety of research studies have examined topics at the group level of analysis rather than exclusively at the individual level of analysis. For example, while empowerment has largely been investigated as an individual-level motivation construct, researchers have begun to study team empowerment as a means of understanding differences in group performance. Similar research has focused on elevating the level of analysis for personality characteristics and cooperative behaviour from the individual level to the group level.

Another research trend is an increasing focus on personality as a factor in individual- and group-level performance. This stems from the movement toward more organic organization designs, increased supervisory span of control, and more autonomous work designs. All of these factors serve to increase the role that personality plays as a determinant of outcomes such as stress, cooperative or deviant behaviour, and performance.

Personality traits that are related to flexibility, stress hardiness, and personal initiative are also the subject of research. Examples of these personality traits include a tendency toward individualism or collectivism, self-monitoring, openness to experience, and a proactive personality. Forms of behaviour that are constructive and change-oriented in nature are also studied. These forms of behaviour are proactive in nature and act to improve situations for the individual, group, or organization. Examples of these behaviors include issue selling, taking initiative, constructive change-oriented communication, innovation, and proactive socialization.

Other topics of interest in the field of organizational behaviour include the extent to which theories of behaviour are culturally bound, unethical decision-making, self-management and self-leadership, and work/family conflict.

ORGANIZATIONAL DESIGN AND PROCESSES

Organizational Behaviour scientists have conducted extensive studies on job definitions and the tasks a job comprises. They have looked at how each job fit into different groups within the organization, a process called departmentalization. The researchers have studied managerial spans of control, i.e., the number of people an individual manager can manage most effectively. The process required that researchers reduce to its most basic level each task performed and then find ways to perform jobs more efficiently and effectively.

Many researchers have suggested viable ways that organizations could restructure jobs and relationships to stimulate job satisfaction and productivity simultaneously. They have devised better communications programs, identified the elements that create stress, and explained how it could be better managed.

Organizational Behaviour scientists performed extensive studies on company cultures and climates with an eye to upgrading employees' quality of life in the workplace. They have sought ways to include more people in the managerial and decision-making processes. Their suggestions have included such techniques as quality circles and participative management programs.

Quality circles, which are team approaches to identifying and resolving work-related problems, became popular in some businesses. So, too, did participative management efforts, which gave a wider variety of people opportunities to comment on—and implement—new ideas in the workplace. One prominent organizational Behaviour scientist, William Ouchi, recommended that American companies integrate more Japanese management concepts into their management practices. His approach became known as Theory Z. The ideas promulgated by organizational Behaviour scientists have caught on in managerial circles. Not surprisingly, not all of the programs can be used by all companies. If there is one thing that researchers have recognized, it is that no two companies are alike.

To compensate for the dissimilarities, behavioural scientists reformed detailed cultural profiles to determine which programs fit individual companies' needs. These profiles have illustrated the importance of culture in the field of organizational Behaviour. Researchers have examined how company cultures control individual and group Behaviour, promote innovation, foster personnel commitment, and so on.

Organizational Change

Another subject of special interest to organizational Behaviour scholars is how change affects people in an organization and how the process of change can be managed to maximize its success and minimize unintended disruptions. Change is compelled by many sources: social and demographic trends, economic cycles, competition, technology, and politics and regulation, to name a few. Scholars distinguish between change that is incremental and ongoing, sometimes called first-order change, and change that is radical and episodic, termed second-order change. While each form can have both positive and negative consequences, radical changes are commonly seen as requiring the most caution and skill at pulling off. For example, one of the most visible trends in corporate America since the 1980s has been the rise of sudden mass layoffs at large corporations, or downsizing. This clearly represents one of the largest kinds of changes a company might face, and its scope affects not only the workers who lose their jobs but also those who remain.

Researchers have found that downsizing can have both positive and negative effects on the employees who stay on. In some cases, for example, layoffs can induce employees to work harder and engage in other Behaviours that benefit the company. One obvious explanation is that these workers might fear losing their jobs if they don't improve their performance, but there are likely other reasons as well, such as a move to fill a performance vacuum left by the departing workers. Still, other workers may respond by diminishing their performance; they may be demoralized by the corporate policies and may lower their mental and emotional investment in their jobs.

However, studies in organizational Behaviour suggest that all of these responses aren't inevitable. Scholars have suggested that the way in which the company goes about managing the change, in this case, the events leading up to and following downsizing, can have a significant effect on how employees react. This is not to say all negative reactions can be eliminated, but that there is a good chance they can be reduced. In the downsizing example, taking actions that foster trust in the management (such as open communication or demonstrating objective and consistent criteria for decision making) and that increase employee feelings of empowerment (letting workers have a say in some aspects of change) have been posited as methods of reducing some of the negative shocks of massive organizational change. Similar principles apply to managing other forms of organizational change.

More broadly, scholars like psychologist Kurt Lewin have identified basic models for managing change in organizations. In Lewin's widely cited three-step process, outlined in his 1951 classic *Field Theory in Social Science,* management must first "unfreeze" the status quo in the organization, facilitate a move to a new set of practices or environment, and then solidify or "refreeze" the new practices or environment into a permanent state. The process of unfreezing the current status involves introducing new policies or initiatives that begin to actively move employees away from the old way of doing things and/or removing policies or practices that tie them to the old. The second step, the shift to the new practices, is the formal implementation of the changes, for example, reorganizing a division or closing a branch office. Third, during refreezing management must solidify the changes by ensuring all the policies and practices are now geared toward maintaining the new equilibrium, and not throwbacks to the supplanted practices or lingering transition measures that create an atmosphere of instability or uncertainty.

ORGANIZATIONAL PSYCHOLOGY AND HUMAN RESOURCE MANAGEMENT

Although there are quite a few overlapping areas between Organizational Psychology and Human Resource Management (HRM), there are fundamental differences between us. The first and perhaps the most obvious difference between us is the knowledge foundation. As psychologists, we base our work heavily on science. All work has to be backed up by scientific evidence and statistics is always in our toolbox.

In contrast, HRM is essentially a business study which emphasizes more on the practical side, with less focus on the scientific side. Moreover, in addition to working on overlapping areas, we work on different levels. Organizational Psychologists focus more on the design and development of procedures, tools and principles while HR professionals work more on the operational level, such as implementation of selection systems and applying training principles in real training scenarios.

INTERNATIONAL ORGANIZATIONS: ROLE AND SIGNIFICANCE

Strategic management, corporate responsibility and stakeholder management Integrating corporate responsibility principles and stakeholder approaches into mainstream strategy: a stakeholder-oriented and integrative strategic management framework.

Since the early 1990s, corporate responsibility issues have attained prominence in the political and business agenda. The need for a more pro-active role by states, companies and communities in a development process aimed at balancing economic growth with environmental sustainability and social cohesion has motivated the following three interlinked business movements:

1. Corporate social responsibility (CSR).
2. Corporate sustainability.
3. Worldwide reforms on corporate governance.

CSR and corporate sustainability involve assessment of the company's economic, social and environmental impact, taking steps to improve it in line with stakeholder requirements and reporting on relevant measurements. Corporate governance reflects the way companies address legal responsibilities and therefore provides the foundations upon which CSR and corporate sustainability practices can be built to enhance responsible business operations.

The CSR and corporate sustainability movements are building an impressive momentum with support from governments and the investment community through socially responsible investing (SRI) and associated corporate sustainability indexes. There is no doubt that businesses are doing far more than ever before to tackle the sustainability challenge by recognizing their social responsibilities, reducing their environmental impacts, guarding against ethical compromises, creating governance transparency and becoming more accountable to their stakeholders. However, it is widely recognized that CSR and corporate sustainability as business practices remain isolated from mainstream strategy and therefore mainstreaming has become the key challenge for the corporate responsibility movement. Theoretical developments in the field of business in society have focused in two areas, the ethical and accountability responsibilities and the stakeholder approaches to strategic management. The stakeholder theory provides the foundations of a strategic view of corporate responsibility issues and advocates a single strategic management framework. However, stakeholder approaches can be regarded as another strand of strategic management theories and do not attempt to define a single strategic management framework, which is the objective of this paper. The motivation for the paper is therefore to establish a strategic management framework that could contribute from a methodological perspective to charting ways for corporate responsibility mainstreaming.

The baseline of the proposed framework is the 4CR classification of strategic management theories against criteria of value, responsiveness and responsibility.

The main theories included in the 4CR classification are:

- industrial organization/environmental approaches;
- resource based view (RBV) and related theories of core competencies and dynamic capabilities;
- business networking and relational perspectives;
- knowledge view of the firm;
- corporate responsibility and sustainability; and
- stakeholder approaches.

A reference model for stakeholder-oriented integrative strategic management is derived from the 4CR classification illustrating the interaction of the above theories in developing a single strategic management capability. The concepts for advantage-creating knowledge and advantage-creating stakeholder relations are developed according to resource based theory, and a baseline descriptive mathematical model is outlined specifying their composition and clarifying key interactions between constituent elements. To resolve the issues surrounding the impact of corporate social responsibility strategies on performance we differentiate between the instrumental elements of stakeholder approaches that are integrated in the value and responsiveness dimensions of strategic management and become an integral part of competitive strategy. The ethical aspects or intrinsic elements of stakeholder approaches are dealt with in the responsibility dimension enabling integration through contextual links with the competitive dimensions.

The Value Dimension of Strategic Management

In general, a firm's profitability depends jointly on the attractiveness of its industry/markets and its success in creating more value than its competitors. A recent survey by McGahan and Porter indicate that industry accounts for 19 percent of profit variations while the competitive position accounts for 32 percent and a large component of 43 percent represents variation that cannot be accounted for by any systemic influence.

The traditional focus of strategic management to position the company where it can leverage its resources to deliver superior economic value (perceived customer benefits and cost) is addressed in a complementary way by industrial organization/environmental and resource based theories. Environmental based strategies focus on market characteristics and examine how best a company can configure its value chain to obtain a competitive advantage (Porter, 1980, 1985). Resource based theories address how companies can perform activities within the value chain more efficiently utilizing firm-specific resources which must valuable, rare, imperfectly imitable and non-substitutable, the so called VRIN criteria. Firms adopting a resource-based approach begin the strategy process by identifying their core resources, how they can be leveraged and developed to achieve the corporate mission, cost efficiency and differentiation strategies.

From the beginning of the 1990s resource related strategies were elaborated through the concept of leveraging core competencies and distinctive capabilities to exploit economies of scope. Core competencies represent what a company does better than any competitors and are based on the concept of resource recombination or in other words on the collective knowledge and learning capacity in the organization. A distinct characteristic of core competencies is that it can be leveraged widely in many products and markets. Strategies for developing core competencies are frequently combined with networking and knowledge management strategies. Resource based strategies will identify networking requirements regarding relation-specific assets and complementary assets.

Resource based strategies will also determine the knowledge requirements for core competencies in the context of networking strategies and organizational design. It is has been suggested that the resource based theory may be too narrow by concentrating on the acquisition and protection of critical resources and that knowledge of how resources are brought together, coordinated, integrated, and put into use is the essence of the successful firm. More specifically, productivity is dependent on the learning capabilities of the firm (learning curve) with the obvious implications on value. Networking strategies should combine a "competence" perspective for the acquisition and development of knowledge and capabilities with a perspective of "governance", for the management of "relational risks" and the minimization of transaction costs. The management of networking risks and the development of knowledge based capabilities is dependent on the relational view of the organization which is addressed both by industrial network theory and stakeholder approaches to strategic management. From a value perspective, instrumental stakeholder approaches view stakeholders as controlling resources that can facilitate or slow down the implementation of strategies and therefore must be managed to create competitive advantage. Development of special relations to support advantage-creating resources such as employee motivation, customer loyalty, influence on sector regulation, local license to operate, etc. are dependent on stakeholder instrumental strategies aimed at trust development.

Trust is a key enabling condition for stakeholder management and can be sub-divided into:

- Competence trust (confidence in the capacity of other actors to perform);
- Business trust (confidence in reliability of transactions); and
- Emotional trust (personal confidence based on personal relationships).

Under current macro-economic developments trust is seen as a moderating mechanism facilitating coordination of expectations and interactions between economic actors.

By considering the industry attractiveness in the value dimension, responsibility-driven self-regulation and responsibility strategies to meet investor and consumer demands become important elements of the strategic positioning of the company. With regard to the latter, strategic responsibility positioning should be based on:

- Understanding stakeholders' perceptions on the company's responsibility strategies and performance in relation to competition;
- Consumers' clusters of ideal points on green products and competitor positions in specific industries; and
- Investors' clusters of ideal points on responsible behaviour and competitor positions.

The Responsiveness Dimension of Strategic Management

In recent years there is strong interest on "dynamic strategies" associated with enhanced organizational responsiveness. Dynamic strategies can be subdivided into:

- Those associated with flexibility and agility (reconfigurable processes and products, integration technologies, shareable services, resource pools) addressed by core competencies and business networking strategies; and

- Those associated with detection and reaction speed addressed by dynamic capabilities and learning/innovation strategies.

Dynamic capabilities represent a firm's ability to integrate, build and reconfigure competences to address rapidly changing environments and include business intelligence capabilities for scanning and interpreting new technological fields and new markets. Dynamic capabilities can be characterized as trajectories of competence development combining flexibility constrained by the firm's history which makes them tacit and idiosyncratic. Dynamic capabilities are needed both to integrate and reconfigure resources and to allow the firmto acquire and release resources (Eisenhardt and Martin, 2000).

Dynamic capabilities are closely linked to the firm's inter-organizational relationships, which are idiosyncratic and difficult for competitors to imitate and to substitute and they allow a firm to adapt to changing opportunities and challenges by tapping into a broad and diverse base of network resources. Networks vary in terms of the structure and relational characteristics such as pattern of ties, nodal diversity or variation in the mix of relationships. We can identify two distinct categories of networks reflecting the theory of mechanistic and organic management systems. Mechanistic networks are characterized by rules, stability, formal standardization, specialization and loyalty.

Organic networks are characterized by loose and adaptive links governed by mutual adjustment, participative knowledge and commitment to progress. Generally, mechanistic networks are more suitable for value strategies where organic networks are best suited for responsiveness strategies. Arguably companies need to adopt a layered model for business networking comprising of an inner layer representing long term alliances linked to value strategies, a number of intermediate layers of progressively looser relations and an outer layer comprising of ''on demand'' service providers linked to responsiveness strategies. Each layer may be characterized by different quality of relations and strategic convergence requirements that should be reflected in the corresponding stakeholder engagement strategies.

Beyond flexibility addressed by networking strategies, responsiveness is dependent on the learning and innovative capacity of the organization. As companies are under continuous pressure to improve their products and services, learning is ultimately ''the only sustainable source of competitive advantage''. Empirical evidence suggests that firms survive longer depending on learning capacities and on the rate of learning that intrinsically supports innovation. Organizational learning depends on the ''capacity for knowledge absorption'' by the members of knowledge networks and their ''collaboration motivation'' which can be facilitated by stakeholder engagement strategies.

Stakeholder engagement is closely related with the concepts of social capital described by OECDC as "... networks, together with shared norms, values and understandings which facilitate cooperation within or among groups". Social capital can be defined by characteristic properties along the following three dimensions:

1. The structural quality of a relationship referring to the structure of the social network in which the relationship is embedded.
2. The relational quality of the relationship associated with the levels of mutual trust and reciprocity.
3. The cognitive quality of the relationship reflecting the levels of common understanding and shared values and goals.

Responsiveness is also facilitated by transparency as advocated by responsibility strategies as it encourages broad stakeholder participation in risk management processes aimed at early identification of risks and vulnerabilities and even contribution in corrective and mitigation actions.

Organizational change and development

Many of these are based on the 'narratives', 'stories' and 'lessons' offered by various reflective research-informed change agents, including managers, trainers and developers, who have been successful in bringing about beneficial organizational change either in their own organization or in host organizations.

The Key Insights Gained Include

- The significance placed on 'communicating with all stakeholders for the purpose of securing common ownership, commitment and involvement';
- The pivotal importance of 'securing the active commitment, involvement and participation of senior to middle managers' and particularly 'top management';
- The need to be 'clear, consistent and open with regard to what you are seeking to achieve, setting clear strategic objectives and sharing the vision';
- The importance of 'recognizing and addressing the real problems or root causes of problems, including the cultural dimensions';
- The importance of 'giving enough time for the OCD programme to take root and succeed';
- The importance of the 'contribution that the HR function can make and the strategic role it can play in bringing about transformational change';
- The need to recognize 'the role of learning in the change management process and the need for a no blame culture';

- The value of 'being reflective';
- The emphasis and importance placed on 'the value of conducting internal research as part of change agency practice'.

The latter two insights are particularly significant. For most of those who contributed the case histories, reflection was a legitimate component of their change agency practice which they made an integral and explicit part of the change process. Furthermore, many wished they had spent even more time up front of their change projects carrying out research to understand better the organizational context, particularly the cultural aspects, in order to form a stronger foundation upon which to build their change programmes and developments.

The implementation of evidence-based practice

This example relates to the world of nursing and healthcare management. Some of the case studies presented in this work relate strongly to change management, facilitation and learning issues in contexts, settings and situations similar to those faced by managers and HRD practitioners in other types of organization. At heart it is the belief that 'the implementation of good quality research is likely to have improved outcomes for patients and is therefore important for quality patient care'. The conceptual framework presented by the authors suggests that 'successful implementation of research into practice is a function of the relation between the nature of the evidence, the context in which the proposed change is to be implemented, and the mechanisms by which the change is facilitated'. As much attention needs to be given to preparing the context and choosing the facilitation method as to testing the evidence. Four case studies are presented of varying degrees of quality from low to high relating to the evidence, the context and the facilitation respectively.

The most successful implementation seems to occur when evidence is high; when the context is receptive to change with sympathetic cultures and appropriate monitoring and feedback mechanisms, and when there is appropriate facilitation of the change, using in a complementary way the skills of both external and internal facilitators. The framework could be used as a tool by HRD practitioners for implementing research findings or engaging in research activities as part of their change agency practice. Additionally it provides a useful reminder of the importance of giving sufficient attention to the process issues of change which call for high levels of facilitation skill and change agency expertise.

HRD through professional partnerships

As already mentioned various authors in the UK have called for more research informed approaches to human resource development and management development. Others have argued the case for more internal research in support of organizational change programmes and organizational learning. In the USA Swanson (1997) advocates that HRD professionals should 'advance their professional practice by becoming truly expert practitioners' through what he calls 'backyard research'. Jacobs (1997) strongly advocates HRD collabourations between organizations and universities. However, these should be 'professional partnerships' in which the 'partners' recognize that HRD scholars and HRD practitioners enter such partnerships with their own respective goals.

Thus, in 'HRD professional partnerships', there is a dual goal to advance the HRD field and improve the organization through the findings and application of rigorous internal research. Building upon the ideas of Jacobs, and a number of tentative ideas shared by a group of HRD academics and practitioners attending the 1997 Annual Conference of the University Forum for HRD, a 'conceptual framework' has been devised to illustrate the connection between 'HRD professional partnerships' and the 'HRD research-practice gap.

The narrow outside 'boxes' to the left and right of the model are there to remind us that the joint research effort is not a 'service contract' but a 'collabourative partnership'. The narrow outside boxes at the top and bottom of the model illustrate the connection between the respective 'stakeholders' who are jointly involved in the active 'processes' of research and consultancy. These need to be relevant, rigorous, robust and ethical if they are to lead to 'outcomes' of maximum value to the interested parties.

The large box to the left of centre of the model endeavours to illustrate 'professional partnerships' in which HRD scholars from universities, in partnership with HRD practitioners, conduct internal organizationally related research to academic standards. At the centre of this box is the notion of the 'reflective research-informed/evidence-based' practitioner. The large box at the centre of the model draws attention to the cyclical nature of the processes for conducting internal research and consultancy respectively. These are similar and follow a 'common' sequence of stages from entry to reporting.

The outcomes from the research/consultancy activities as illustrated in the large box to the right of centre of the model are perceived as being mutually reinforcing. At the outset of an HRD intervention the reflective research-informed/evidence-based HRD practitioner uses 'best evidence' to support his or her decisions. This might mean building a 'research' component into the HRD strategy for the specific purpose of using empirical evidence from internal organizational research to further inform, shape and measure the required HRD intervention and thereby enhance the professional practice. Building sufficient rigour into the research with the help of an HRD scholar in a professional partnership arrangement will give the necessary 'academic credentials' required to ensure the credibility and acceptance of the research by people inside the organization, and also impart value in terms of its contribution to the advancement of knowledge.

This concept of collabourative 'professional partnerships' for generating internal partnership research, and the processes involved, bear similarity to the notion of 'co-operative research' as advocated and practised within the healthcare sector. To get 'research into practice' Sang draws attention to a 'virtuous cycle' of co-operation that needs to exist from beginning to end of the research process involving the initiators, commissioners, designers, planners, implementers and evaluators.

This HRD professional partnership was set within the Anglia Region of HM Customs and Excise (HMCE), which at the time was one of fourteen executive units comprising HMCE within the UK. The partners in this instance included Dick Shepherd, the regional head of 'Anglia', Margaret Reidy his internal research officer/HRD consultant, plus the author and Professor Jim Stewart from Nottingham Trent University.

The aim of the partnership was to help bring about radical change in the management culture of the organization through HRD initiatives based on the findings of rigorous internal academic research. The research programme included, amongst other activities, an extensive 'ethnographic' longitudinal case study on the changing culture of the organization. It also comprised a complementary empirical research study into the criteria of managerial and leadership effectiveness using critical incident technique and statistical analytic methods for processing the data.

The partnership comprised two strands, the one concerned with the 'ethnographic' research, the other with the study of managerial effectiveness. The 'ethnographic' research became coincidentally the focus of a PhD/MPhil study programme undertaken by the research officer. Hence this strand of the partnership was partly contractual for the doctoral studies component and non-contractual for all of the other aspects. The managerial effectiveness strand to the partnership differed from the 'ethnographic' strand in that it was wholly voluntary and non-contractual with each partner entering the 'partnership' with quite different yet complementary goals. It should be mentioned that in the 'Anglia partnership' the internal HRD practitioner, Margaret Reidy, carried out most of the field research, but the other stages of the research programme were done jointly.

At the time of his appointment as regional head of Anglia in 1991, Dick Shepherd found himself in a region which, whilst productive, was working with a 'command and control' style of management. However, to reflect the changing organizational environment where year on year demands to deliver more for less were being made by the department, the management style needed to be changed. Furthermore, to cope effectively with the various change programmes he anticipated would be imposed 'top-down' from above, and those he intended initiating himself, he concluded a new cultural infrastructure was required. He found though that change was slow to happen due to the effects of 'cultural lag', a term first coined by Bate (1996).

He realized he needed to understand better the resilient but no longer relevant culture of his organization so as to know how best to change it. Hence he commissioned an ethnographic longitudinal research study from Margaret Reidy on culture and cultural change that was designed to help inform, shape and measure the changes he had set his mind to bring about. In the main his early change initiatives were a success in terms of changing the organizational structure. However, the desired changes in the management culture were only partly achieved as revealed by the ethnographic study. A large proportion of managers persisted in managing in the traditional ways of the Civil Service.

At the beginning of 1995, Shepherd decided to address again the issue of changing the management culture. However, he wanted to know with a greater degree of certainty the type of managerial behaviours that were proving particularly effective within the changing organization which therefore needed to be encouraged and promoted, and conversely those behaviours that were least effective which needed to be discouraged or eliminated. Furthermore, he and Margaret Reidy were curious to know whether a different research methodology would substantiate the longitudinal 'ethnographic' research findings.

Hence a second strand of the HRD professional partnership was formed focusing on a complementary research programme into managerial and leadership effectiveness. This latter research, and its application to inform and shape the range of HRD interventions used to bring about significant change in the management culture of 'Anglia'. In summary, the initial research revealed six 'positive' criteria relating to managerial effectiveness within 'Anglia', and twelve 'negative' criteria relating to managerial ineffectiveness.

The criteria are rich and robust in that they are underpinned by behavioural statements which are relevant in terms of the inherent language and culture of 'Anglia', and have been piloted and tested through a number of diverse tools. A further research study was carried out focusing specifically on team leaders with the purpose of identifying criteria of leadership effectiveness. It was based on twenty of the 'positive' leadership-specific behavioural statements obtained from the managerial effectiveness research, and used the same data processing methods.

Dick Shepherd presented the preliminary findings from the critical incident stage of the research to his managers at his 1995 Annual Management Conference. The results were well received with people agreeing that the identified behaviours did exist. These were then discussed in syndicate workshops with some of the revealed behavioural problems being addressed. Various managers and team leaders carried the results back to their offices, and ran similar workshops with their own people in order to address those problem issues affecting them. Subsequent monitoring of the culture changes that had taken place as a result of the research-based HRD interventions revealed marked increases in the incidence of 'positive' managerial behaviours, and reductions in the 'negative'. However, many problems remained with certain managers still exhibiting attitudes and behaviours associated with ineffective management as defined by the 'negative' criteria. Hence it was concluded additional effort was required to effect further change in the management culture. The reasons why the initial findings had not had a bigger impact was that some people did not relate the 'negative' behaviours to themselves, although they accepted that in general such behaviours were a major problem for the organization. The strict codes of confidentiality and anonymity as applied when conducting the research meant none of the observed critical incidents and behaviours reported in the findings were attributed to any persons in particular. Hence it was too easy for some people to believe that other managers elsewhere in the organization were the ones exhibiting the negative behaviours. Some managers were obviously reluctant to analyse their own behaviours in relation to the research findings.

This created a barrier to further cultural change. Therefore a different approach was needed that would encourage and enable managers and team leaders in the organization to relate the 'positive' and 'negative' criteria to their own behaviours. The approach used was based on the concepts of self-analysis, 360-degree feedback and action learning, using a range of 'framework tools' focusing on different criteria and problem issues identified by the managerial and leadership effectiveness research. Team-effectiveness workshops were set up for particular team leaders (managers) and their respective teams, and these were facilitated initially with the help of Margaret Reidy.

Through the process of action learning, participants at the workshops were helped to translate and transfer to themselves not only the positive findings of the research, but also the negative findings that required personal remedial action as revealed by the 360-degree feedback process. This team effectiveness/action learning workshop approach enabled people to obtain feedback from colleagues without risk of compromising their positions or relationships within the organization. It allowed them to work through problems in a supportive climate and learn from them, and led to meaningful change on a personal, team and organizational level. Subsequent workshops became self-generating and self-facilitating.

The research-informed/evidence-based HRD practice outlined above, which took place between 1995 and 1998, was highly successful in engaging the active interest and commitment of 'Anglia' people to the process of strategic change. Managers went much further in their thinking than had been the case with previous organizational change programmes. In the past 'Anglia' people had not always responded well to certain organizational change initiatives, particularly those involving consultants using external research or adapted 'off the shelf' OD instruments that failed to 'ring true'. In this case they were willing to move forward with cultural change brought about through the strategically led and research-informed/evidence-based HRD interventions initiated by Dick Shepherd.

This was because the internal research findings presented an accurate picture of the actual realities of managerial life as it existed, and also 'struck a chord' with people. But the perceived value of this research-informed/evidence-based HRD practice stemmed particularly from the attributes of the research resulting from the 'Anglia' HRD professional partnership, namely its academic rigour and credentials, the strict codes of anonymity and confidentiality that were applied, its relevancy and the sense of ownership it engendered. In the case of the 'Anglia' cultural change programme the contribution of the internal research was pivotal and of crucial importance. As Dick Shepherd said, 'it was of enormous value in bringing about the culture change, and gave me the confidence and courage to proceed with the change programme'.

Several lessons can be drawn from the examples outlined above. There are strong arguments that strategically led research-informed/evidence-based HRD practice can become a central plank of any HRD strategy for helping to bring about beneficial organizational change and development. However, this is unlikely to become commonplace if most HRD practitioners remain constrained at the margins of the organization, rather than at its centre. The question is how might HRD professionals become centrepiece players on the organizational stage? Certainly this will not happen unless and until line managers overcome the five OCD 'failings', and unless and until HRD people increase significantly their competency and credibility. Herein lies a major challenge for those who educate and train managers, trainers and developers, particularly university academics who teach on professional qualification programmes such as the MBA and Master's degrees in HRD and HRM.

They should be making key contributions towards such developments as:

- Ensuring that the organizational/business leaders and managers they teach do fully understand the significance of investing in appropriate HRD (and HRM) effort when initiating and implementing organizational change programmes. This might mean changing the way HRD/HRM is taught in business schools. Greater emphasis should be placed on helping practising managers recognize not only the importance to themselves of becoming more skilled as change agents and research-informed/evidence-based reflective practitioners, but also on the value of co-operative or partnership research and professional partnerships.

- Ensuring HRD practitioners develop the skills required to operate effectively and with competence, confidence and credibility at strategic levels within organizations. This includes helping them develop expertise as internal consultants, change agents, strategic organizational facilitators, and as research-informed/evidence-based reflective practitioners.
- Doing more applied research themselves, focused towards enhancing professional HRD practice as well as advancing the field of HRD knowledge.
- Working collabouratively with their current and past students and other research-active HRD practitioners, preferably within HRD professional partnerships and other co-operative or partnership research arrangements.
- Recognizing the potential of such partnerships for generating academically rigorous HRD research that can be of relevance and interest to HRD practitioners.

A key message for those readers who are HRD practitioners is the need at least to become a reflective research-informed professional; and then to embark upon a journey towards becoming an evidence-based practitioner, emulating what other professionals do in the healthcare professions. HRD professional partnerships or co-operative research arrangements with HRD academics are one means of enhancing professional HRD practice through research.

There is also an important message to be drawn from the above examples for top managers and business/organizational leaders. They need increasingly to recognize the value of research-informed/evidence-based HRD for bringing about beneficial organizational change and development. However, as an HRD-orientated manager, trainer, or developer it may fall to you, the reader, to ensure this message 'strikes home' at the top of your own organization. This may prove an essential requirement if you are to maximize your contribution to organizational effectiveness and helping to bring about beneficial organizational change and development.

VALUES AND ASSUMPTIONS WITHIN THE FIELD

In *Collective Bargaining and Industrial Relations,* Kochan suggested that an important factor distinguishing industrial relations from its contributing disciplines and related applied areas of study (e.g., human resources) is a distinctive set of values and assumptions. These include the following propositions:

1. Labour is more than a commodity. That is, unlike inanimate factors of production such as machinery and raw materials, the work of human beings raises questions about the impact of work and work relations upon employees, questions that are societal concerns. Some industrial relations scholars (such as Roy J. Adams, in an 1992 article in *Labour Studies Journal)* take this assumption a step further in arguing that a society cannot be truly democratic if it does not provide mechanisms by which employees can influence their working lives, i.e., a means for industrial democracy.
2. There are inherent conflicts of interest between employers and employees not only in terms of economic matters (e.g., wages versus profits), but also in terms of inherent friction in superior-subordinate relations.
3. There are large areas of common interests between employers and employees despite their conflicting interests, and important interdependencies (e.g., firms need workers and workers need jobs). These compel employers and employees to resolve their conflicting interests for the sake of mutual benefits.
4. There is an inherent inequality of bargaining power in most individual employer-employee relationships, and thus collective representation of employees (e.g., unions) is often necessary to establish true freedom of contract. That is, it is not sufficient to argue that since employer and employee are each legally free to establish or terminate an employment relationship, that they are then on equal footing.
5. Pluralism—the notion that there are multiple competing interest groups in society, each with valid interests. Thus in the workplace and in the larger society the goals of workers, employers, and society should be accommodated in an equitable balance. This contrasts with the often implicit assumption in business areas that the goals of the firm or its shareholders are supreme. Similarly, it contrasts with economists' stress on efficiency as a supreme goal, although some labour economists (such as Richard B. Freeman and James L. Medoff, authors of *What Do Unions Do?)* have updated and expanded upon earlier arguments for the efficiency of collective voice mechanisms (e.g., collective bargaining and other forms of worker representation) relative to individualistic market mechanisms (e.g., the worker's choice to enter or exit an employment relationship).

Some of these assumptions (e.g., inherent conflict of employer-employee economic interests) can be traced at least as far back as the 19th century and the work of German political philosopher Karl Marx (1818-1883); in fact, some regard Marx as the intellectual father of industrial relations. In the United States, however, the "Wisconsin School" of institutional economics, led by John R. Commons (1862-1945) and Selig Perlman (1888-1959) in the early 20th century, rejected Marx's prediction of pathological conflict escalating into inevitable class warfare between workers and capitalists and the ultimate demise of capitalism. Instead, Commons and his followers argued that collective bargaining and legislation could temper the excesses of capitalism, allowing workers and management to resolve their conflicts for the sake of greater common interests within the capitalist economic system. Commons is generally regarded as the intellectual father of American industrial relations.

INDUSTRIAL RELATIONS SYSTEMS MODEL

The dominant paradigm or conceptual framework for the study of industrial relations is the "Industrial Relations Systems" model advanced by Dunlop in his book of the same name. The concept of a system is applied in the sense that industrial relations, according to Daniel Quinn Mills, author of*Labour-Management Relations,* consists of the "processes by which human beings and organizations interact at the workplace and, more broadly, in society as a whole to establish the terms and conditions of employment." In other words, certain inputs (e.g., human labour, capital, managerial skill) from the environment are combined via alternative processes (e.g., collective bargaining, unilateral management decisions, legislation) to produce certain outcomes (e.g., production, job satisfaction, wage rates). Consistent with the definitions of industrial relations noted above, the study of industrial relations and the systems model focus on outcomes most closely related to the interaction of employees and employers and the "web of rules" concerning employment that they and their organizations, along with government, establish to govern employer-employee relations. Thus production per se is a system outcome, but not a principal focus of industrial relations. It has been noted that the industrial relations system concept may fall short of the definition of a system in the physical or biological sciences, but nonetheless the concept has proved useful and endured. Dunlop, in *Industrial Relations Systems,* noted that industrial relations systems can be thought of as being embedded in broader social systems. In *Collective Bargaining and Industrial Relations,* Kochan observed that like any complex social system, industrial relations systems are best understood by identifying and analysing their various components and how they interact with one another to produce certain outcomes. The major components of the industrial relations system are:

1. The actors (workers and their organizations, management, and government).

2. Contextual or environmental factors (labour and product markets, technology, and community or "the locus and distribution of power in the larger society" [from Dunlop's *Industrial Relations Systems]).*
3. Processes for determining the terms and conditions of employment (collective bargaining, legislation, judicial processes, and unilateral management decisions, among others).
4. Ideology, or a minimal set of shared beliefs, such as the actors' mutual acceptance of the legitimacy of other actors and their roles, which enhance system stability.
5. Outcomes, including wages and benefits, rules about work relations (e.g., standards for disciplinary action against workers), job satisfaction, employment security, productive efficiency, industrial peace and conflict, and industrial democracy.

The basic purposes of the industrial relations systems concept are to provide a conceptual framework for organizing knowledge about industrial relations and for understanding how various components of an industrial relations system combine to produce particular outcomes (and hence why outcomes vary from one setting to another or over time). Thus for example, wage rates for a particular group of workers might be understood as reflecting the interactions of their unions with management via collective bargaining within the constraints of a particular market, technological, and community environment.

The precise specification of system components may vary with the level of analysis and from one system to another. For example, when applied to a particular work site, legislation may be best understood as an environmental constraint upon the immediate parties to the employment relationship (workers, management, and possibly unions). But when speaking of a nation's industrial relations system or systems, legislation can be viewed as a process by which the parties (via government) establish terms and conditions of employment or the rules workers and management must follow in establishing those terms and conditions. As another example, when comparing industrial relations systems at a given level of analysis, the roles of the various actors may differ. Unions may play a critical role in one system, and virtually no role in another. In some national systems (e.g., within certain Latin American countries), other actors such as the military or organized religious institutions may play influential roles. The nature of actor roles may also vary across industries within a nation, perhaps as best illustrated by public sector employment, where government is also the employer.

5

Organization Psychology and Industrial Relations

Hugo Munsterberg created the field of industrial psychology with the publication of his text Psychology and Industrial Efficiency in 1913. He argued for the scientific study of human behaviour to identify general patterns and to explain individual differences. Interestingly, Munsterberg saw a link between scientific management and industrial psychology. Both increased efficiency through scientific work analysis and through better alignment of individual skills and abilities with the demands of various jobs.

Munsterberg suggested the use of psychological tests to improve employee selection, the value of learning theory in the development of training methods, and study of human behaviour in order to understand what techniques are most effective for motivating workers. Much of our current knowledge of selection techniques, employee training, work design, and motivation is built on Munsterberg's work.

The Magna Of Labour

Following the stock market crash of 1929, the United States and much of the world's economy entered the Great Depression. To help relieve the effects of the depression Labour force, President Franklin D Roosevelt supported the Wagner Act, which was passed in 1935. This act recognized unions as the authorized representatives of workers, who would be able to bargain collectively with employers in the interests of their members. The Wagner Act would prove to be the Magna Carta of labour. It legitimized the role of trade unions and encouraged rapid growth in union membership.

In response to this legislation, managers in Industry became much more open to finding new ways to handle their employees. Having lost the battle to keep unions out of their factories, the management tried to improve the working conditions and seek better relations with its workforce. A set of studies done at Western Electric's Hawthorne plant would be the prime stimulus for the human relations movement that swept American industry from the late 1930s through the 1950s.

Moon Lighting By Employees: Blue Moon To Full Moon

Wages and salaries are provided to the employees for their service or contribution to the job and organizations. Organizations also pay dearness allowance to take care of the decline in purchasing power of the employee due to rise in cost of living. Similarly, a number of other allowances are provided to the employee. Further organizations also provide various fringe benefits to enhance the living standards of the employees. Despite all these allowances and benefits, employees feel that their wages are low, allowances are inadequate and fringe benefits are insufficient. They feel that the employers enjoy the increased profit and that they are being exploited by the employer.

Consequently they agitate for hike in wages, allowances and benefits so as to improve their living standards. But a few employees in most of the organizations realize that all their demands cannot be met by their organization alone. Hence, they depend either on some other organizations for part-time job, part-time business or take up a business or start an industrial unit in order to earn more money and become much stronger financially. This type of activity i.e. taking up another part-time job or business or industrial unit simultaneously with that of the original job is known as Moon Lighting by Employees (double jobbing).

Blue Moon

Employees in future will demand the management for hike in wages and benefits. The management will also respond positively to the employees demand. Some employees will be satisfied with the increased in wages and benefits and adjust their expenses with the level of wages and benefits from time to time willingly. Some employees will not be satisfied with the level of wages and benefits and will not go for second job in future because of their in ability in getting a second job. Such type of employees will have a conflict with the organizational wage level as this category of employees need a second job for additional income and it will not be available to them. Thus, their efforts to earn additional income through second job will not bear any fruit. Such type of efforts and the consequent result may be called Blue Moon Lighting by employees.

Full Moon Lighting

Employees in some professions/occupations find relatively free time whereas employees in some organizations generally feel that their income from the job is almost negligible, compared to their expectations. Some employees (deserve their) have friends or relatives earning huge money more than their salary. Similarly, some employees view that their friends or relatives with lower educational qualifications and abilities enjoy better social status due to their ownership of and earning from business or industry.

Employees who realize that their jobs are almost negligible from the point of view of social status, venture to start a business unit/industrial unit. They spend most of their time and resources in starting, developing, expanding and diversifying their business or industrial units. They keep on staying on the job as it will be useful for them as a shock absorber in times of need. Their financial and social position will almost be determined by the second occupation. The extent of second jobbing may be known as Full Moon Lighting by employees.

Effect of Moon Lighting of HRM in Future

Moon lighting by employees affects almost all the functions of human resources management. The effects of moon lighting would be mostly negative and it possesses challenges to the HR manager. Presently very limited number of employees does moon lighting. But the number of employees who will do moon lighting will go on increasing due to change in employee values and expectations.

Managements will have to take all possible care in selection process about the possibility of moon lighting by the prospective candidates. Moon lighting will affect human resources development as employees would not be interested in the human resources development as planned by the organizations. Employees will go on demanding for hike in wages and other benefits. The moon lighting will be increased i.e. from dark to full moon and expended to dark moon lighting employees if the management does not accept the demand of the employees.

The relations between the superior and subordinate will be affected adversely in case of moon lighting by sub-ordinates. The disciplinary procedure in that case becomes worse. Managements will face a challenge in motivating the moon lighting and non-moon lighting employees due to varying values, aspirations and goals. It reduces the interest of employees in participative management, quality circles etc. Thus, different degrees of moon lighting by employees will affect Human Resources Management in future adversely. It will become a challenging task to the Human resources managers.

Coverage Of HRM Policies

Policies are made for all the areas of an organization at the top level which give impetus for growth, discipline, productivity of an industry or business. There will be a policy for the entire organization and policy for each and every functional areas say Human Resources, Production, Materials Management etc., These policies act as a management guidelines to the functional heads who can discharge their responsibilities with clarity.

Policies are formulated in such areas which are repetitive in nature. They may cover the following areas:

- Organizational policies including general company policies.
- External policies having their impact on the organizational functioning.
- Internal policies of the organization which guide the internal relations among different units of the organization both vertically and horizontally.
- Centralized policies which guide the relations among different units of the company located in various geographical areas.

INDUSTRIAL RELATIONS SYSTEMS

The dominant paradigm or conceptual framework for the study of industrial relations is the "Industrial Relations Systems" model advanced by Dunlop in his book of the same name.

The concept of a system is applied in the sense that industrial relations, according to Daniel Quinn Mills, author of Labour-Management Relations, consists of the "processes by which human beings and organizations interact at the workplace and, more broadly, in society as a whole to establish the terms and conditions of employment." In other words, certain inputs (e.g., human labour, capital, managerial skill) from the environment are combined via alternative processes (e.g., collective bargaining, unilateral management decisions, legislation) to produce certain outcomes (e.g., production, job satisfaction, wage rates).

Consistent with the definitions of industrial relations noted above, the study of industrial relations and the systems model focus on outcomes most closely related to the interaction of employees and employers and the "web of rules" concerning employment that they and their organizations, along with government, establish to govern employer-employee relations. Thus production per se is a system outcome, but not a principal focus of industrial relations.

It has been noted that the industrial relations system concept may fall short of the definition of a system in the physical or biological sciences, but nonetheless the concept has proved useful and endured.

Dunlop, in Industrial Relations Systems, noted that industrial relations systems can be thought of as being embedded in broader social systems. In Collective Bargaining and Industrial Relations, Kochan observed that like any complex social system, industrial relations systems are best understood by identifying and analysing their various components and how they interact with one another to produce certain outcomes.

The major components of the industrial relations system are:

- The actors (workers and their organizations, management, and government).
- Contextual or environmental factors (labour and product markets, technology, and community or "the locus and distribution of power in the larger society" [from Dunlop's Industrial Relations Systems]).
- Processes for determining the terms and conditions of employment (collective bargaining, legislation, judicial processes, and unilateral management decisions, among others).
- Ideology, or a minimal set of shared beliefs, such as the actors' mutual acceptance of the legitimacy of other actors and their roles, which enhance system stability.
- Outcomes, including wages and benefits, rules about work relations (e.g., standards for disciplinary action against workers), job satisfaction, employment security, productive efficiency, industrial peace and conflict, and industrial democracy.

The basic purposes of the industrial relations systems concept are to provide a conceptual framework for organizing knowledge about industrial relations and for understanding how various components of an industrial relations system combine to produce particular outcomes (and hence why outcomes vary from one setting to another or over time). Thus for example, wage rates for a particular group of workers might be understood as reflecting the interactions of their unions with management via collective bargaining within the constraints of a particular market, technological, and community environment. The precise specification of system components may vary with the level of analysis and from one system to another. For example, when applied to a particular work site, legislation may be best understood as an environmental constraint upon the immediate parties to the employment relationship (workers, management, and possibly unions). But when speaking of a nation's industrial relations system or systems, legislation can be viewed as a process by which the parties (via government) establish terms and conditions of employment or the rules workers and management must follow in establishing those terms and conditions.

As another example, when comparing industrial relations systems at a given level of analysis, the roles of the various actors may differ. Unions may play a critical role in one system, and virtually no role in another. In some national systems (e.g., within certain Latin American countries), other actors such as the military or organized religious institutions may play influential roles. The nature of actor roles may also vary across industries within a nation, perhaps as best illustrated by public sector employment, where government is also the employer.

Criticisms Of The Industrial Relations Systems Model

Although it has endured, the industrial relations systems concept has been criticized and challenged. Criticisms have included charges that it is too static, failing to specify how change occurs in industrial relations; that its treatment of ideology is too simplistic; and that it is too deterministic or does not encourage sufficient appreciation for strategic choices made by the actors.

All of these criticisms have been embodied in recent writings arguing that U.S. industrial relations have been undergoing profound transformations in recent years. Kochan, Harry C. Katz, and Robert B. McKersie-the authors of The Transformation of American Industrial Relations-although not rejecting the systems concept entirely, argue that as it has been widely understood, the systems concept has not prepared us to appreciate the nature and extent of the transformation taking place. In particular, they stress how the strategic choices of management to avoid and oppose unions (both legally and illegally), often in conjunction with decisions to open or close facilities or locate production abroad or in areas where unions are weak, have fundamentally altered U.S. industrial relations.

They note for example, that in the 1950s, when unions represented roughly one-third of U.S. workers, the unionized sector of the economy was often the leader in introducing workplace innovations, including innovations in employment terms and work methods. Further, that level of unionization was sufficiently high to provide a compelling model (or perhaps threat) for nonunion firms, such that they tended to follow the lead of the unionized sector. By the 1980s, however, innovation came to be associated more with the nonunion sector, and with unionization falling, the power of the unionized sector as a model to be emulated by nonunion firms was diminished in tandem.

For example, although unions themselves represent a form of employee participation, many of the recent innovations in employee participation at the workplace level (e.g., employee involvement programmes, team concepts, quality circles, employee empowerment, etc.) are more closely associated with the nonunion sector. In addition, Kochan and his coauthors stress that there are multiple levels of interaction between employers and employees-strategic (e.g., top executives' decisions to open or close facilities), functional (e.g., collective bargaining), and workplace (e.g., day-to-day supervisor-subordinate relations)-arguing that the industrial relations systems conception has tended to encourage excessive preoccupation with the functional level and thereby neglect of the other levels.

During the same time, public policy on employment matters had shifted from a reliance on collective bargaining (and markets) to more of an emphasis on individual worker rights established by statute and judicial decisions. Equal employment opportunity laws and judicial decisions narrowing the notion of employment-at-will (the notion that employer and employee are free to enter or terminate an employment relationship at any time for good reason, bad reason, or no reason in the absence of a formal contract) are prominent examples of this trend. Reflecting its temporal origins, Dunlop's industrial relations systems concept had tended to portray or least be perceived as portraying collective bargaining as the principal mechanism for setting employment terms, although this is not inherent in the industrial relations systems concept. By the 1980s and 1990s, this tendency (or interpretation) was clearly open to question, if not clearly inaccurate.

Although not denying change, several scholars have argued that even though major transformations in industrial relations may be occurring, they are not inconsistent with traditional understandings of industrial relations or the systems concept. For example, in his essay "Industrial Relations as a Strategic Variable," which was published in Human Resources andthe Performance of the Firm, David Lewin noted that many managerial decisions that have been called strategic choices can easily be viewed as managerial responses to environmental imperatives.

Thus to the extent that increased domestic and foreign competition put cost-cutting pressures on employers, these can be seen as strongly influencing employer choices to avoid and oppose unions as well as influencing other employer choices about how to organize production to improve quality and minimize costs. In a recent study of possible industrial relations system transformation in several countries, which was published in Industrial and Labour Relations Review, Christopher L. Erickson and Sarosh Kuruvilla noted that the "transformation debate" persists partly because there is no clear consensus on what constitutes transformation.

THE TRANSFORMATION OF INDUSTRIAL RELATIONS

This changing public policy was partly responsible for a significant transformation of industrial relations in many countries. A major element of the changing landscape of industrial relations has been the almost universal decline in trade union membership and influence, accompanied by a decline in the scope of bargaining and strikes, particularly in the private sector. Other factors contributing to this have been the increasing internationalization of the economy, growth of the service sector, use of computers and other new technologies, and constraints on public spending and on public services. Coinciding with this union decline, increasing attention has been given to new forms of human resource management (HRM) practices associated with the so called High Performance Organization Model (or'high involvement management'), many of which were pioneered in large non-unionized US firms such as IBM. Nonetheless, any supposition that HRM is substituting for trade unions is not supported by the evidence, and certainly elements of both co-exist in many organizations in a variety of counties.

Increasing salience in both policy making and academia has also been given to alternative forms of representation to trade unionism, notably works councils which, as legally constituted in some European countries, are independent from management. This has also fuelled a renewed interest in comparing experiences across countries, particularly in the light of the emphasis in political theory on varieties of capitalism, e.g., coordinated and liberal market economies. Through studying these and other developments the field has moved well beyond its past over-emphasis on trade unions. Employee voice is no longer equated with trade unions.

PRINCIPLES OF SOUND INDUSTRIAL RELATIONS

Maintenance of sound industrial relations is as crucial and difficult as that of human relations. Hence, the following principles should be followed to maintain sound industrial relations:

- Recognition of the dignity of the individual and of his right to personal freedom and equality of opportunity.
- Mutual respect, confidence, understanding, goodwill and acceptance of responsibility on the part of both employer, management and workers and their representatives in the exercises of the rights and duties in the operation of the industry.
- Similarly, there has to be an understanding between the various organisations of employers and employees who represent the management and workers.

SCOPE OF INDUSTRIAL RELATIONS

The scope of industrial relations include:

- Relationship among employees between employees and their superiors or managers.
- Collective relations between trade unions and management. It is called union-management relations.
- Collective relations among trade unions, employers associations and government.

Three actors of industrial relations

According to John T. Dunlop, Industrial societies necessarily create industrial relations defined as the complex of interrelations among workers, management and government.'

Thus three major participants or actors of industrial relations viz., workers and their organisations, management and government are identified.

- *Workers and their organisations*: The total worker plays an important role in industrial relations. The total worker includes working age, educational background, family background, psychological factors, social background, culture, skills, attitude towards others work etc. Workers' organisations prominently known as trade unions. The main purpose of trade unions is to protect the workers' economic interest through collective bargaining and by bringing pressure on management through economic and political tactics.
- *Employers and their organisations*: Employer is a crucial factor in industrial relations. He employs the worker, pays the wages and various allowances, regulates the working relations through various rules, regulations and by enforcing labour laws. He expects the worker to follow the rules, regulations and laws. He further expects them to contribute their resources to the maximum. The difference between the demands of worker and employer results in industrial conflicts.
- *Government*: Government plays a balancing role as a custodian of the nation. Government exerts its influence on industrial relations through its labour policy, industrial relations policy, implementing labour laws, the process of conciliation and adjudication by playing the role of a mediator etc. It tries to regulate the activities and behaviour of both employees organisations and employers' organisations.

EVOLUTION OF INDUSTRIAL RELATIONS IN INDIA

In India the industrial relations have been seen through the following three stages:

- Occupations in India
  - Labour in medieval India
  - Guilds and union.
- Industrial Relations in India
  - Early British Rule
  - 1st World War to Pre-Independence Period
  - Post independence period.

Occupations in Ancient India

In those days, the prime occupation in India was "Agriculture". Trading was of second importance. Manual service formed the third area of preference. Majority of the states were ruled by kings. India was greatly advanced in the industrial field, this is evident from the "Kautilya's Arthashastra". This gives a comprehensive picture of the organisations and functions of the social and political institutions in ancient India.

The caste system had great influence on the development and progress of these industries and occupation. The concept of caste systems was originally based on the transfer of skills and specializations which ultimately led to standardization of professions. The "Atarvana" Veda divides the community into four categories:

- Kshatriya
- Vaishya
- Shudra
- Arya

The following professions become hereditary:

Goldsmiths, weavers, potters, blacksmiths, carpenters, hunters, charioteers, architects, sculptors, armourers. Persons engaged in these occupations become separate communities.

- *Labour Medieval India*: The caste system unified a number of persons belonging in particular occupations and formed the basis of occupational guilds. Indian works of art and crafts were badly ruined with the foreign invasions, which lasted 700 years. These artisans gradually lost the traditional skills. This led to the state that there was no difference between a slave and these artisans. The situation improved only after restoration of law and order under the Mughals. Under Akbar, government factories operated in Agra, Lahore, Fatehpur and Ahmedabad, where employees could develop respective art. A large number of occupations were also carried on by small manufacturers and traders in their cottages mostly on a hereditary basis. A majority of artisans lived in the fringe of starvation.
- *Guilds and Unions*: From early days, craftsmen and workers felt the need of being united. Different terms such as Gana and Vrat as in "Rigveda" Sheshthi in Aitareya Brahmana; Gana and Ganapati in Vajasaneyi Samhita; Sreni in Arthashastra and Puga, Gana, Vrat, Shremi and Sangha have been used to indicate what Katyanyana calls group.

These unions gradually gained strength and were helpful not only in the evolution of arts but were powerful centers of arts in themselves. Only responsible persons could become their members. The union followed democratic principles. In event of a dispute between the president and the members, the king intervened and brought about conciliations.

Kautilya has given a good description of the unions of employees, craftsmen or artisans. According to him the work of unions should be controlled by the board of 3 directors, members should pay the entrance fee to the president and the profits earned by the unions should be equally distributed among their members.

Almost every craft, profession or occupation had its own union which was called "Shreni". Every "Shreni" included about 1000 members. The Shreni elected its chief who was called the "Pramukha" or "Jyeshta". These guilds and corporations wielded considerable political power and influence.

Industrial Relation in India

However due to the autocratic regime of the Muslim rulers, the economic conditions of the employees was deplorable. Labourers could be forced to leave home to work on wages, as per the "Forman" of the emperor or the Governor, as the case may be. There were no organisations of the workers during the Mughal rule which could deal with the difficulties and problems of the members.

The wages, if paid were very meager and insufficient for a day meal too. They were also paid in the form of old, used and tattered clothes and such other articles, when the emperor and his officials dealt harshly with the workers cordial relations between layout and capitol could not be expected to exist. Commercial character of the East India Company did not change the conditions of the workers. The underdevelopment of the economy continued even under the British rule. But collective relations in industry were modeled on the British pattern. In fact the growth of industries in different parts of the country was based on the need for good industrial relations.

- Early British Rule: There was not much if scope for industrial development in India during the early British rule. India was expected to be colonial market for British goods till the second half of the 19th Century. A cotton mill was established in Bombay and Calcutta. The workers were to work in subversive and deplorable conditions, while they were exploited by their contractors. Their relations had been strained and the workers abstained themselves from work. As a result, many disputes rose.

Mining industry also started slowly. Tata Iron and Steel industry had been established in Jamshedpur, which produced on a moderate scale. Engineering and railway workshops, iron and brass foundries etc had also been developed in a moderate way prior to World War-I.

The modern industry in India owes a great deal to the initiative of the Europeans. However the workers were not satisfied with the working conditions and the worker-management relations were not cordial. Hence the Factories Act of 1881 was passed which gave an impetus to the worker's approach for redressal.

- *World War-I*: This was period of Boom for all employers. With the rising prices, the profit also went up enormously. The wages of the workers, however did not keep pace with this tendency. The economic distress brought workers together and an organised working class movement began in the country. The unrest among the workers found an outlet in increased strike actions among which the one at Ahmedabad and other at Chennai are famous. During this period, as a result of ILO influence, various laws were enacted (Workmen's compensation act -1923, the trade unions act-1926 and the Trade disputes act - 1917)

During the second war, employers made enormous profits. The workers demanded a share in them. Bonus and dearness allowance were granted to them but as money wages did not increase in proportion to the rise in prices, the government tried to check dissatisfaction of workers and consequential strike activity by prohibiting strikes under the emergency rules.

- *Post Independence Era*: Immediately after independence, in the interests of the national economy, it was considered necessary to put a stop to strikes and lockouts that interrupted production. A tripartite conference was adopted, giving paramount importance to the maintenance of industrial peace. The minimum wages act, the factories act and Employees State insurance Act were all enacted 1948.

Post independence industrial relations were very much influenced by the pre-independence industrial environments and labour management relations. Industrial unrest and shattered worker management relations prevailed everywhere when India became independent in 1947. Government has emerged as an arbitrator between management and workers. During the second five year plan, certain norms, mechanisms and practices were evolved which formulate the need of minimum wage, wage boards, guidelines on rationalization, code of discipline, code of conduct, scheme for workers participation in management.

Future of Industrial Relations in India

- The first is the issue of strengthening collective bargaining by trying to determine a sole bargaining agent for negotiation. The state of Maharashtra has already passed a law for the creation of a sole bargaining agency in every unit and industry. Collective Bargaining is advocated where the parties involved have a fuller understanding. This will help to arrive at a speedier settlement of disputes between themselves.
- The second issue relates to the gaps that are occurring as a result of the variations that occur in Central and State legislation as far as labour matters is concerned. In India, labour falls under the Concurrent List

though NCL has made a recommendation for forming a common labour code, which is yet to be adopted. Adoption of this recommendation will go a long way in solving some of the problems that India's legislation process in facing.

- Another issue is that of worker's participation in management. India has already experienced working of many forms of worker participation schemes but none of them seems to have made any headway. The reasons for the failure of these schemes need to be probed into.

Its strategic importance extends beyond the limited frontiers of union-management relationship and overlaps with the future prospects for Indian democracy on one hand, and the basic concepts and assumptions of economic development on the other. The set of strategic choices must be made in the midst of economic and political difficulties that the country is undergoing.

APPROACHES TO INDUSTRIAL RELATIONS

In its stricter sense, the term "industrial relations" means relationship between management and workmen in a unit or an industry. In its wider connotation, it means the organisation and practice of multi-pronged relationships between workers and management, unions and workers, and the unions and managements in an industry. Dale Yoder defines it as a "whole field of relationship that exists because of the necessary collaboration of men and women in the employment process of an industry."

Tead and Metcalfe observed that "industrial relations are the composite result of the attitudes and approaches of employers and employees towards each other with regard to planning, supervision, direction and coordination of the activities of an organization with a minimum of human efforts and frictions with an animating spirit of cooperation and with proper regard for the genuine well-being of all members of the organization."

According to Allan Flanders, "the subject of industrial relations deals with certain regulated or institutionalized relationships in industry. Personal or in the language of sociology, "unstructured" relationships have their importance for management and workers, but they lie outside the scope of a system of industrial relations." Professor Clegg defines industrial relations in the broadest terms as encompassing the rules governing employment together with the ways in which the rules are made and changed and their interpretation and administration." To put it simply, industrial relations is that part of management which is concerned with the manpower of the enterprise. It is, thus, the relation created at different levels of the organisation by the diverse, complex and composite needs and aspirations and attitudes and approaches among the participants. It is a highly complex and dynamic process of relationships involving not only employees and managements, but also their collective forums and the State. In an organisation, these relationships may be personal and informal at one end, and may be highly institutional with legally prescribed structures and procedures, at the other end.

The four main parties who are actively associated with any industrial relations system are the workers, the managements, the organisations of workers and managements, and the State. Fundamentally, the term industrial relations refers to an organised relationship between two organised parties representing employers and employees regarding matters of collective interest. With the growth of professional management, the industrial relations scene is being represented by the representatives of both the employers and the employees. But the scope of industrial relations cannot merely be confined to common labour-management relations or employer-employee relations. It is a comprehensive and total concept embracing the sum total of relationships that exists at various levels of the organisational structure.

More specifically, it connotes relations among workers themselves within the class of employees, relations among the managements within the managerial class, and relations between the two distinct classes of workers and management. It denotes all types of inter-group and intragroup relations within industry, both formal and informal. It consists of a complex network of relations that arise out of functional interdependence between workers and managements and between industrial organisations and society. Industrial relations is a social concept because it deals with social relationships in different walks of life. It is also a relative concept because it grows and flourishes or stagnates and decays in accordance with the economic, social and political conditions prevailing in a society and the laws made by the state to regulate them. The advances made in the field of science and technology also influence the state of industrial relations. There is greater divergence in industrial relations systems as a result of the divergent economic, social, political and cultural environments.

Objectives

Apart from the primary objective of bringing about sound and healthy relations between employers and employees, industrial relations aim:

i) to facilitate production and productivity;

ii) to safeguard the rights and interests of both labour and management by enlisting their co-operation;

iii) to achieve a sound, harmonious, and mutually beneficial labour management relations;

iv) to avoid unhealthy atmosphere in the industry, especially work, stoppages, goslows, gheraos, strikes, lockouts; and

v) to establish and maintain industrial democracy.

The state endeavours to correct, through effective industrial relations, an imbalanced, disordered and maladjusted social and economic order with a view to reshaping the complex socio-economic relationships following technological and economic progress. It also controls and disciplines the parties concerned and adjusts their conflicting interests. In this process, it protects some and restrains others, depending upon the situation.

According to Kirkaldy,5 industrial relations in a country are intimately connected with the form of its political government; and the objectives of an industrial organisation may vary from purely economic to purely political ends. He divides the objectives of industrial relations into four categories:

i) improvement in the economic conditions of workers in the existing state of industrial management and political government;
ii) control exercised by the state over industrial undertakings with a view to regulating production and promoting harmonious industrial relations;
iii) socialisation or rationalisation of industries by making the state itself a major employer; and
iv) vesting of a proprietary interest of the workers in the industries in which they are employed.

The industrial relations objectives must follow the determination of business objectives which they should be intended to facilitate. In this context, the industrial relations policies and practices should not negate its intentions in other areas. For instance, if a company wishes to encourage voluntary retirement, its salaries, pensions, and working conditions should not encourage its employees to stay at all costs.

Approach

The problems posed in the field of industrial relations cannot be solved within the limits of a single discipline, and hence it is bound to be inter-disciplinary in approach. It is an interdisciplinary field that includes inputs from sociology, psychology, law, history, politics, economics, accounting and other elements of management studies. Industrial relations, then, has a dual character, it is both an interdisciplinary field and a separate discipline in its own right. It is much more of an art than it is a science. Industrial relations is largely an applied field concerned with practice and the training of practitioners rather than with theory and measurement. It is thus related to the basic social sciences as engineering is to the physical sciences or medicine is to the biological sciences.

Any problem in industrial relations has to be approached on a multi-disciplinary basis, drawing from the contributions of the above disciplines. The causes of an industrial dispute may be, by nature, economic, social, psychological or political or a combination of any of them. Labour economics provides an economic interpretation of the problems growing out of employer-employee relationship. Industrial sociology explains the social background of the workers, which is essential for the understanding of industrial relations. Industrial psychology clarifies certain concepts and provides empirical tools in areas such as recruitment, placement, training, fatigue and morale. For instance, attitudes and morale surveys are powerful tools to discover causes of industrial strife and to evolve methods for their prevention. Labour laws and their interpretation by tribunals and courts contributes to the growth of industrial jurisprudence. Application of quantitative analysis and labour statistics throws light on the exact state of industrial relations during a particular period. Political aspects also assume importance in industrial relations, particularly in a developing economy dominated by centralised planning. In fact, the growth of industrial relations as a scientific discipline depends upon the extent to which it integrates the contribution of established disciplines in the social sciences. There is no country where industrial relations is entirely a matter of tradition or custom nor is there a country where the employers, the workers or their organisations and the government do not at all interact to build up the country's industrial relations system. It has been a mixture of traditions, customs and a web of action, reaction and interaction between the parties. The industrial relations system may be conceived at different levels, such as national, regional, industrial and workplace. The concept of the system has been influential in establishing industrial relations as a discipline in its own right. The concepts of the system approach are operationally definable. An industrial relations system may be defined as comprising the totality of power interactions of participants in a workplace, when these interactions involve industrial relations issues. It is viewed as an integral and non-separable part of the organisational structure and its dynamics. An industrial relations system includes all the individuals and institutions that interact at the workplace. Regardless of the level at which the system exists, an industrial relations system can be viewed as having three components: (1) a set of individuals and institutions that interact; (2) a context within which the interaction takes place; and (3) an output that serves to govern the future relationship of the parties. The components of industrial relations system are:

i) Participants: The participants in the industrial relations sphere are composed of duly recognised representatives of the parties interacting in several roles within the system.
ii) Issues: The power interactions of the participants in a workplace create industrial relations issues. These issues and the consequences of power interactions find their expression in a web of rules governing the behaviour of the parties at a workplace.

iii) Structure: The structure consists of all forms of institutionalised behaviour in a system. The structure may include collective procedures, grievances, and settlement practices. Legal enactments relevant to power interactions may also be considered to be a part of the structure.

iv) Boundaries: In systems analysis, it is possible to find an issue which one participant is totally indifferent to resolving while, at the same time, the other participant is highly concerned about resolution of the same. These issues may serve to delimit systems boundaries.

At least there are three marked features of the systems approach. They are:

i) Inter-disciplinary Character: Some theorists regard the systems approach to be universally applicable to all human relationships, in small or large units. Its flexibility of application in the behavioural sciences has been aptly demonstrated.

ii) Suitability to Work Organisation and their Sub-systems: The adaptability of the systems approach to organisation is also a frequently discussed trait. This springs from the fact that organisations, and to some extent their sub-systems, are rational and purposeful.

iii) Dynamic Aspects: A systems approach is oriented towards the study of interactions and changing relations.

GLOBALIZATION AND INDUSTRIAL RELATIONS

The pressures on traditional IR models are not all due to globalization, as we shall see, but many of the changes taking place can be traced to globalization. it is not always easy to disentangle the causes and effects of globalization. However, it would probably be true to say that globalization is represented by the opening up of markets due, in large measure, to foreign direct investment consequent upon the lowering of investment barriers in practically all countries; by the liberalization of trade, and by the deregulation of financial markets in consequence of which governments increasingly have little control over the flow of capital across borders. All this implies the dominance of the market system, facilitated by the collapse of alternative economic (and in many cases political) systems. There is also a direct link between globalization and information technology (IT). Rapid technological change and reduction in communication costs have facilitated the globalization of production and financial markets. At the same time globalization stimulates technology through increased competition; it diffuses technology through foreign direct investment. As aptly observed:

"Together, globalization and IT crush time and space."

These developments have had further effects such as:

- Democratization and pressures for more labour rights in countries where such rights have been restricted
- More liberalization and deregulation
- Competition for investment
- Increased economic independence of nations
- Capital, information and technology flows are on the increase
- Internationalization of enterprises and creation of mergers and alliances
- Customer-driven (and not product-driven) global and local markets, but at the same time segmented markets
- Competitiveness increasingly based (not on low wages or natural resources) on knowledge/innovation, skills and productivity. The success of global companies is to a large extent dependent on their ability to organize (within and between organizations) across national boundaries information, money, people and other resources.

Employer Responses and Implicationsfor Industrial Relations

Among the responses of employers are the following:

- Moving production overseas to reduce costs and to facilitate sensitivity to local and regional market requirements.
- Contracting out and out-sourcing. It is an important rationale of out-sourcing that it, on the one hand, enables an enterprise to concentrate on its core competencies, and on the other hand, it makes service work more productive. For example, in the USA, outsourcing of functions in hospitals not directly related to the work of doctors and nurses (care of patients) has substantially increased the productivity of the hospitals, and provided new opportunities for service employees. "Outsourcing is needed not just because of the economics involved. It is required equally because it gives opportunities, income and dignity to service work and service workers."
- More part-time and temporary work (especially among women, the elderly and students)
- Introduction of new technology
- Pushing for a more deregulated and flexible labour market
- More emphasis on productivity and quality
- Greater employee involvement in the design and execution of work
- Shifting the focus of collective bargaining from the nation/industry level to the enterprise level. Employers are of the view that issues relevant to the employment relationship such as work re-organization, flexible working hours and contractual arrangements, and pay for performance and skills, are increasingly workplace-related, and should therefore be

addressed at the enterprise level. In the USA collective bargaining has, with some exceptions, been very much at the enterprise level; in the UK there is a marked shift towards enterprise bargaining; and the trends in Continental Europe are also in that direction. In many Asian countries outside Australia and New Zealand, the relatively little collective bargaining has been mostly at the enterprise level. In New Zealand negotiation has in the 1990s been almost entirely decentralized, and in Australia the trend is in the direction of decentralization.

- Exceptionally (in the USA) employers have reduced terms of employment through 'concession bargaining' when firms have been in financial difficulties.
- Downsizing the workforce.

One important response has been the introduction of flexibility in the employment relationship to increase the capacity of enterprises to adapt rapidly to market changes. This has involved measures such as

- Flexible working hours
- Part-time work
- Different types of employment contracts to the standard ones familiar to collective IR
- Flexibility in functions, so that employees who are multi-skilled are not confined to the performance of only one task. They can cover up for absenteeism, and make some jobs redundant.
- Flexible pay which involves some component of pay being dependent on performance, whether of the company, a group or the individual.

Globalization has, through technology diffusion, substantially increased the introduction of new technology. This, as well as the need for flexible adaptation to market changes, have led to the re-organization of production systems and methods of work, such as the following:

- Reduction of narrow job classifications and demarcation lines between managers and workers, accompanied by skills enhancement needed to perform jobs with a broader range of tasks.
- Increasing areas for worker involvement in the conception, execution and control of work.
- A greater focus on workplace relations and policies and practices conducive to better motivation and performance such as information-sharing and two-way communication.

These responses have increased the necessity for employers to make more investments in skills training, to offer incentives to employees to improve their skills, and for workers to take upon themselves some responsibility for their own development. The competition generated by globalization and rapid technological changes accompanied by shorter product life have, while destroying countless jobs in industrialized countries, created opportunities for multi-skilled and easily trainable workers, and for the most significant group of emerging employees - the knowledge worker. Knowledge and skills have become the most important determinants of investment, employment opportunities, productivity and quality and of flexibility.

The impact globalization and information technology have had on each other has made work more mobile, capable of being performed in different parts of the world without the need to actually set up physical facilities in other countries. Other changes in the nature of work and workers are being brought about partly by globalization, but not entirely because of it. For instance, it is arguable whether globalization is solely responsible for the growing service sector, and it does not account for the rapid influx of women into the workforce. Be that as it may, some of the changes which have a fundamental impact on traditional IR include the following:

- The expanding service sector at the expense of the manufacturing sector in industrialized and rapidly industrializing countries
- More advanced and skilled workforces
- The rapid influx into the workforce of women who will, in some countries, occupy more than half the emerging jobs
- An increasing number of people who will not be working in an organization, though they will be working for an organization
- The decreasing number of people working under 'permanent' contracts of employment, and the proliferation of other types of work arrangements such as part-time and temporary work, home work and contract work. Thus traditional IR has been challenged to accommodate different types of employment contracts, and different types of pay systems to reward performance and skills.

Competitive Advantage and Industrial Relations

The push for competitive advantage render it necessary for IR, without abandoning its earlier function of providing mechanisms to secure a fair distribution of the gains of economic performance, to also develop a strategic perspective which promotes the goal of competitiveness. This implies an IR system not only from the point of view of bargaining, conflict resolution, basic rights and so on, but also from the point of view of contributing to enterprise performance on which the welfare of employees also depends.

Viewing IR from the perspective of competitive advantage involves distinguishing between competitive and comparative advantage. Whether it is economies or enterprises that truly compete in the global marketplace is a complex issue. But certainly the overall national environment of which IR is a part, contributes to the competitiveness of industries and enterprises. However, as pointed out by Michael Porter, there is "no accepted definition of competitiveness. To firms competitiveness (means) the ability to compete in world markets with a global strategy."On the other hand, to some politicians it signifies a positive balance of trade, while to some economists it means a low unit cost of labour adjusted for exchange rates.

Comparative advantage of a country is based on the greatest advantage (or the least disadvantage) a nation has in relation to its trading partners. Where this advantage depends on a natural resource (e.g. oil) and wages rise to a level similar to that of competitors, the comparative advantage is lost. Dependence on low skilled low cost labour renders it impossible to add value to the particular advantage or resource. Where the investment in education and skills development has been low or inappropriate, moving to more value-added activities becomes difficult, if not impossible.

Competitive advantage, by contrast, is based on the ability to add value to the advantage or resource. High and appropriate investment in education and skills enables the absorption of higher wages, which are compensated or off-set by higher productivity/quality and the capacity to innovate and introduce technological change. Today, of the many factors on which competitiveness is based,people are a key factor. Their contribution to competitiveness is conditioned by their literacy, type and quality of education, their skills, motivation, work attitudes, value systems and quality of life.

If, therefore, employers do not see IR as contributing to strategic management objectives, they will continue to view the techniques of HRM as being more relevant to their objectives, as a way of individualizing the employment relationship and keeping decision-making within the enterprise. Hence the issue - to be covered elsewhere in this Paper - of harmonizing IR and HRM.

Management and Industrial Relationsn

These developments impact not only on IR. Technology, information and the imperatives of succeeding in the global marketplace are transforming the way enterprises are managed as well as management objectives themselves. The much closer relationship between management and IR needs to be recognized - principally because both must focus on people and IR at the workplace level.

Industrial relations systems and practices are shaped by the three main actors - governments, workers/unions and employers/employers' organizations. In Asia, for instance, governments have had a significant impact on IR. In Continental Europe unions in some countries (Germany and the Nordic countries) have had a major influence on shaping IR. In the UK the Thatcher governments had a significant influence in changing the direction of IR. In the USA it has been more employer-driven. However, it has been too infrequently appreciated by IR specialists that IR are shaped to a large extent by the way enterprises are managed, and that when fundamental changes occur in management they create changes in IR as well.

This is particularly so in the context of globalization; many of the changes taking place in IR - indeed the increasing shift from collective IR to more enterprise (and in some cases, individual) focused IR - are spurred by employers. It is significant that the collective standardized model of IR evolved during the era of the classical model of the enterprise which itself sought standardization at the expense of creativity and innovation.

Therefore in this context it is useful to note two important - and diametrically opposite - theories about management. The first and earlier theory is to be found in the scientific management school, which viewed the worker as a mere cog in the organizational structure. Since, according to Taylor, the worker does not possess creative ability let alone intelligence and wisdom, the elements of a human-oriented management system which promotes sound industrial relations such as communication, consultation and participation, found no place in the theory.

The hallmarks of organizations based on this model are centralized and clear lines of authority, a high degree of specialization, a distinct division of labour, numerous rules pertaining to authority and responsibility, and close supervision. This concept of management can be seen as an ideal breeding ground for an industrial relations system based on conflict rather than on cooperation.

The opposite theory, appropriately styled the human relations school, had as one of its earliest and celebrated exponents, Douglas McGregor. He gave an impetus to the development of a management theory which focused on the human being as part of an enterprise, which, in turn, was viewed as a biological system, rather than as a machine. Human relations, trust, delegation of authority, etc. were some of the features of this theory. In the preface to his classic.

The Human Side of Enterprise McGregor underlined the necessity to learn "about the utilization of talent, about the creation of an organizational climate conducive to human growth... This volume is an attempt to substantiate the thesis that the human side of enterprise is 'all of a piece' - that the theoretical assumptions management holds about controlling its human resources determine the whole character of the enterprise. They determine also the quality of its successive generations of management."

Two basic realities of an organization in McGregor's model is the dependence of every manager on people under him and the potential of people to be developed to match organizational goals. He therefore postulated that people are not by nature resistant to change in an organization, and that people have the potential to be developed and to shoulder responsibility. As such, management's main task is to organize business in such a way as to match people's goals with organizational ones. McGregor believed that the dynamism for organizational growth is found in the employees of the organization. It could be said that in McGregor's Theory Y (as it is called) is to be found the essence of human-oriented management and workplace industrial relations systems. The events noted in the succeeding paragraphs which are compelling enterprises to pay greater attention to the human factor in management, serve to vindicate McGregor's basic theory propounded as far back as 1960, if not earlier.

However, subject to exceptions (such as Japan in Asia) most large enterprises continued to be dominated by hierarchies. This is reflected in the classic "strategy, structure, systems" (the three Ss) of modern corporations, vividly expressed by two writers:

"Structure follows strategy. And systems support structure. Few aphorisms have prevented western business thinking as deeply as these two. Not only do they influence the architecture of today's largest corporations but they also define the role that top corporate managers play."

As explained by Bartlett and Ghoshal, in this concept of an enterprise top level managers see themselves as the designers of strategy, the architects of structure, and the managers of systems. The impact of the three Ss was to create a management system which minimized the idiosyncracies of human behaviour, emphasized discipline, focus and control, and led to the view that people were "replaceable parts".

The basic flaw - particularly in the context of today's globalized environment - of this concept is that it stifled the most scarce resource available to an enterprise: the knowledge, creativity and skills of people. Successful enterprises have now moved away from this corporate design, and their philosophy, which has transformed corporations enabling them to compete in the new competitive environment, consists of the following:

"First, they place less emphasis on following a clear strategic plan than on building a rich, engaging corporate purpose. Next, they focus less on formal structural design and more on effective management processes. Finally, they are less concerned with controlling employees' behaviour than with developing their capabilities and broadening their perspectives. In sum, they have moved beyond the old doctrine of strategy, structure, and systems to a softer, more organic model built on the development of purpose, process and people."

Those enterprises which have effected a successful transformation to a more 'people-focused' organization recognize that the information necessary to formulate strategy is with their frontline people who know what is actually going on, whether it be in the marketplace or on the shopfloor. The chief executive officer, for instance, can no longer be the chief architect of strategy without the involvement of those much lower down in the hierarchy.

How do these developments relate to enterprise level labour relations? In essence, they heighten the importance of the basic concepts of information sharing, consultation and two-way communication. The effectiveness of the procedures and systems which are established for better information flow, understanding and, where possible, consensus-building, is critical today to the successful managing of enterprises and for achieving competitiveness. As such, the basic ingredients of sound enterprise level labour relations are inseparable from some of the essentials for managing an enterprise in today's globalized environment. These developments have had an impact on ways of motivating workers, and on the hierarchy of organizations. They are reducing layers of management thus facilitating improved communication.

Management today is more an activity rather than a badge of status or class within an organization, and this change provides it with a wider professional base. The present trend in labour relations and human resource management is to place greater emphasis on employee involvement, harmonious employer-employee relations and on practices which promote them. One of the important consequences of globalization and intense competition has been the pressure on enterprises to be flexible. Enterprises have sought to achieve this in two ways. First, through technology and a much wider worker skills base than before in order to enhance capacity to adapt to market changes. Second, by introducing a range of employee involvement schemes with a view to increasing labour-management cooperation at the shop floor level, necessary to achieve product and process innovation.

Achieving flexibility does not depend on the absence of unions. Organizational flexibility "depends upon trust between labour and management. It implies that workers are willing to forego efforts to establish and enforce individually or through collective action susbtantive work rules that fix the allocation of work, transfer among jobs, and workloads. Organizational flexibility also implies that workers are willing to disclose their proprietary knowledge in order to increase labour productivity and the firm's capacity for innovation."

Manufacturers in Japan and Germany were more successful than those in, for example, Britain and France in achieving this flexibility. The two former countries after World War II institutionalized labour-management consultation. Many organizations have successfully transformed themselves to promote the role of trust. In strategies involving the use of technology and promotion of innovation, employees are a critical factor. The requirement of organizational flexibility and its industrial relations and human resource implications have had a major impact on the way organizations are structured (less hierarchical), how authority within the firm is exercised (less unilateral), and on how decisions are arrived at and work organized (through information sharing and consultation, transfer of more responsibility to employees and cooperative methods such as team work).

Traditional assumptions that efficiency is achieved through managerial control, technology and allocation of resources have given way to the view that efficiency is the result of greater involvement of employees in their jobs, teams and the enterprise. Organizations which have made this shift tend to reflect the following characteristics: few hierarchical levels; wide spands of control; continuous staff development; self managing work teams; job rotation; commitment to quality; information sharing; pay systems which cater to performance rewards and not only payment for the job; generation of high performance expectations; a common corporate vision; and participative leadership styles. It hardly requires emphasis that achieving most of these requires training. In Asia too there is a keen awareness in the business community that radical changes are necessary to sustain Asia's dynamic growth. The point is well made by a noted Asian: The earlier generation's recipe for success hinged on hard work, smart moves, the right business and political connections, monopolies, protectionist barriers, subsidies, access to cheap funds and, in many cases, autocratic leadership and a docile labour force.

The 'global village' is this system's nemesis... the new 'Global-Asian' manager has to exercise greater levels of leadership than before, and balance this with being an entrepreneur, modern manager and deal-maker skilled at public relations. To this has to be added coaching, team-building and motivating the company, the ability to visualize, plan strategically, market and re-engineer products and services, and the belief in a customer driven culture.

None of these shifts is feasible without a substantial change in traditional models of dealing with people in an enterprise.

The Multinational Dimension

Globalization has substantially increased the influence of multinationals (MNEs) on the IR environment. A few figures indicate their importance in the global economy:

- From about 7,000 MNEs in 1969, the number has increased to over 37,000 today
- Though employing directly less than 2% of the world's labour force, they account for one-third of the world's private sector assets, and have world-wide sales of US $ 5.5 trillion, which is marginally less than the USA's GDP in 1993.

- In 1995 foreign direct investment was in the region of US $318 billion, with the USA receiving US $60 billion and the UK US $30 billion.

What is significant about the increased presence of MNEs, especially in developing countries, is that governments are competing to attract them and are prepared to change the environment (including the IR environment) to achieve this objective. This gives the MNEs the opportunity to spur changes which have commenced - for instance, in economies in trasnition. The point is graphically made by the well-known former CEO of Asean Brown Boveri, Percy Barnevik: Global companies speed up the adjustment. We don't create the process, but we push it. We make visible the invisible hand of global competition.

FUTURE ISSUES FOR INDUSTRIAL RELATIONS

Continuing Relevance of Industrial Relations

In a globalized environment with businesses, money and people moving with relative ease across borders, the relentless pursuit of competitive advantage at the expense of all else, the disruption of social relationships and stability, the rapid outdating of knowledge, skills and technology, with learning being a life-long pursuit, and increasing job insecurity, the only certain factor is change and its rapidity.

Poverty worldwide is nowhere near reduction to minimal levels, and on the contrary, is increasing. Many of the benefits of recent changes have benefited a few, and in many countries income gaps are widening, rather than narrowing. It has been suggested by eminent writers that the world may well be heading towards over-production of goods, food shortages, and environmental degradation. Before we dispense with institutions or systems which have contributed to social stability, it is worthwhile assessing their continued relevance. Industrial relations is one such.

IR is no doubt undergoing needed changes, but it is by no means irrelevant. Its major contribution was that it facilitated distributive justice and thereby contributed to social stability. Western Europe is probably the best example of an IR system which was underpinned by its social market principles and, by concerning itself with distributive justice and equity, raised the living standards of the majority, thus providing decades of relative social stability.

If, as many employers claim, the labour market in that region is too regulated in the context of the changed environment, this does not imply a total abandonment of the system, but only its reform. In fact when we speak of changes in IR in many countries, it does not always imply a radical change, but rather a change of emphasis. For instance, the idea of negotiation on which collective bargaining is based, continues to be valid even if the trend is towards decentralized bargaining. Nor is there anything in HRM that contradicts the value of negotiation. HRM undoubtedly poses a challenge to IR as we have seen. But a democracy and pluralism are based on the recognition of different interest groups within a society, each acting as a check and balance in relation to the other to prevent a centralization of power. A system which provides some external regulation of the behaviour of groups must therefore be necessary. Since HRM is enterprise-focused, there is a need for a system which can deal with issues which arise in the external labour market.

At last for those who have no individual bargaining power - and they constitute the majority of the world's working population - traditional IR institutions such as freedom of association, collective bargaining, minimum employment terms (e. g. age of employment, force labour, safety and health, holidays), social security and dispute settlement mechanisms continue to be relevant. Policies need to be formulated on these matters and applied across society. The fact that some traditional IR features may need to be changed, does not imply that they are irrelevant; the need for a greater enterprise focus does not imply the absence of a national focus as well.

IR institutions continue to have the following relevance:

- Collective bargaining, even if it be at the enterprise level, can still help to reduce inequalities in negotiating power
- Freedom of association provides the foundation for the recognition that employees have rights.
- Industrial peace needs to be ensured both by addressing it at the enterprise level, any by providing in the event of their failure, safeguard mechanisms external to the enterprise such as conciliation, courts or tribunals.
- Processes such as tripartism are needed to ensure that the relevant parties have the opportunity to influence labour policy and legislative outcomes.
- The boundaries of action within which parties may act need to be set.
- Social protection through minimum standards may often be required, whether they relate to children or women, safety and health or superannuation.

Current And Future Issues

In these circumstances the issues which IR will be called upon to address, in particular in Asia, need to be identified. Employers are now compelled to view IR and HRM from a strategic perspective; in other words, not only from the traditional viewpoint of negotiating terms and conditions of employment and performing a personnel and welfare function. IR and HRM are directly relevant to competitiveness, and how they are managed will impact on enterprise performance, e.g. its productivity and quality of goods and services, labour costs, quality of the workforce, motivation, prevention of disputes and not only their settlement, and aligning employee aspirations with enterprise objectives.

Minimum Wages

In countries which have a legal minimum wage three employer concerns are evident. The first is that minimum wage levels sometimes tend to be fixed on extraneous considerations (e.g. political), or on inadequate data needed to define the level of wages. The second concern is that such instances have an adverse effect on competitiveness in the global market and on employment creation where the minimum wage is fixed above a certain level (much of the controversy relates to what that level is). Therefore many employers prefer to see the minimum wage, if there is to be one at all, as a'safety net' measure to uplift those living below the poverty line. The third concern relates to increases in minimum wages not being matched by productivity gains which would help to offset increased labour costs.

Flexible/Performance Pay

Many employers, and even some governments, wish to review traditional criteria to determine pay levels such as the cost of living and seniority. Pay system which are flexible (i.e based on profitability and productivity) so as to be able to absorb business downturns and also reward performance, are receiving considerable attention. One major problem in this regard is how employees and their organizations can be persuaded to negotiate on pay reform. The objectives of pay reform will not be achieved unless reforms are the result of consensual agreements and are a part of a larger human resource management strategy and change in human resource management systems.

"We now pay workers not for output produced, nor even for labour input provided, but simply for time spend on the job." Traditionally wages and pay have been determined through government regulation, minimum wage determination, negotiation with unions, decisions of arbitration and labour courts and the individual contract of employment. The factors or criteria which have influenced pay and pay increases have included profit (but generally unrelated to individual or group performance). Job evaluation, seniority, cost of living, manpower shortage or surplus, negotiating strength of the parties and skills.

Performance measures such as productivity or profit related to the performance of a group has been of less importance in determining pay increases. Though skills have been reflected in pay differentials, pay systems have been seldom geared to the encouragement of skills acquisition and application. Industrialized countries have built their competitive advantage not around low wages, but around clusters of competitive industries in which high earnings and standards of living have been sustained through improved technology, productivity and quality. Many Asian countries now recognize that high technology; productivity and low earnings cannot be combined and sustained over a long period of time.

Many Asian employers are now seeking to sustain their competitiveness through pay increases which are more related to performance measures as a way of absorbing increased labour costs, while at the same time rewarding and motivating employees. Japan, Singapore and the Republic of Korea, for example, have succeeded in moving to high value-added and technology-based or service activities partly because they had invested in skills development and accepted the fact that higher earnings (in Singapore partly through a flexible pay system) are an essential strategy for entry into the knowledge-based industries of the future.

Increases in real earnings have been made possible because investment in education and skills contributed to productivity enhancement which, in turn, created the capacity to absorb higher earnings. In the 1980s Singapore made a deliberate shift to a high wage economy in order to encourage entry into high value-added activities. Productivity increases are necessary to sustain higher earnings; at the same time there cannot be a long term productivity growth without an increase in real wages.

Traditional pay systems for non-executive staff have generally been characterized by standardization across and within sectors (e.g. government, particular industries) and within enterprises. So long as employers were competing mainly in domestic markets which were protected from foreign competition - in some cases leading to monopolies - the effects of standardization on considerations such as performance, recruitment and retention of good staff, etc. were less felt. Indeed, standardization, while being equitable from the point of view of employees, benefited employers as well by reducing competition based on labour costs.

With the gradual opening up of economies to world trade and foreign investment, local employers are now compelled to compete with enterprises with sophisticated technology, more productive ways of providing goods and services, and the advantage of being global players. In many instances these foreign enterprises are able to attract the best local talent on terms and conditions beyond the capacity of many local enterprises to pay. With the acceleration of the process of globalization, accompanied by the movement of former centrally planned economies towards market economies, governments and private enterprises have had to compete in the global market by developing competitive advantages, which are affected by costs and quality.

Productivity increase as the measure of performance at the national and enterprise levels, with quality as an intrinsic part of productivity, is becoming the goal of many developing countries as well - now pushed to the forefront by the forces of globalization and the collapse of economic systems which were alternatives to a market economy. Economies which are seeking to progress from low cost manufacturing to highly-skilled and technology-based production need pay systems which not merely recognize skill differentials (as standard pay systems do), but also provide an incentive to acquire skills and multi-skills facilitated by years of careful and correct investment in education and training.

In the area of IR, collective bargaining outside the enterprise is seen by employers as achieving distributive justice in the sense of equality, with outcomes often being based on the bargaining strength of the parties. It is increasingly viewed as contributing little to productivity and performance. The outcomes often leave employers with little or no capacity to make further payments on account of performance under a scheme. The movement towards decentralization of collective bargaining has been the result of the need to address efficiency and performance issues at the enterprise level. It is natural that with decentralization employers would seek ways to introduce performance criteria into wage increases.

The increase in atypical forms of employment (e.g. homework) which cannot consistently or always be supervised, has also influenced the search for alternative forms of pay. Traditionally increased earnings were secured and performance rewarded partly through promotions. With limitations on higher positions in the context of organizations becoming less hierarchical in the future, relating part of pay increases to performance would be a way of rewarding performance, other than through promotions. In these circumstances pay systems are increasingly forming a part of human resource management initiatives to achieve enterprise-level objectives and strategies, with more attention being paid to how they fit into the overall human resource management policies of enterprises.

These developments have several implications for pay systems. Employers (and some governments) see that pay increases need to be more than matched by productivity increases if competitiveness is to be achieved or maintained. The relationship between pay, productivity, skills and inflation were understood quite early in Asia by Japan as well as by the newly industrialised economies. Some other South-East Asian countries have also come to appreciate this relationship.

The pressure in the Asia-Pacific region for the recognition of performance criteria in pay determination has not come only from employers. In Singapore the government initiated the move to flexible pay. In Malaysia the government drew attention in 1988 to the desirability of introducing a flexible pay system. In Fiji the government has been exploring the feasibility of introducing performance pay into the public service, while encouraging employers to do likewise. The Minimum Wage Board in Papua New Guinea has, since the early 1990s, been required to relate minimum wages to performance criteria in place of indexation. In recent years the wage determination system in Australia has encouraged employers and unions to negotiate a part of wage increases in the context of productivity and productivity-related improvements. The fundamental shift of industrial relations to the enterprise level and the individualization of the employment relationship in New Zealand have provided ample scope for performance-related pay. Therefore it is increasingly recognized that performance and skills criteria need to be injected into pay determination; that it cannot be achieved through centralized or macro-level pay determination; and that changes have to be negotiated at the enterprise level. In these circumstances, a major concern for employers will be to negotiate pay systems which

- Achieve a strategic business objective;
- Are flexible in that their variable component could absorb downturns in business and reduce labour costs;
- Are oriented towards better performance in terms of productivity, quality, profit, etc.;
- Are capable of enhancing workers' earnings through improved performance;
- Are capable of reducing the incidence of redundancies in times of recession or poor enterprise performance through the flexible component of pay;
- Are able to reward good performance without increasing labour costs, and
- Are able to attract competent staff.

The types of schemes which fall within the description of performance pay are varied. Broadly speaking, they consist of schemes designed to share or distribute the financial results of enterprise performance with or to employees. In essence, performance pay is based on paying the worker for his or her value, rather than the value of the job. Such schemes fall into four broad categories:

- Individual-based or based on individual performance, such as incentive schemes and sales commissions.
- Profit-sharing which applies to all or most of the employees.
- Gain-sharing measured by a pre-determined formula, applicable to all groups of employees. The performance measure may be profit or some other objective such as productivity.
- Employees share ownership schemes.

A Positive Change in Human Relationships

Many respondents referred to a change in human relations such as: 'It has led to a most positive approach to interpersonal relations'; 'Cooperation with parents has been improved. Teacher-learner relationship has so much improved and all these improved the performance and standard of the school and 'The human relationships between staff members improved dramatically which in turn resulted in a big happy staff. Their productivity increased compared to that before'. Some learners also referred to less conflict among staff members as explained by these comments: 'Because of my ideas of resolving conflict, most of the problems are being resolved at school'; and 'There has been a major reduction in conflict in my school'.

Some respondents referred to the impact of sharing their knowledge. 'Our school has improved a lot since I have started sharing my learning experience with my colleagues and persuaded them to try to implement what I have learnt in dealing with certain issues'; and 'The knowledge I gained and shared helped a great deal in improving my school'. The types of improvement are explained in the following comments: 'The image of the school has changed tremendously'; 'The working rate has improved in my school. There is commitment in the promotion of the culture of teaching and learning'; 'Teachers are enthusiastic about their work. Team spirit and cooperation are enhanced. The culture of teaching and learning is established'; 'My school is now being administered in a more professional way. All the stakeholders are able to be accountable in executing their duties.

Teachers now understand their professional obligations and the role they have to play in developing the school for the benefit of the entire community'; 'We are now able to work in unison'; 'Our school has improved as regards the quality of management and in terms of performance. We are now among the best schools in the circuit'. The latter comment concerning their outstanding performance was also confirmed by two other respondents: 'Today the department and parents are admiring the organisation of the school. The school turns to be a model school in the area. I am still on the way to develop the school'; and 'The senior management team are equipped with skills and knowledge in managing the school effectively. Now our school is one of the best in our district'.

In a predictable world education and training programmes can be organised and implemented so that staff may acquire the necessary skills. These acquired skills will, however, be the possession of the individual. According to the knowledge management, paradigm learning depends on the interaction of people and not a possession of an individual. Furthermore, the social nature of learning allows for people to meet one another, gives them time to do so and tells them that talk and the sharing ideas are valued.

The structure and processes established in the module reflect its commitment to education practice as well as the theory and principles of knowledge management. The module also links with socially constructed models of knowledge management that view people and learning issues as central to knowledge management. Judging by the learners' generally overwhelming positive response to their learning, learners learnt to solve organisational problems, which are significant not only to themselves but also to the organisation.

Furthermore, the module reveals some resemblance to McAdam and McCreedy's knowledge management model, which identifies four phases of knowledge management in the organisation: knowledge construction, knowledge dissemination, knowledge use and knowledge embodiment. According to the learners, they developed new skills, created new insights and exchanged their views and experiences in meetings, workshops and informal interactions in the school/organisation. This in turn has had an influence on the development of the school/organisation. The intervention used in the learning material therefore extended each learner's repertoire of knowledge and skills and helped learners to develop themselves and the organisation. Learners accordingly gained mastery of the field of HRM and quality management in education.

In the learning process, the three goals were met: knowledge building; skills development; and self-awareness. These included processes of consultation, idea generating methods, group decision-making and problem-solving strategies, oral persuasion and how to conduct effective group meetings. By intergrating and applying knowledge and skills in the learning material links between theory and practice have been achieved. The channeling of the learning material towards real life problems experienced by learners meant that their involvement held far more significance and relevance for them as individuals and as staff members of a school/organisation.

Since this has been an exploratory study on knowledge management in an education management module, it is necessary to expand the study to determine the perceptions of other role players concerning their acquired knowledge and skills and the development of the school/organisation. Since the world of work has changed, learners should be prepared for higher levels of knowledge and skills, not only in the curriculum, but also in the professional and personal qualities required in the transformed work place. These qualities include aspects such as autonomous, self-organising, networking, innovative, creative and to access sources for skills required to perform a given task.

A major work of knowledge management is to establish a learning environment in which people (learners) are able to conduct all sorts of learning activities and share knowledge with other people in the organisation. Different learning activities serve different sharing functions and it is important to master each sharing function in order to enhance the performance of knowledge management in an organisation.

Employing a knowledge management philosophy in designing a module is challenging because it is necessary to understand and manage the relationship between knowledge and the social contexts that shapes knowledge. Although public institutions and administrative processes have been subjected to a virtually uninterrupted string of reform movements dating back to 1883, the personnel function in particular has been regarded as a "work in progress". Persistent efforts to improve the performance of public personnel systems represent a phenomenon that is largely attributable to pervasive dissatisfaction with the field's traditional preoccupation with narrow techniques and the overly enthusiastic enforcement of regulations. Anyone who is remotely familiar with its history is painfully aware of the poor reputation that public personnel management (PPM) or human resource management (HRM) has traditionally endured, and the endless streams of innovations that have been proposed as remedies.

With the dawn of the new century, pressures for change have seldom been more intense. PPM's (as well as the rest of public management's) world has been rocked repeatedly in recent years. Fiscal crises, a brooding and hyper-critical public, and stunningly rapid movement in the personnel system's environment (highlighted by technological advances and momentous shifts in the labour force) have exacerbated the field's traditional problems and fueled renewed calls for reform. The United States workforce has changed dramatically in terms of age, gender, ethnic and racial composition, family structure, and job expectations. The so-called "reinvention movement" encapsulates many of the contemporary reform themes, including demands that PPM become more flexible and responsive to the needs of line managers, as well as to customers.

These general sentiments find expression in a variety of reform proposals from such groups as the Volcker Commission (1989) and the Winter Commission (1989), and were singled out for special attention in Vice President Gore's National Performance Review (1993). The reform proposals that emerge from these documents include an enormous number of both vague and specific recommendations dealing with virtually every HRM technique and every personnel office responsibility. Taken together, the HRM-related recommendations are particularly insistent on (1) enhancing management discretion in personnel management; (2) increasing the flexibility and responsiveness of PPM systems; (3) improving public sector performance; and (4) adopting private-sector staffing techniques. These themes are typically included in the widespread assertion that HRM needs to become more strategic in its focus and operation.

HRM certainly has not been indifferent to such demands in the past. Witness the important adjustments that occurred in the field during the 1970s and 1980s. There is much greater attention to measuring and enhancing employee and organizational performance; equal employment opportunity and affirmative action policies designed and implemented by personnel offices have contributed greatly to the diversity of the public workforce; staffing techniques have become more sophisticated; employee benefit systems have expanded; and job designs and processes have become more creative. These modifications in the practice of HRM represent incremental modifications—not fundamental or revolutionary change.

Due in part to the reform culture that now dominates public administration, however, HRM is presently experiencing a near revolution in its operating practices. Cherished techniques are reportedly being abandoned, and a profusion of new approaches to the HRM function is taking hold within the personnel profession. Pervasive control techniques are yielding to a consultative role for the personnel office. HRM is purportedly being viewed as a strategic staff enterprise aligned with organizational values, mission, and vision. Personnel functions are being decentralized to lower levels of public organizations. Change appears to be occurring so quickly that it almost has become necessary to learn a new language as terms and acronyms are coined to reflect developments in the field. Whereas most personnelists today will immediately recognize such expressions as "C.A.T." and "360-degree evaluation," these terms would likely have generated only a quizzical expression from personnel administrators just a few short years ago.

Clearly, the rate of change within the field presents personnelists with both opportunities and daunting challenges. Merely keeping pace with technological developments is difficult enough, but the HR profession is also expected to referee many of the ideological struggles that prevail in the broader political community. Public personnel managers are called upon not only to be efficient, but also to promote social agendas such as equal employment and equity. In addition, they are asked to defend the merit system against political assault; to make the civil service accountable to the public; and to adhere to the values of professionalism, while at the same time encouraging greater levels of responsiveness to executive leadership. Simply stated, the HRM field is asked to respond to a wide array of pressures and demands, many of which do not necessarily complement one another (or, which are in obvious conflict). In light of these societal pressures, unrelenting "reform" of the public personnel function may be viewed as a reflection of the fact that so much is expected of our HR professionals.

In order to assess the past and future pace of change within PPM, we decided to ask the individuals who (putatively, at least) are most intimately acquainted with human resource management in government for their opinions concerning the present and anticipated status of public personnel systems. More specifically, the memberships of two large groups of personnel professionals—the International Personnel Management Association (IPMA) and the Section on Personnel and Labour Relations (SPALR) of the American Society for Public Administration (ASPA)—were surveyed. Respondents were asked to evaluate the current (in 1998) significance of 80 personnel techniques and activities, and then to project how important those same techniques and activities will be to PPM in the year 2008.

The purpose of this exercise was to examine the extent to which the field has already altered its traditional practices in response to pressures for reform, and to provide an informed forecast of what additional changes are in the offing during the next decade. In addition to providing an interesting snapshot of the perceived state of modernization within PPM, the results reflect a considerable amount of agreement among personnel professionals concerning the expected direction of further change.

Although the conventional wisdom relating to major reform themes tends to be reinforced in the respondents' forecasts (for example, most tend to agree that the explicit goals of reinvention, along with newly fashionable techniques, will be reflected in personnel practices), not all of the popularly-accepted fads within the personnel field received a ringing endorsement. Based on the attitudes and beliefs of this particular group of expert respondents, the expected prospects for reform in a few areas of PPM look relatively bright, while other change initiatives do not yet appear to have captured the imagination of the nation's public personnel professionals.

Because much of the professional literature tends toward advocacy (or even boosterism), there is no shortage of material covering the supposed benefits of emergent personnel techniques. Proponents of the latest staffing strategy, scheduling innovation, benefit plan, or novel approach to performance evaluation fill a significant portion of the space available in many of the field's journals. This is especially prevalent among the more applied professional outlets, but it also characterizes a substantial portion of the content of the academic publications. All one needs to do in order to formulate a tentative list of developments in the personnel field is to peruse the annual indexes of a handful of journals.

Most of this best practices literature consists of a descriptive overview of someone's pet personnel technique, often supplemented with a case study demonstrating the innovation's effectiveness in a real-world setting. By informing other practitioners about potentially beneficial approaches to the personnel function, this type of literature almost certainly encourages the diffusion of innovation and thereby serves an important professional objective.

A smaller body of literature consists of research that is intended to evaluate the true impact of various personnel techniques. Instead of accepting the benefits of a new personnel strategy at face value, the technique is empirically examined (with wildly varying levels of rigor) in order to identify both its intended and unintended effects.

Excellent examples of this type of evaluative study abound. Recent issues of Public Personnel Management, for instance, include a comprehensive analysis of performance evaluation practices in municipal government, coupled with a look at their perceived utility, and a thoughtful treatment of the relative effectiveness of various types of diversity programs. One of the most comprehensive collections of research findings on the full array of personnel techniques can be found in Siegel's (1989) symposium, "Learning from Personnel Research: A Report 1963-1988." The symposium essentially constitutes a compendium of research findings covering all of the primary personnel functions.

Although this type of literature is important for the understanding and appreciation of various approaches to personnel reform, it plays no role in the current study. Our objective is more modest, in that we merely wish to report the opinions of personnel professionals as to the perceived utility of a comprehensive list of personnel functions and techniques. We assume the endorsement of trained and educated experts reflects their faith in a technique's effectiveness.

The body of literature that is most relevant to this study attempts to predict future developments within HRM. There is a long tradition of personnel system forecasting, a significant portion of which focuses on either the environmental challenges facing the field or the impairments that may impede HRM's ability to meet its organizational and societal obligations. Sayre's essay prompted much introspection among personnel professionals during the succeeding decades, leading to such works as Cecil Goode's (1958) famous report on the research frontiers in personnel administration. Goode was one of the first (if not the first) commentators to predict that population shifts, technological advances, and increased professionalism would require massive adjustments within personnel offices.

Similar predictions occurred periodically thereafter, as exemplified by Chester Newland's (1984) examination of the "crucial issues" that would shape personnel policy in future years. Many of Newland's issues echo Goode's earlier work, including the observations that government growth, concerns for societal equity, automation, and the rapid influx of women into the labour force would present serious challenges to the personnel profession. Newland also identified several more recent phenomena that could not have been anticipated by Goode. These included the emergence of productivity as a major concern in business and government, the loss of public confidence in government, the fragmentation of political units and processes, and the advent of increased federal involvement in the personnel function. Other researchers soon fine-tuned this list, adding such topics as the aging of the workforce and dramatic changes in social values and motivational traits.

The most recent iterations of this research genre include the various Workforce 2000 reports, the work of the National Commission on the State and Local Public Service, and the growing body of reinvention literature specifying an explicit reform agenda for HRM. A chief focus of this reform literature is that the underlying values of public personnel systems need to be altered. Responsiveness and flexibility are the new watchwords, while the bureaucratic tendencies of traditional merit systems are under attack in almost all quarters. The reform movement also includes a long list of detailed recommendations, including the decentralization of personnel operations, elimination of central job registers, enhanced discretion over the assignment and utilization of civil servants, less rigid pay and classification schemes, and experimentation with new incentive and bonus systems to spur productivity. Many of the specific personnel techniques that are included in the survey have arisen, at least in part, in response to these pervasive calls for a more flexible and innovative approach to HRM.

Whereas generic prescriptions and predictions concerning the roles and functions of personnel management are fairly common, empirical studies and detailed forecasts concerning personnel practices are comparatively rare. One of the most sophisticated efforts occurred in 1972, when John Parker employed the Delphi technique to assess expert opinions about the expected state of PPM in the year 2000. His findings reflect both the promise and the hazards of long-range forecasts. Parker's panel of experts correctly predicted many important developments, including the decline of civil service commissions, the movement away from rank-in-job classification, the increase in staffing flexibility, the advent of contracting out, and the decline of paper and pencil examinations.

The experts were less prescient in several other areas, however, having predicted that by the year 2000 "union organizations will represent public service employees in 95 percent of all jurisdictions in the United States" and that "the prestige of public employment will have attained parity with that of employment in the private sector". A related vein in the literature arises from a small number of surveys that probe the policy inclinations of high-level personnel managers. Hays and Kearney (1992), for example, examined how state personnel directors were coping with the demands of Workforce 2000 in a complex environment characterized by competing values and demands.

The policy directions that emanated from this demanding context included a strong emphasis on social equity considerations and an abiding interest in protecting the merit system, in conjunction with a determination to facilitate executive leadership and efficient management. Examination of the policy priorities of the same group of state HRM professionals by Grady and Hunt (1993) found that state personnel priorities during the 1990s were expected to be dominated by cutback management and modifications in compensation and benefits programs. Another small body of research, stemming from the view that personnel offices have gradually become much more significant actors in the management hierarchy, examines how front-line personnel managers allocate their time among the various personnel functions, and to what extent they are significantly involved in formulating personnel policies for their respective organizations.

An early study of a U.S. Air Force installation found that the personnel managers were heavily engaged in such substantive areas as recruitment, promotions, incentive programs, health and safety, and grievance handling. The survey also concluded that the personnel professionals were blocked from active participation in labour planning, job design, and strategic planning. A more comprehensive federal study conducted a few years later revealed that personnel budgets were being spent almost entirely in just three traditional areas of employment: classification, compensation, and general administration. Thus, it was concluded that the expansive role envisioned for personnel offices had not yet permeated public organizations at any level.

Perhaps the closest parallel to this research project is the International Personnel Management Association's annual "Personnel Programme Inventory" (PPI). This inventory is intended to identify the major policy concerns and operational practices of the IPMA's agency members. Instead of probing the respondents' attitudes about the importance of various personnel techniques, however, the inventory's primary focus is to develop a descriptive snapshot of the agencies' personnel systems. The questionnaire addresses organizational characteristics, mission statements, the content of personnel procedures, and the jurisdiction's policy profile (for example, a list of the topics that are covered in the personnel manual, and any programs that are in effect). No effort is made to assess the relative importance of various topics, except for the fact that the IPMA asks jurisdictions to prioritize their "most pressing demands".

In summary, there is little existing research that is completely analogous to that which is reported here. Futuristic forecasts abound, but few are based on survey data from expert populations. Thus, this research project offers a more sweeping and better-informed look at the current and potential status of public personnel management than has previously existed. A survey instrument was developed by the authors and pretested by human resource managers in federal, state, and local government.

The instrument was administered in a two-wave mailing to two populations: (1) the entire 1998 United States membership of the American Society for Public Administration's (ASPA) Section on Personnel and Labour Relations (SPALR) (N=421); and, (2) personnel directors in federal, state, and local government listed in the 1997 membership directory of the International Personnel Management Association (IPMA) (N=563). Academics who were not included among the SPALR mailing list but who were members of IPMA were also included in the survey. The assumption was that elite members of the human resource management community who participated in these professional organizations by attending conferences, reading professional materials (including SPALR's Review of Public Personnel Administration and IPMA's Public Personnel Management), and formally interacting with their professional peers would be more able and likely to pay attention to and think about trends in the profession than other personnelists.

An important delimitation of this nominal group research is, of course, that the "experts" who have been surveyed are reporting nothing more than their aspirations for the field. That is, critics might legitimately allege that, instead of identifying actual trends in the field of HRM, the personnel professionals are simply wishing out loud. They are speculating on the directions that they hope HRM reform will take, not on empirically verifiable phenomena. This dilemma is an inevitable cost of expert inference research, but it is a risk that we are both willing and anxious to take. Because no other group of apparent experts is better positioned to make informed judgments, the opinions of IPMA and SPALR members are the best available indicators of probable trends in public sector HRM.

Out of the total sample of 984, there were 295 responses—108 from SPALR (26 percent) and 187 from IPMA (33 percent). The total response rate was 30 percent, which is typical for a survey of this type and for surveys administered in this particular professional community (IPMA, 1997).(1) Indeed, our response rate was superior to that of the IPMA's official Personnel Programme Inventory, which rarely exceeds a 25 percent rate of return. The 1997 inventory, for example, is based on a response rate of 23 percent (345 of 1,489 agency members).

The organizations that supplied the sample populations had a small number of dual members (including both authors of this article) whose names were deleted from the IPMA listing before mailing. Also, approximately 30 foreign members of SPALR were deleted from the distribution list. Generally, the demographic characteristics of the two organizations are similar, although SPALR had a greater percentage of academics (about 50 percent) than IPMA (about 3 percent [due to the culling process noted above]). For this reason, SPALR respondents reported higher levels of formal education than IPMA members. (The mean SPALR respondent had an education level somewhere between a master's degree and a Ph.D., while the average IPMA personnel director indicated some graduate work but less than the master's degree).

Otherwise, the two groups of survey respondents closely resembled one another in age, human resource management experience, government experience, gender, and unionized setting. For purposes of analysis, the groups were merged. Any differences in responses were attributed primarily to employment sector and education rather than to professional organization membership. The merged group of respondents was 59 percent male, a proportion that was somewhat surprising considering that the doors to the human resource management profession have long been open to women. Seventy-five percent of all respondents were in the 40-59 age range. The respondents were highly educated, seasoned professionals.

Ninety-two percent were college graduates, 63 percent held advanced degrees, and 23 percent reported having a doctorate or jurisprudence degree. Forty-four percent indicated 20 or more years of human resource management experience and 80 percent had 10 or more years in the profession. Similarly, 45 percent had worked in government 20 years or more and 78 percent had worked 10 or more years in the public sector. Only a very small number of respondents were self employed (3 percent) or employed in the private, nonprofit, or federal sectors (5 percent), generally reflecting the membership characteristics of the two organizations.

The largest number of respondents were working in local government (61 percent), followed by those working in a college or university (21 percent), and state government (11 percent). Thus, a large majority of respondents (81 percent) were employed in local government or in institutions of higher education. Every state and region of the country is represented in the responses, although the southern and midwestern states are overrepresented relative to the Northwest and Northeast. Finally, a majority (51 percent) reported working in a unionized setting.

Survey Results There were three parts of the survey. In the first portion, respondents were presented with a list of personnel functions and activities, some of them conventional and some relatively new. They were asked the importance of these functions and activities to the practice of human resource management today (1998), and what they believed their importance would be one decade later, in 2008. Respondents were instructed to consider the survey questions from the perspective of HRM generally, rather than in relation to their specific employers and places of work. The HRM functions and activities were organized into six categories: Staffing and selection, compensation-pay, compensation-benefits, performance appraisal, labour relations and collective bargaining, and job design and processes. Likert-type scales with five possible choices ranging from very important (value of 1) to very unimportant (value of 5) accompanied each category. The resulting show the order of importance for each variable in 1998 and in 2008.

The difference of means for each set of variables is also reported. Fifteen items related to employee staffing and selection in 1998 and 2008 were presented to the respondents. Ranking in the first three positions in order of importance today are: use of temporary workers, performance testing, and reductions in force. One decade later, respondents expect computer-assisted testing will rank first, followed by use of temporary workers, and performance testing. Examination of the differences of mean scores indicates anticipation of significant change for most staffing and selection items. The use of resume databases is expected to experience the greatest change in importance (+1.077). Computer matching of job applicants to positions is also anticipated to be of much greater importance in the future (+.996).

Significantly declining in importance are the use of paper and pencil exams, the rule-of-three, and, mercifully, reductions in force. This provides the first indication—confirmed throughout the remainder of the survey findings—that human resource management will be technologically driven in the next decade.

When viewed broadly, these trends reflect phenomena that are often referenced in the contemporary HRM literature. Continuing calls for a strategic approach to HRM are evident in the respondents' underlying assumptions that there will be (or has been) a reduction in the surplus workforce. Relatedly, there will be less of a need for reductions in force and retirement incentives. Moreover, the age-old control mentality of HRM activities is expected to yield, at least in part, to a concentration on technological applications and a greater concentration on such concerns as the organizational "fit" of the employee and team memberships. In other words, the reinvention themes of decentralization, employee empowerment, and a more relevant application of the HRM functions are implicit in the response pattern.

The greatest changes occur in team-based pay, skill-based pay, and bonuses. The expected changes are dramatic, with traditional cost of living adjustments declining from first to last in importance, and the various performance-based pay approaches leaping ahead. Merit pay, skill-based pay, and bonuses rank highest in 2008. The use of cost of living adjustments, rated first in importance in 1998, drops to last on the list. Ten benefits and approaches for distributing benefits are next compared for the two time periods. Defined pension plans are expected to experience a precipitous drop from first to last in importance.

Respondents believe that the other nine benefits will gain salience over the next 10 years, suggesting that benefits will become a larger portion of the total compensation equation in the future. Elder care, cafeteria benefits, defined contribution pension plans, and child care are predicted to grow the most in importance. The extraordinary surge in the elder care variable is undoubtedly in recognition of the aging U.S. population, as the average life span is extended through medical and health care technology. Interestingly, women respondents, who are generally affected more directly and personally by benefits plans than men, are more sanguine about the prospects for health care, child care, cafeteria-benefit plans, and elder care, reflecting perhaps their hopes, as well as their convictions. These trends, once again, collectively point to a more strategic approach to HRM in the future. By concentrating on pay and benefit programs that are relevant to a changing workforce, personnelists are obviously planning on staying a step ahead of environmental trends.

A discordant note, however, is sounded by the view that employee recognition is expected to decline in importance relative to other types of benefits. This highly tentative finding may mirror the respondents' recognition that the public sector may become (or is becoming) less of a "special" place to work. By responding to externally-imposed pressures for efficiency (ad nauseam), over time less attention may be paid to the intrinsic facets of the public employment. The widespread use of performance appraisals is predicted to continue, ranking first in importance for both years. Generally, new performance-assessment techniques such as peer evaluations, client evaluations, appraisals by subordinates, team-based evaluations, and the all-inclusive 360-degree approach are anticipated to leap ahead of such traditional approaches as rating scales and checklists. Nonetheless, the application of traditional evaluation formats, including rating scales, checklists, and the forced-choice method, will continue to be widespread.

As in the case of compensation variables, women tend to attach greater importance than men do to innovative and less traditional techniques for both time periods. The faculty-heavy SPALR respondents indicate greater faith in peer evaluation (understandably) and are also quite optimistic about client, subordinate, and 360-degree rating schemes. It is also interesting to note that respondents in unionized settings project less utilization of the newer, less conventional approaches to performance appraisal.

Overall, the response pattern indicates less union impact on management and the budget and greater use of alternative methods for resolving labour-management disputes. Labour-management partnerships maintain their importance in both time periods, as do alternative dispute resolution techniques; the use of both is expected to grow in the future. The use of management consultants for labour-relations activities, which has been in ascendancy for at least a decade already, will also gain further currency. Union impacts on pay and benefits, contract disputes, and union constraints on management are believed to be in decline, although the mean differences are not statistically significant. When responses are broken down by unionized and non-unionized settings, some divergence is noted.

Those in union settings show greater adherence to the view that organized employees exercise an important impact on pay and benefits presently, but that this effect will decline in the next decade. Respondents in unionized settings also project that the use of alternative dispute resolution will become much more important in the future, compared to the nonunion set of respondents who think that alternative dispute resolution is highly important now and will remain so.

The last set of PPM activities in this section of the survey asked respondents to assess 13 job design and process variables. Results indicate significant growth in innovative and technology-driven strategies for redesigning and reengineering jobs. Only job security and position classification, ranked in the top two positions for 1998, will decline significantly in importance by 2008. Respondents believe that the remaining items will gain salience, led by the virtual office, and followed by job sharing, automated customer service, job enlargement, job rotation, cross training, mentoring, and broadbanding of position classes.

Previously established patterns are once again observable in the data, including the intensified influence of technology on human resource management in the future, and women respondents' greater affinity for non-traditional approaches and techniques. In sum, the data continue the expected trend toward flexibility, while also emphasizing performance objectives that have become so dominant in the contemporary HRM dialogue.

The second major part of the survey asked respondents to evaluate the amount of personnelists' time dedicated to various human resource management activities today, and the nature of their anticipated time commitments one decade hence. Substantial retooling of today's human resource managers will be needed, and the teaching of new skills and abilities will be required. Staffing responsibilities will continue to command an important time commitment from human resource managers, as will responding to agency and department heads, administering benefits, and managing information. Respondents expect quite a bit more attention will be given to monitoring contracts and outsourced functions, training and employee development activities (projected to become number one in importance), managing incentive programs for employees, mastering HRM software, measuring performance, managing diversity, and brokering conflict. Position classification will be significantly less important.

Little or no difference in time commitments is predicted for staffing, responding to agency and department heads, benefits administration, pay administration, and developing HRM policy—all of which, however, maintain relatively high overall ratings for the two time periods. Functions and activities of less importance in terms of time commitments, and generally expected to remain so, involve responding to requests from elected officials, processing grievances, engaging in collective bargaining, and administering labour contracts. The expected relative decline in importance of union-related tasks could be related to increased outsourcing of collective bargaining activities, a conviction that public sector unions will diminish in effectiveness, or, perhaps, a belief that progress in implementing participative mechanisms will reduce friction between the traditional combatants. The final section of the survey asked respondents to turn their attention to the values operating in their own personnel offices, both today and one decade ahead. A list of eight primary personnel values frequently identified in the literature was presented, along with brief definitions for each of the values. Respondents expressed remarkable consistency, and (interestingly) all values were projected to gain importance. Two possible explanations can be offered for this finding. First, one might conjecture that today's personnelists are unwilling to loosen their grasp on the past. The implication is that even as HRM changes dramatically in many of its procedures, approaches, and emphases, it will remain firmly rooted in its traditional values.

An alternative, but not entirely inconsistent, explanation is that all of the values that were delineated in the survey are regarded as being virtuous. It would therefore be unlikely that the respondents would forecast the downgrading of any particular value, be it professionalism, responsiveness, equity, or the like. This phenomenon raises the troublesome query as to whether or not today's HRM experts are sufficiently appreciative of the trade-offs and conflicts that are inherent in personnel reform. One might wonder how the pursuit of political responsiveness can be expected to have no adverse effects on professionalism or merit, for example. A more detailed analysis of the independent variables, including a factor analysis, is planned to determine if the data can be sufficiently massaged to provide a better explanation for the value perspectives of our respondents.

Insofar as the specific results are concerned, equity was placed at the top of the list for both time periods, confirming the abiding significance of public sector human resource management's commitment to the just and fair treatment of all employees, regardless of gender, race, and other individual characteristics. Holding on to second place was efficiency, defined as trying to minimize waste and maximize productivity. The high placement of this, the most recent addition to the matrix of HRM values, is an indication of how deeply the reinventing government philosophy and its business mentality have penetrated human resource management in government.

Professionalism, defined as helping to upgrade the expertise, ethics, and professional values of employees, was ranked third for both time periods, and executive leadership (implementing the chief executive's agenda) placed fourth.

With the exception of equity, the salience of the first four values was expected to increase significantly in salience by 2008. Although their relative rankings varied only slightly between the two time periods, representativeness (maintaining a diverse workforce), merit, political responsiveness (to external groups, including legislators and the public), and neutral competence (protecting merit system employees from political influences) were all projected to be of even greater importance in the respondents' personnel offices in the future.

Interestingly, university faculty was the only group to anticipate a decline in the emphasis of any values. They predict a reduced emphasis on representativeness and neutral competence, a phenomenon that might be explained by the fact that most criticism of reinvention arises within the academic community. Whereas the fundamental goals of reinvention appear to have been embraced enthusiastically by most practitioner audiences, many academic treatments of the topic worry aloud about the "Theory X" mentality that is inherent in reinvention. Since the underlying premises of the current reform movement are based on not-too-complimentary perspectives of public workers, and since much of the reform agenda constitutes an effort to "deprivilege" civil servants, it is not unreasonable to expect academicians to express concerns arising from the potential politicization of merit systems.

6

Organization Development Planning in Industry

Organization development (OD) is a planned, organization-wide effort to increase an organization's effectiveness and viability. Warren Bennis has referred to OD as a response to change, a complex educational strategy intended to change the beliefs, attitudes, values, and structure of organization so that they can better adapt to new technologies, marketing and challenges, and the dizzying rate of change itself. OD is neither "anything done to better an organization" nor is it "the training function of the organization"; it is a particular kind of change process designed to bring about a particular kind of end result. OD can involve interventions in the organization's "processes," using behavioural science knowledge as well as organizational reflection, system improvement, planning, and self-analysis.

The term "Organization Development" is often used interchangeably with Organizational effectiveness, especially when used as the name of a department within an organization. Organization development is a growing field that is responsive to many new approaches including Positive Adult Development. At the core of OD is the concept of organization, defined as two or more people working together toward one or more shared goal(s). Development in this context is the notion that an organization may become more effective over time at achieving its goals.

OD is a long range effort to improve organization's problem solving and renewal processes, particularly through more effective and collaborative management of organizational culture, often with the assistance of a change agent or catalyst and the use of the theory and technology of applied behavioural science. Although behavioural science has provided the basic foundation for the study and practice of organizational development, new and emerging fields of study have made their presence known. Experts in systems thinking, leadership studies, organizational leadership, and organizational learning (to name a few) whose perspective is not steeped in just the behavioural sciences, but a much more multi-disciplinary and inter-disciplinary approach have emerged as OD catalysts. These emergent expert perspectives see the organization as the holistic interplay of a number of systems that impact the process and outputs of the entire organization. More importantly, the term change agent or catalyst is synonymous with the notion of a leader who is engaged in doing leadership, a transformative or effectiveness process as opposed to management, a more incremental or efficiency based change methodology.

Organization development is a "*contractual relationship* between a *change agent* and a *sponsoring organization* entered into for the purpose of *using applied behavioural science and or other organizational change perspectives*in a *systems context* to *improve organizational performance* and the *capacity of the organization to improve itself*". Organization development is an ongoing, systematic process to implement effective change in an organization. Organization development is known as both a field of applied behavioural science focused on understanding and managing organizational change and as a field of scientific study and inquiry. It is interdisciplinary in nature and draws on sociology, psychology, and theories of motivation, learning, and personality.

INTERVENTIONS

"Interventions" are principal learning processes in the "action" stage of organization development. Interventions are structured activities used individually or in combination by the members of a client system to improve their social or task performance.

They may be introduced by a change agent as part of an improvement program, or they may be used by the client following a program to check on the state of the organization's health, or to effect necessary changes in its own behaviour. "Structured activities" mean such diverse procedures as experiential exercises, questionnaires, attitude surveys, interviews, relevant group discussions, and even lunchtime meetings between the change agent and a member of the client organization. Every action that influences an organization's improvement program in a change agent-client system relationship can be said to be an intervention.

There are many possible intervention strategies from which to choose. Several assumptions about the nature and functioning of organizations are made in the choice of a particular strategy. Beckhard lists six such assumptions:

1. The basic building blocks of an organization are groups (teams). Therefore, the basic units of change are groups, not individuals.
2. An always relevant change goal is the reduction of inappropriate competition between parts of the organization and the development of a more collaborative condition.

3. Decision making in a healthy organization is located where the information sources are, rather than in a particular role or level of hierarchy.
4. Organizations, subunits of organizations, and individuals continuously manage their affairs against goals. Controls are interim measurements, not the basis of managerial strategy.
5. One goal of a healthy organization is to develop generally open communication, mutual trust, and confidence between and across levels.
6. People support what they help create. People affected by a change must be allowed active participation and a sense of ownership in the planning and conduct of the change.

Interventions range from those designed to improve the effectiveness of individuals through those designed to deal with teams and groups, intergroup relations, and the total organization. There are interventions that focus on task issues (what people do), and those that focus on process issues (how people go about doing it). Finally, interventions may be roughly classified according to which change mechanism they tend to emphasize: for example, feedback, awareness of changing cultural norms, interaction and communication, conflict, and education through either new knowledge or skill practice. One of the most difficult tasks confronting the change agent is to help create in the client system a safe climate for learning and change. In a favorable climate, human learning builds on itself and continues indefinitely during man's lifetime. Out of new behaviour, new dilemmas and problems emerge as the spiral continues upward to new levels.

In an unfavorable climate, in contrast, learning is far less certain, and in an atmosphere of psychological threat, it often stops altogether. Unfreezing old ways can be inhibited in organizations because the climate makes employees feel that it is inappropriate to reveal true feelings, even though such revelations could be constructive.

In an inhibited atmosphere, therefore, necessary feedback is not available. Also, trying out new ways may be viewed as risky because it violates established norms. Such an organization may also be constrained because of the law of systems: If one part changes, other parts will become involved. Hence, it is easier to maintain the status quo. Hierarchical authority, specialization, span of control, and other characteristics of formal systems also discourage experimentation. The change agent must address himself to all of these hazards and obstacles. Some of the things which will help him are:

1. A real need in the client system to change
2. Genuine support from management
3. Setting a personal example: listening, supporting behaviour

4. A sound background in the behavioural sciences
5. A working knowledge of systems theory
6. A belief in man as a rational, self-educating being fully capable of learning better ways to do things.

A few examples of interventions include team building, coaching, Large Group Interventions, mentoring, performance appraisal, downsizing, TQM, and leadership development.

WORKFORCE PLANNING

Strategic Workforce Planning is the business process for ensuring that an organization has suitable access to talent to ensure future business success. Access to talent includes considering all potential access sources (employment, contracting out, partnerships, changing business activities to modify the types of talent required, etc.). By talent is meant the skills, knowledge, predisposition and ability to undertake required activities including decisions making. Strategic Planning considers the business risks concerning insufficient, disrupted, mis-deployed talent on the organization's business priorities. Workforce planning is considered an iterative discipline. The cycle of workforce planning includes filling resource requests, analysing resource utilization, forecasting capacity, managing and identifying the resources (human) to fill that capacity, and then re-starting the cycle.

Strategic Workforce Planning is analogous to the treasurer role which is concerned with ensuring the organization has suitable access to working capital. This role also looks at multiple sources for access and similar risks to those mentioned above.

One of the more restrictive and potentially dangerous assumptions is that Strategic Planning is only about talent in the form of employees. Hiring is a strategy for accessing talent and will often be the superior one. However, the use of employees to meet talent needs carries with it unique risks that can be mitigated using alternative access sourcing arrangements. Regardless of the access source used, insightful assessment of the strategy's attendant business risk is prudent.

The process for starting out Strategic Workforce Planning is link with the organization's strategy. This means identifying the critical talent needs that if not met can materially adversely impact business success. Once the business risks are fully appreciated then attention turns to schedule and timing. Assessing current internal capability and assessing its relative position when it will be called upon in the future. Speculating on future sourcing options and identifying the preferred sourcing option. Implementation and execution follow. Attention to periodically reviewing the "sanity" of the current plan is prudent.

PLANNING IDENTIFICATION AND VERIFICATION

This is about identifying the range of obligations relating to employment and verifying compliance. To maintain legal compliance, enterprises must identify and understand the award(s) and workplace, project or other agreements (approved under Federal or NSW legislation) to which they are bound. They must also meet employment laws regarding their employees. This includes compliance with the industrial relations requirements outlined in the:

- NSW Government Code of Practice for the Construction Industry
- Accompanying Implementation Guidelines, and
- Project agreements - NSW Government Code of Practice for the Construction Industry process.

Industrial Relations Risk Identification and Management Planning

This is about mainstreaming industrial relations management into project management activities. It requires an identification and analysis of potential industrial relations risks for the enterprise and the project and developing and implementing responses as appropriate to their impact.

Managing industrial relations risk is an integral part of good management and should be integrated with project planning and delivery. The objective of risk management is to identify and analyse risks and manage their consequences In this way the efficient management of the enterprise and the project will be optimised, and delays minimised through:

- Early identification of industrial relations issues
- Establishing well-defined lines of communication within the enterprise and with all project participants including subcontractors and other contractors
- Clearly defined roles and responsibilities for industrial relations and for project participants
- Preparation of contingency plans to minimise potential adverse impacts,
- Communication with workers and unions.

The four steps in the risk management process are:

- *Assessment:* This is about identifying the industrial relations issues that will be relevant to the enterprise and the project. This includes a review of the prevailing industrial relations environment, the requirements in the tender documents and the:
- *Risk analysis:* This involves:
  - Identifying the sources of industrial relations risk that might impact on the project
  - Assessing the potential likelihood and consequences of each risk (ie. minor, moderate or major).

- Identifying those risks that will require management attention, particularly moderate or major risks.

A risk ranking table provides a graphic presentation of risk classes and assists in planning and management.

As a working definition:

- Minor risks can be accepted or ignored
- Moderate risks are either likely to occur or to have high impacts, but not both.

  Management measures should be specified for all moderate risks.
- Major risks are those risks with both a high likelihood of arising and a high impact. Those risks will require close management attention, and the preparation of a risk action plan.

Examples of sources of risk:

- Planning stage
- Location
- Capability of contractor
- Capability of project personnel
- Capability of service providers
- Legislation, regulations and standards
- Competing deadlines
- Client endorsement
- Costs

Project procurement and contracts delivery stage:

- Contractor, subcontractor capability
- Contractor, subcontractor performance
- Delays - eg. weather, industrial disputes
- OHS&R disputes
- Construction methods

Construction or maintenance

- Compliance controls
- Industrial action
- OHS disputes

Human factors

- Operator error
- Sabotage
- Vandalism

Natural events

- Weather
- Fire
- Other

Organisational

- Resource shortages
- Operational policies
- Management capabilities and practices
- Personnel skills
- Occupational health, safety and rehabilitation management
- Industrial relations management
- Work practices

Risk response planning:- This is about:

- Outlining the management measures developed in response to the industrial relations risks identified, and
- Nominating those measures most likely to ensure efficient project delivery.

If a project agreement is foreshadowed by a tenderer in its IR Strategy and the tenderer is awarded the tender, a business case as outlined in the Project agreements-NSW Government Code of Practice for the Construction Industry process must be submitted and approved by the Principal.

Ideally, this process should be finalised with the Project IR Plan.

Contingency Planning

This is about making sure that contingency plans and procedures are in place to minimise adverse impacts.

Contingency plans can include, but are not limited to:

- Consultation and communication strategy (internal and external)
- Details of actions to be taken in the event of incidents such as:
  - Grievances
  - Inclement weather
  - Threatened industrial action
  - Actual industrial action, and
  - Other unforeseen risks.

Implementation Resources

This is about the resources necessary to implement the IR Strategy and the Project IR Plan.

The resources essential to the implementation of the IR Strategy and the Project IR Plan should be defined.

These include human, physical (eg. facilities and equipment) and financial resources. In allocating resources, the enterprise can develop procedures to track the benefits as well as the costs of its industrial relations management activities at both the enterprise and project level.

Accountability and Responsibility

This is about defining the responsibilities of all personnel whose roles can affect the industrial relations performance of the enterprise and on projects.

Personnel at all levels should be accountable, within the scope of their responsibilities, for industrial relations management performance in support of the IR Strategy and the Project IR Plan.

A management representative should be nominated as responsible for implementing the enterprise's IR Strategy and the Project IR Plan.

By clearly spelling out the responsibilities and authorities of personnel for specific tasks relating to industrial relations management, there should be no doubt as to who is responsible for taking decisions, and for acting on grievances and disputes. As a minimum, the following responsibilities and tasks must be addressed.

INDUSTRIAL RELATIONS MANAGEMENT ISSUES

- Defining industrial relations management commitment, priorities and targets.
- Defining the responsibilities of personnel for industrial relations management matters.
- Allocating human, physical and financial resources adequate to meet these requirements.
- Ensuring compliance with, and keeping abreast of changes to, awards and other legal obligations relating to employment.
- Acquiring and disseminating industrial relations management information.
- Planning and conducting training in industrial relations management, including induction for employees, subcontractors and other contractors.
- Developing and implementing procedures.
- Assessing and monitoring subcontractors' ability to comply with industrial relations laws and their employment obligations, and
- Monitoring workplace and management practices to continually improve industrial relations management performance.

Industrial Relations Strategy

These responsibilities, authorities and tasks must be clearly documented and communicated so that all personnel on the project will know:

- What industrial relations risks are involved in the project, and
- What action plan and management measures are proposed to manage these risks.

Subcontractors

This is about nominating the measures that will be implemented to assess subcontractor

compliance with their industrial relations and employment obligations. Contractors must be able to demonstrate:

- The measures they will take to select subcontractors who comply with industrial relations laws and employment obligations
- How dealings with subcontractors and other contractors is to be managed, and
- How ongoing subcontractor compliance with industrial relations requirements is to be monitored and assessed.

Selection and Industrial Relations Management

A contractor may maintain a panel of preferred subcontractors with sound, responsible and effective industrial and employee relations management practices a contractor may require verification of compliance, in the preceding twelve months, with all employment and legal obligations including:

- Payment of remuneration to employees
- Annual leave
- Long Service Payment Scheme registration
- Workers' compensation insurance (including self-insurance arrangements)
- Superannuation fund membership and contributions
- Over-award payments (eg. redundancy fund contributions) a contractor may require that subcontractors develop and implement a Project IR Plan which is compatible with the Contractor's Project IR Plan. Implementation of the plan and performance would be reviewed during the life of the subcontractor's contract with the contractor.

INDUSTRIAL RELATIONS STRATEGY

An IR Strategy is an expression of an enterprise's capacity to develop and implement a sound industrial relations management plan which ensures that industrial relations issues and risks are identified, assessed and managed. The IR Strategy should demonstrate the integration of industrial relations requirements with the normal procedures, practices and performance standards of the enterprise.

It involves an enterprise:

- Developing a policy statement on industrial relations management that has the total support of management

- Defining responsibilities for industrial relations management within the enterprise
- Identifying resources and procedures for implementing required industrial relations management measures
- Having planning processes and procedures in place that enable identification of potential industrial relations issues and facilitate the development of measures to minimize impacts
- Outlining methods used to assess the capacity of subcontractors to understand and comply with their industrial relations responsibilities, and
- Establishing procedures to review and monitor the implementation of measures which support the IR Strategy and to initiate corrective action when required.

The detail and scope of an IR Strategy will depend on the size, nature and scale of the enterprise and its projects.

What is a Project IR Plan?

A Project IR Plan is the implementation of the IR Strategy accepted with the successful tender response which confirms the specific industrial relations commitment, responsibilities, planning, implementation, and management strategies that will be applied to the particular project. It must address the key elements in the following section in detail. The Project IR Plan must be submitted by the contractor with information to verify compliance with employment obligations and will be reviewed before it is accepted by the government agency, before site works begin.

The Project IR Plan will be subject to Project IR Plan Implementation Reviews throughout the duration of the contract. Each Review will examine the extent to which the tractor has implemented the Plan on the project.

Key Elements of an Industrial Relations Strategy

An acceptable Industrial Relations Strategy must clearly address the following key elements.

Commitment and Management Responsibility

This is about confirming the enterprise's commitment to industrial relations management and defining its policies and objectives. It spells out the responsibilities for industrial relations management. The policy statement can really only be articulated after the planning elements have been finalised.

Senior management must demonstrate its commitment to improving its industrial relations management performance at both the enterprise and project levels by developing an industrial relations management policy statement.

Ongoing commitment and leadership from the top is expected and is vital to the effectiveness and success of the enterprise's IR Strategy and the Project IR Plan. An enterprise's industrial relations management policy statement:

- Has the full support and commitment of the chief executive officer and senior management
- Defines the enterprise's industrial and employee relations policies, objectives and targets
- Identifies those responsible for the management of industrial relations matters, compliance with industrial and employment obligations and the initiation of corrective action
- Outlines communication processes with workers, unions, other contractors and subcontractors on industrial relations issues, and
- Outlines measures for assessing subcontractors' ability to comply with industrial relations and employment obligations.

MANAGEMENT OF INDUSTRIAL OBJECTIVES AND RELATIONS

The objectives of managements, the ways in which enterprises are managed to achieve these objectives and the human resource management (hereinafter referred to as "HRM") and industrial relations (hereinafter referred to as "IR") initiatives in this regard, are affected by pressures, many of which are exerted by globalization. Changes in IR practices (rather than in institutions and systems) such as increased collective bargaining at enterprise level, flexibility in relation to forms of employment as well as in relation to working time and job functions have occurred as a result of such factors as heightened competition, rapid changes in products and processes and the increasing importance of skills, quality and productivity.

These factors have also had an impact on HRM policies and practices. In managing change, the key elements include employee involvement in effecting change, greater customer orientation, and ensuring that the skills of employees are appropriate to the production of goods and the provision of services acceptable to the global market. As such, managing people in a way so as to motivate them to be productive is one important objective of HRM. The implications and consequences of globalization include the following:

- Countries are more economically interdependent than before, particularly in view of foreign direct investment interlocking economies, as well as increased free trade. The inability of economies to be 'self-sufficient' or 'self-reliant' or 'self-contained' has been accompanied by a breakdown of investment and trade barriers.
- Governments are increasingly less able to control the flow of capital, information and technology across borders.

- There has been de-regulation of financial and other markets, and the integration of markets for goods, services and capital such as the European Community.
- It has led to the de-nationalization of enterprises and the creation of global companies and global webs.
- Production of goods and services acceptable to the global market, and the convergence, to a great extent, of customer tastes across borders determined by quality.
- The need to achieve competitiveness and to remain competitive in respect of attracting investment, goods and services. This means, inter alia, the necessity for high quality skills at all levels to attract high value-added activities, as distinct from cheap labour low value-added ones, and improvements in productivity.

Enterprises driven by market pressures need to include in their goals improved quality and productivity, greater flexibility, continuous innovation, and the ability to change to respond rapidly to market needs and demands. Effective HRM is vital for the attainment of these goals. Improved quality and productivity linked to motivation can be achieved through training, employee involvement and extrinsic and intrinsic rewards. The growing interest in pay systems geared to performance and skills reflects one aspect of the increasing significance of HRM in realizing management goals and a gradual shift from collectivism to the individualisation of pay.

In such pay systems a critical attraction is the possibility of achieving these goals without increasing labour costs but at the same time increasing earnings. Realizing management goals and managing change need employee involvement, commitment and training, employee participation, cooperation and team-work - all important HRM initiatives and activities. The dominant position towards which HRM is moving points to a "change in power relations and highlights the supremacy of management. The management prerogative is rediscovered but in place of command and control the emphasis is on commitment and control as quality, flexibility and competence replaces quantity, task and dumb obedience. To put it another way: the managerial agenda is increasingly focused on innovation, quality and cost reduction. Human resource management makes more demands on employees, work is intensified.... there is less room for managerial slack and for indulgency patterns.

From a purely HRM perspective, one writer has identified the following six factors as accounting for the increasing interest in and resort to HRM practices:

- Improving the management of people or utilizing human resources better as a means of achieving competitive advantage.

- The numerous examples of excellence in HRM have created an interest in such models.
- The traditional role of personnel managers has failed to exploit the potential benefits of effective management of people; neither did personnel management form a central part of management activity.
- In some countries the decline of trade union influence has opened the way for managements to focus on more individual issues rather than on collectivist ones.
- The emergence of better educated workforces with higher individual expectations, changes in technology and the need for more flexible jobs have, in turn, created the need to incorporate HRM into central management policy.
- Many important aspects of HRM such as commitment and motivation emanate from the area of organizational behaviour, and place emphasis on management strategy. This has provided an opportunity to link HRM with organizational behaviour and management strategy.

The Theory Of The Conflict

In considering the relationship between HRM and IR, two central concerns are: in what way does HRM pose a challenge to IR and how can conflicts between the two, if any, be reconciled so that they can complement each other? This section concerns itself with the first of these two issues. In considering the issue, it is necessary to identify the broad goals of each discipline. The goals of HRM have already been identified in the previous section. It remains to consider some of the basic objectives of IR, which could be said to include the following:

- The efficient production of goods and services and, at the same time, determination of adequate terms and conditions of employment, in the interests of the employer, employees and society as a whole, through a consensus achieved through negotiation.
- The establishment of mechanisms for communication, consultation and cooperation in order to resolve workplace issues at enterprise and industry level, and to achieve through a tripartite process, consensus on labour policy at national level.
- Avoidance and settlement of disputes and differences between employers, employees and their representatives, where possible through negotiation and dispute settlement mechanisms.
- To provide social protection where needed e.g. in the areas of social security, safety and health, child labour, etc.
- Establishment of stable and harmonious relations between employers and employees and their organizations, and between them and the State.

IR is essentially pluralistic in outlook, in that it covers not only the relations between employer and employee (the individual relations) but also the relations between employers and unions and between them and the State (collective relations). IR theory, practice and institutions traditionally focus more on the collective aspect of relations. This is evident from the central place occupied by labour law, freedom of association, collective bargaining, the right to strike, employee involvement practices which involve unions, trade unionism and so on. HRM deals with the management of human resources, rather than with the management of collective relations. There is of course a certain measure of overlap. Individual grievance handling falls within the ambit of both disciplines, but dispute settlement of collective issues more properly falls within the scope of IR. Policies and practices relating to recruitment, selection, appraisal, training and motivation form a part of HRM.

Team-building, communication and cooperation, though primarily HRM initiatives, have a collectivist aspect. Thus joint consultative mechanisms are as much IR initiatives, which may (as in Japan) supplement collective bargaining. But IR has not, in regard to team-building for instance, developed any techniques or theories about how to achieve it; in fact, it is not a focus of attention because it implies a potential loyalty to the enterprise through the team and is seen as conflicting with loyalty to the union. IR has a large component of rules which govern the employment relationship. These rules may be prescribed by the State through laws, by courts or tribunals, or through a bipartite process such as collective bargaining. HRM differs in this respect from industrial relations in the sense that it does not deal with such procedures and rules, but with the best way to use the human resource through, for example, proper selection and recruitment, induction, appraisal, training and development, motivation, leadership and intrinsic and extrinsic rewards.

Thus "at its most basic HRM represents a set of managerial initiatives." Four processes central to a HRM system - selection, appraisal, rewards and development- leave only limited room for IR as a central element in the human resource system. "Based on theoretical work in the field of organizational behaviour it is proposed that HRM comprises a set of policies designed to maximise organizational integration, employee commitment, flexibility and quality of work. Within this model, collective industrial relations have, at best, only a minor role."

A discernible trend in management is a greater individualisation of the employer-employee relationship, implying less emphasis on collective, and more emphasis on individual relations. This is reflected, for instance, in monetary and non-monetary reward systems. In IR the central monetary reward is wages and salaries, one of its central themes (given effect to by collective bargaining) being internal equity and distributive justice and, often, standardisation across industry. HRM increasingly places emphasis on monetary rewards linked to performance and skills through the development of performance and skills-based pay systems, some of which seek to individualise monetary rewards (e.g. individual bonuses, stock options, etc.).

HRM strategies to secure individual commitment through communication, consultation and participatory schemes underline the individualisation thrust, or at least effect, of HRM strategies. On the other hand, it is also legitimate to argue that HRM does not focus exclusively on the individual and, as such, does not promote only individual employment relations. Though much of HRM is directed at the individual,

"at the same time there is a parallel emphasis on team work, whether in the form of quality circles or functional flexibility, and above all, on the individual's commitment to the organization, represented not just as the sum of the individuals in it, but rather as an organic entity with an interest in survival. The potential conflict between emphasizing the importance of the individual on the one hand, and the desirability of cooperative team work and employee commitment to the organization, on the other, is glossed over through the general assumption of unitarist values..: HRM stresses the development of a strong corporate culture -not only does it give direction to an organization, but it mediates the tension between individualism and collectivism, as individuals socialised into a strong culture are subject to unobtrusive collective controls on attitudes and behaviour."

Some of the tensions between IR and HRM arise from the unitarist outlook of HRM (which sees a commonality of interests between managements and employees) and the pluralist outlook of IR (which assumes the potential for conflict in the employment relationship flowing from different interests). "It is often said that HRM is the visual embodiment of the unitarist frame of reference both in the sense of the legitimation of managerial authority and in the imagery of the firm as a team with committed employees working with managers for the benefit of the firm."

How to balance these conflicting interests and to avoid or to minimize conflicts (e.g. through promotion of negotiation systems such as collective bargaining, joint consultation, dispute settlement mechanisms within the enterprise and at national level in the form of conciliation, arbitration and labour courts) in order to achieve a harmonious IR system is one central task of IR. The individualization of HRM, reflected in its techniques which focus on direct employer-employee links rather than with employee representatives, constitutes one important difference between IR and HRM. It has been observed that:

"The empirical evidence also indicates that the driving force behind the introduction of HRM appears to have little to do with industrial relations; rather it is the pursuit of competitive advantage in the market place through provision of high-quality goods and services, through competitive pricing linked to high productivity and through the capacity swiftly to innovate and manage change in response to changes in the market place or to breakthroughs in research and development... Its underlying values, reflected in HRM policies and practices, would appear to be essentially unitarist and individualistic in contrast to the more pluralist and collective values of traditional industrial relations."

How does HRM more specifically challenge IR and trade unions, though HRM is not per se anti-union and its central themes are not necessarily inconsistent with unionism ? First, HRM does not focus, as does IR, on collective bargaining, which is a central institution in IR. However, collective bargaining should not be understood only in the narrow sense of negotiation of terms and conditions of employment leading to a formal agreement. It should be viewed as a process, and as including all mechanisms introduced to arrive at a consensus on matters affecting the two social partners, even if they do not result in formalised agreements. If viewed in this way, it reduces the conflict between HRM and IR within this area. A second area in which HRM is said to pose a challenge to unions is on the issue of flexibility- critical in HRM but traditionally absent as a factor in IR where a degree of standardisation for purposes of internal equity has been an objective of unions and of IR. Here the scene is undergoing considerable change.

There is today a major thrust towards achieving flexibility in the labour market on matters such as functions, working time, pay and types of contracts. Unions are being compelled to 'participate' in these changes as an alternative to being marginalized. The trend towards greater decentralization of collective bargaining has compelled viewing issues more from a workplace perspective. It has provided an opportunity for unions in countries with a high rate of unionization to be involved in issues other than wages and related ones, such as technology introduction, new work processes and organization, It involves, on the one hand, the willingness of employers to deal with unions on such matters (which they have to be willing to do in high union-density enterprises), and on the other the willingness of unions to cooperate on legitimate measures to achieve competitiveness -especially where the employees themselves are willing to do so -and to adapt to the realities of the workplace.

A third - and perhaps the principal challenge - emanates from employee loyalty and commitment, which are central objectives of HRM. The issue here is whether dual allegiance is possible i.e. commitment to the goals and values of the organization, and to contribute to its success on the one hand, and commitment to the trade union on the other. It is at this point that IR becomes a critical factor. In principle there should be no antithesis, because trade unionism need not (and should not) be conflictual in approach and attitude. Much of the empirical evidence drawn from the USA indicates that in a workplace with a cooperative IR system dual loyalty is possible, but that it is not possible in one where a cooperative climate is absent or minimal. In some of the larger unionised corporations in Japan, this conflict of loyalty is less felt.

Traditional IR and trade unionism can be challenged in other ways - that is, other than through anti-union activity. Downsizing the labour force as a HRM initiative to achieve competitiveness and offering monetary incentives to employees to improve productivity could create IR tensions, especially if the union has not been involved in the process. A similar result may occur when an employer, without seeking to dismantle existing IR practices, establishes other mechanisms and practices such as direct communication and consultation systems, small group activities, employee share option schemes and so on without involving the union.

The unitarist approach of HRM and the pluralist tradition of IR, though regarded by some as incompatible, are not regarded in the same light by others. There are three issues involved here. The first is whether the pursuit of HRM policies such as employee involvement and commitment, two-way communication and small group activities, and the integration of HRM policies in corporate objectives and strategies pose a challenge to central IR institutions such as collective bargaining and to unionism. The second is whether such HRM policies are pursued consciously as a union avoidance strategy. The third is whether HRM and IR are necessarily incompatible or whether there is scope for their co-existence.

David E. Guest points out that HRM, which is an American concept, "finds its fullest expression in a number of well-known and successful American companies." He points out that research indicates that the established model of HRM is often found in a non-union company. Referring to the research done by one writer, he states:

He notes that in almost all the companies he looked at the HRM policies came first, often encouraged by the values of a powerful CEO, preceding any considered non-unionism. In many cases, remaining non-union has subsequently become a policy goal. On the basis of the companies he studied, this has a number of cost implications. Personnel policies must be sufficiently good and sufficiently integrated and reinforced by line management practice to avoid giving grounds for union organising. Foulkes found that most of the companies he studied paid above average rates. They also provided mechanisms for individual expression of grievances and were likely to monitor reactions to personnel policies through the communication system and the use of attitude surveys. All of these practices are to be found in a company like IBM which provides the best known model of HRM but which is also what Bassett refers to as the 'ultimate non-union company'.

This does not mean that HRM is anti-union or that unions have no role to play in HRM, but rather that effective HRM policies and practices are sometimes either used as a union avoidance strategy or else it can have that effect.

Three very influential scholars have put forward the view that there is a role for union involvement in HRM, and point to companies (such as the General Motors Saturn plant) which have involved unions in the move towards HRM, and by so doing unions have facilitated this move.

Such an involvement, if it is to take place, would require, in many countries, a substantial change of attitude on the part of both management and unions. David E. Guest remarks however:

If a new set of practices can be introduced, it is not clear what role is left for the union. The most likely one is that of policing management practices and dealing with grievances which seem almost inevitable with repetitive production line work and persisting pressures to increase productivity. By implication, management is not practising effective HRM and the door is left open for the unions to play a role.

At the annual meeting of European employers' organizations, held in Bordeaux in 1993 the compatibility of new trends in HRM with the traditional IR systems was considered. The following summary is indicative of the growing attitude of employers in many industrialized market economies:

"The key to competitiveness is quality. And quality depends more on the commitment of individuals than on their acquired technical skills; more on the way these individuals behave and their team spirit than on the passive execution of orders received. Regulations - be they internal to the enterprise or imposed by the legislator - plague innovation and have a negative effect on motivation. Good human resource management lies in the behaviour of each employee within an enterprise... It applies to individual men and women... The classic approach to industrial relations is entirely different, with its peculiarity being collective bargaining - which, by definition, does not consider the individual but the mass.

The status of a worker is defined by a few general criteria, such as his professional category and possibly his seniority and his age. Remuneration, for example, is calculated on the basis of a few simple elements, which do not take into consideration personal behaviour and individual performance. Work provided is considered purely from the quantitative angle. The future of collective bargaining, therefore, depends on the extent to which it can take into account the demands for individualization which modern methods of human resources management imply. This should not of course lead to arbitrariness....... Legislation and regulation imposed by the State should also leave a sufficient margin of flexibility to allow for adaptation."

WORKFORCE ANALYTICS APPROACH

The focus is to analyse current and historical employee data to identify key relationships among variables and use this to provide insight into the workforce they need for the future. Workforce analysis usually includes reviewing employee recruitment, promotion and turnover patterns. In addition the analysis can also include reviewing the age and gender profiles of the workforce. An analytical approach is important as it provides a fact based method of understanding workforce behaviours. Workforce analytics also provides further context to workforce planning efforts by ensuring perceived workforce behaviours are consistent with actual behaviours identified using a more quantitative approach.

Modeling Approach

This approach incorporates forecasting and scenario planning. Forecasting uses quantitative data to create forecasts incorporating multiple what-if and modeling the future. Scenario Planning being the more useful tool where there are uncertainties, therefore incorporating quantitative and qualitative.

Segmentation Approach

Breaking the workforce into segments along the lines of their jobs and determining relevance to strategic intent. Provides a technique for prioritizing.

Steps in Workforce Planning

Though there is no definitive 'Start here' activity for any of the approaches to Strategic Workforce Planning, there are five fundamentals activities that most Workforce Plan models have:

- Environment Scan
- Current Workforce Profile
- Future Workforce View
- Analysis and Targeted Future
- Closing the gaps.

UNDERSTANDING ORGANIZATIONS

Weisbord presents a six-step model for understanding organization:

1. Purposes: The organization member are clear about the organization's mission and purpose and goal agreements, whether people support the organization' purpose.
2. Structure: How do we divide up the work? The question is whether there is an adequate fit between the purpose and the internal structure.

3. Relationship: Between individual, between units or department that perform different tasks, and between the people and requirements of their job.
4. Rewards: The consultant should diagnose the similarities between what the organization formally reward or punished for doing.
5. Leadership: Is to watch for blips among the other boxes and maintain balance among them
6. Helpful mechanism: Is a helpful organization that must attend to in order to survive which as planning, control, budgeting, and other information systems that help organization member accomplish.

Modern Development

In recent years, serious questioning has emerged about the relevance of OD to managing change in modern organizations. The need for "reinventing" the field has become a topic that even some of its "founding fathers" are discussing critically.

With this call for reinvention and change, scholars have begun to examine organizational development from an emotion-based standpoint. For example, deKlerk (2007) writes about how emotional trauma can negatively affect performance. Due to downsizing, outsourcing, mergers, restructuring, continual changes, invasions of privacy, harassment, and abuses of power, many employees experience the emotions of aggression, anxiety, apprehension, cynicism, and fear, which can lead to performance decreases. deKlerk (2007) suggests that in order to heal the trauma and increase performance, O.D. practitioners must acknowledge the existence of the trauma, provide a safe place for employees to discuss their feelings, symbolize the trauma and put it into perspective, and then allow for and deal with the emotional responses. One method of achieving this is by having employees draw pictures of what they feel about the situation, and then having them explain their drawings with each other. Drawing pictures is beneficial because it allows employees to express emotions they normally would not be able to put into words. Also, drawings often prompt active participation in the activity, as everyone is required to draw a picture and then discuss its meaning.

Action Research

Wendell L French and Cecil Bell define organization development (OD) at one point as "organization improvement through action research". If one idea can be said to summarize OD's underlying philosophy, it would be action research as it was conceptualized by Kurt Lewin and later elaborated and expanded on by other behavioural scientists. Concerned with social change and, more particularly, with effective, permanent social change, Lewin believed that the motivation to change was strongly related to action: If people are active in decisions affecting them, they are more likely to adopt new ways. "Rational social management", he said, "proceeds in a spiral of steps, each of which is composed of a circle of planning, action, and fact-finding about the result of action".

Lewin's description of the process of change involves three steps:

"Unfreezing": Faced with a dilemma or disconfirmation, the individual or group becomes aware of a need to change.

"Changing": The situation is diagnosed and new models of behaviour are explored and tested.

"Refreezing": Application of new behaviour is evaluated, and if reinforcing, adopted.

The steps and processes involved in planned change through action research. Action research is depicted as a cyclical process of change. The cycle begins with a series of planning actions initiated by the client and the change agent working together. The principal elements of this stage include a preliminary diagnosis, data gathering, feedback of results, and joint action planning. In the language of systems theory, this is the input phase, in which the client system becomes aware of problems as yet unidentified, realizes it may need outside help to effect changes, and shares with the consultant the process of problem diagnosis.

The second stage of action research is the action, or transformation, phase. This stage includes actions relating to learning processes (perhaps in the form of role analysis) and to planning and executing behavioural changes in the client organization. The feedback at this stage would move via Feedback Loop A and would have the effect of altering previous planning to bring the learning activities of the client system into better alignment with change objectives. Included in this stage is action-planning activity carried out jointly by the consultant and members of the client system. Following the workshop or learning sessions, these action steps are carried out on the job as part of the transformation stage.

The third stage of action research is the output, or results, phase. This stage includes actual changes in behaviour (if any) resulting from corrective action steps taken following the second stage. Data are again gathered from the client system so that progress can be determined and necessary adjustments in learning activities can be made. Minor adjustments of this nature can be made in learning activities via Feedback Loop B. Major adjustments and reevaluations would return the OD project to the first, or planning, stage for basic changes in the program. The action-research model, Lewin's repetitive cycle of planning, action, and measuring results. It also illustrates other aspects of Lewin's general model of change. As indicated in the diagram, the planning stage is a period of unfreezing, or problem awareness. The action stage is a period of changing, that is, trying out new forms of behaviour in an effort to understand and cope with the system's problems. (There is inevitable overlap between the stages, since the boundaries are not clear-cut and cannot be in a continuous process). The results stage is a period of refreezing, in which new behaviours are tried out on the job and, if successful and reinforcing, become a part of the system's repertoire of problem-solving behaviour.

Action research is problem centered, client centered, and action oriented. It involves the client system in a diagnostic, active-learning, problem-finding, and problem-solving process. Data are not simply returned in the form of a written report but instead are fed back in open joint sessions, and the client and the change agent collaborate in identifying and ranking specific problems, in devising methods for finding their real causes, and in developing plans for coping with them realistically and practically. Scientific method in the form of data gathering, forming hypotheses, testing hypotheses, and measuring results, although not pursued as rigorously as in the laboratory, is nevertheless an integral part of the process. Action research also sets in motion a long-range, cyclical, self-correcting mechanism for maintaining and enhancing the effectiveness of the client's system by leaving the system with practical and useful tools for self-analysis and self-renewal.

IMPACT OF INDUSTRIALIZATION

Industrialisatioon (British English) or Industrialization (Canadian & American English) is the process of social and economic change that transforms a human group from a pre-industrial society into an industrial one. It is a part of a wider modernisation process, where social change and economic development are closely related with technological innovation, particularly with the development of large-scale energy and metallurgy production. It is the extensive organisation of an economy for the purpose of manufacturing.

Industrialisation also introduces a form of philosophical change where people obtain a different attitude towards their perception of nature, and a sociological process of ubiquitous rationalisation. There is considerable literature on the factors facilitating industrial modernisation and enterprise development. Key positive factors identified by researchers have ranged from favourable political-legal environments for industry and commerce, through abundant natural resources of various kinds, to plentiful supplies of relatively low-cost, skilled and adaptable labour.

One survey of countries in Africa, Latin America, the Caribbean, and the Middle East and the rest of Asia in the late 20th century found that high levels of structural differentiation, functional specialisation, and autonomy of economic systems from government were likely to contribute greatly to industrial-commercial growth and prosperity. Amongst other things, relatively open trading systems with zero or low duties on imported goods tended to stimulate industrial cost-efficiency and innovation across the board. Free and flexible labour and other markets also helped raise general business-economic performance levels, as did rapid popular learning capabilities.

Positive work ethics in populations at large combined with skills in quickly utilising new technologies and scientific discoveries were likely to boost production and income levels – and as the latter rose, markets for consumer goods and services of all kinds tended to expand and provide a further stimulus to industrial investment and economic growth.

By the end of the century, East Asia was one of the most economically successful regions of the world – with free market countries such as Hong Kong being widely seen as models for other, less developed countries around the world to emulate. The first country to industrialise was Great Britain during the Industrial Revolution.

According to the original sector classification of Jean Fourastié, an economy consists of a "Primary sector" of commodity production (farming, livestock breeding, exploitation of mineral resources), a "secondary sector" of manufacturing and processing, and a "Tertiary Sector" of service industries. The industrialisation process is historically based on the expansion of the secondary sector in an economy dominated by primary activities.

The first ever transformation to an industrial economy from an agrarian one was called the Industrial Revolution and this took place in the late 18th and early 19th centuries in a few countries of Western Europe and North America, beginning in Great Britain. This was the first industrialization in the world's history.

The Second Industrial Revolution describes a later, somewhat less dramatic change that came about in the late 19th century with the widespread availability of electric power, internal combustion engines, and assembly lines to the already industrialised nations.

The lack of an industrial sector in a country is widely seen as a major handicap in improving a country's economy, and power, pushing many governments to encourage or enforce industrialisation.

Economic Effects

In recent years, urbanization of rural areas has increased. As agriculture, more traditional local services, and small-scale industry give way to modern industry the urban and related commerce with the city drawing on the resources of an ever-widening area for its own sustenance and goods to be traded or processed into manufactures.

Research in urban ecology finds that larger cities provide more specialized goods and services to the local market and surrounding areas, function as a transportation and wholesale hub for smaller places, and accumulate more capital, financial service provision, and an educated labour force, as well as often concentrating administrative functions for the area in which they lie. This relation among places of different sizes is called the urban hierarchy.

As cities develop, effects can include a dramatic increase in costs, often pricing the local working class out of the market, including such functionaries as employees of the local municipalities. The almost universal European division into a 'good' west end and a 'poor' east end of large cities developed in this period." This is likely due the prevailing southwest wind which carries coal smoke and other airborne pollutants downwind, making the western edges of towns preferable to the eastern ones. Similar problems now affect the developing world, rising inequality resulting from rapid urbanisation trends. The drive for rapid urban growth and often efficiency can lead to less equitable urban development, think tanks such as the Overseas Development Institute have even proposed policies that encourage labour intensive growth as a means of absorbing the influx of low skilled and unskilled labour. Urbanization is often viewed as a negative trend, but can in fact, be perceived simply as a natural occurrence from individual and corporate efforts to reduce expense in commuting and transportation while improving opportunities for jobs, education, housing, and transportation. Living in cities permits individuals and families to take advantage of the opportunities of proximity, diversity, and marketplace competition.

Environmental Effects

The urban heat island has become a growing concern and is increasing over the years. The urban heat island is formed when industrial and urban areas are developed and heat becomes more abundant. In rural areas, a large part of the incoming solar energy is used to evaporate water from vegetation and soil. In cities, where less vegetation and exposed soil exists, the majority of the sun's energy is absorbed by urban structures and asphalt. Hence, during warm daylight hours, less evaporative cooling in cities allows surface temperatures to rise higher than in rural areas. Additional city heat is given off by vehicles and factories, as well as by industrial and domestic heating and cooling units. This effect causes the city to become 2 to 10° F (1 to 6° C) warmer than surrounding landscapes.. Impacts also include reducing soil moisture and intensification of carbon dioxide emissions.

In his book *Whole Earth Discipline*, Stewart Brand argues that the effects of urbanization are on the overall positive for the environment. Firstly, the birth rate of new urban dwellers falls immediately to replacement rate, and keeps falling. This can prevent overpopulation in the future. Secondly, it puts a stop to destructive subsistence farming techniques, like slash and burn agriculture. Finally, it minimizes land use by humans, leaving more for nature.

Changing Forms

Different forms of urbanization can be classified depending on the style of architecture and planning methods as well as historic growth of areas. In cities of the developed world urbanization traditionally exhibited a concentration of human activities and settlements around the downtown area, the so-called *in-migration*. In-migration refers to migration from former colonies and similar places. The fact that many immigrants settle in impoverished city centres led to the notion of the "peripheralization of the core", which simply describes that people who used to be at the periphery of the former empires now live right in the centre.

Recent developments, such as inner-city redevelopment schemes, mean that new arrivals in cities no longer necessarily settle in the centre. In some developed regions, the reverse effect, originally called counter urbanisation has occurred, with cities losing population to rural areas, and is particularly common for richer families. This has been possible because of improved communications, and has been caused by factors such as the fear of crime and poor urban environments. Later termed *"white flight"*, the effect is not restricted to cities with a high ethnic minority population.

When the residential area shifts outward, this is called suburbanization. A number of researchers and writers suggest that suburbanization has gone so far to form new points of concentration outside the downtown both in developed and developing countries such as India. This networked, poly-centric form of concentration is considered by some an emerging pattern of urbanization. It is called variously exurbia, edge city, network city, or postmodern city. Los Angeles is the best-known example of this type of urbanization.

Rural migrants are attracted by the possibilities that cities can offer, but often settle in shanty towns and experience extreme poverty. In the 1980s, this was attempted to be tackled with the urban bias theory which was promoted by Michael Lipton who wrote: "...the most important class conflict in the poor countries of the world today is not between labour and capital. Nor is it between foreign and national interests. It is between rural classes and urban classes. The rural sector contains most of the poverty and most of the low-cost sources of potential advance; but the urban sector contains most of the articulateness, organization and power. So the urban classes have been able to win most of the rounds of the struggle with the countryside...". Most of the urban poor in developing countries able to find work can spend their lives in insecure, poorly paid jobs. According to research by the Overseas Development Institute pro-poor urbanisation will require labour intensive growth, supported by labour protection, flexible land use regulation and investments in basic services.'

Urbanization can be planned urbanization or organic. Planned urbanization, i.e. planned community or the garden city movement, is based on an advance plan, which can be prepared for military, aesthetic, economic or urban design reasons. Examples can be seen in many ancient cities; although with exploration came the collision of nations, which meant that many invaded cities took on the desired planned characteristics of their occupiers. Many ancient organic cities experienced redevelopment for military and economic purposes, new roads carved through the cities, and new parcels of land were cordoned off serving various planned purposes giving cities distinctive geometric designs. UN agencies prefer to see urban infrastructure installed before urbanization occurs. Landscape planners are responsible for landscape infrastructure (public parks, sustainable urban drainage systems, greenways etc.) which can be planned before urbanization takes place, or afterward to revitalize an area and create greater livability within a region. Concepts of control of the urban expansion are considered in the American Institute of Planners.

ORGANIZATIONAL STRUCTURE TYPES

Pre-bureaucratic Structures

Pre-bureaucratic (entrepreneurial) structures lack standardization of tasks. This structure is most common in smaller organizations and is best used to solve simple tasks. The structure is totally centralized. The strategic leader makes all key decisions and most communication is done by one on one conversations. It is particularly useful for new (entrepreneurial) business as it enables the founder to control growth and development.

They are usually based on traditional domination or charismatic domination in the sense of Max Weber's tripartite classification of authority.

Bureaucratic Structures

Bureaucratic structures have a certain degree of standardization. They are better suited for more complex or larger scale organizations. They usually adopt a tall structure. Then tension between bureaucratic structures and non-bureaucratic is echoed in Burns and Stalker distinction between mechanistic and organic structures. It is not the entire thing about bureaucratic structure. It is very much complex and useful for hierarchical structures organization, mostly in tall organizations.

Post-bureaucratic

The term of post bureaucratic is used in two senses in the organizational literature: one generic and one much more specific. In the generic sense the term post bureaucratic is often used to describe a range of ideas developed since the 1980s that specifically contrast themselves with Weber's ideal type bureaucracy. This may include total quality management, culture management and matrix management, amongst others. None of these however has left behind the core tenets of Bureaucracy.

Hierarchies still exist, authority is still Weber's rational, legal type, and the organization is still rule bound. Heckscher, arguing along these lines, describes them as cleaned up bureaucracies, rather than a fundamental shift away from bureaucracy. Gideon Kunda, in his classic study of culture management at 'Tech' argued that 'the essence of bureaucratic control-the formalisation, codification and enforcement of rules and regulations-does not change in principle.....it shifts focus from organizational structure to the organization's culture'.

Another smaller group of theorists have developed the theory of the Post-Bureaucratic Organization., provide a detailed discussion which attempts to describe an organization that is fundamentally not bureaucratic. Charles Heckscher has developed an ideal type, the post-bureaucratic organization, in which decisions are based on dialogue and consensus rather than authority and command, the organization is a network rather than a hierarchy, open at the boundaries (in direct contrast to culture management); there is an emphasis on meta-decision making rules rather than decision making rules. This sort of horizontal decision making by consensus model is often used in housing cooperatives, other cooperatives and when running a non-profit or community organization. It is used in order to encourage participation and help to empower people who normally experience oppression in groups.

Still other theorists are developing a resurgence of interest in complexity theory and organizations, and have focused on how simple structures can be used to engender organizational adaptations. For instance, Miner *et al.* (2000) studied how simple structures could be used to generate improvisational outcomes in product development. Their study makes links to simple structures and improviseal learning. Other scholars such as Jan Rivkin and Sigglekow, and Nelson Repenning revive an older interest in how structure and strategy relate in dynamic environments.

Functional Structure

Employees within the functional divisions of an organization tend to perform a specialized set of tasks, for instance the engineering department would be staffed only with software engineers. This leads to operational efficiencies within that group. However it could also lead to a lack of communication between the functional groups within an organization, making the organization slow and inflexible.

As a whole, a functional organization is best suited as a producer of standardized goods and services at large volume and low cost. Coordination and specialization of tasks are centralized in a functional structure, which makes producing a limited amount of products or services efficient and predictable. Moreover, efficiencies can further be realized as functional organizations integrate their activities vertically so that products are sold and distributed quickly and at low cost. For instance, a small business could start making the components it requires for production of its products instead of procuring it from an external organization.But not only beneficial for organization but also for employees faiths.

Divisional Structure

Also called a "product structure", the divisional structure groups each organizational function into a division. Each division within a divisional structure contains all the necessary resources and functions within it. Divisions can be categorized from different points of view. There can be made a distinction on geographical basis (a US division and an EU division) or on product/service basis (different products for different customers: households or companies). Another example, an automobile company with a divisional structure might have one division for SUVs, another division for subcompact cars, and another division for sedans. Each division would have its own sales, engineering and marketing departments.

Matrix Structure

The matrix structure groups employees by both function and product. This structure can combine the best of both separate structures. A matrix organization frequently uses teams of employees to accomplish work, in order to take advantage of the strengths, as well as make up for the weaknesses, of functional and decentralized forms. An example would be a company that produces two products, "product a" and "product b". Using the matrix structure, this company would organize functions within the company as follows: "product a" sales department, "product a" customer service department, "product a" accounting, "product b" sales department, "product b" customer service department, "product b" accounting department. Matrix structure is amongst the purest of organizational structures, a simple lattice emulating order and regularity demonstrated in nature.

- Weak/Functional Matrix: A project manager with only limited authority is assigned to oversee the cross-functional aspects of the project. The functional managers maintain control over their resources and project areas.

- Balanced/Functional Matrix: A project manager is assigned to oversee the project. Power is shared equally between the project manager and the functional managers. It brings the best aspects of functional and projectized organizations. However, this is the most difficult system to maintain as the sharing power is delicate proposition.
- Strong/Project Matrix: A project manager is primarily responsible for the project. Functional managers provide technical expertise and assign resources as needed.

Among these matrixes, there is no best format; implementation success always depends on organization's purpose and function.

INDUSTRIAL ORGANIZATION

Industrial organization is a field of economics that studies the strategic behaviour of firms, the structure of markets and their interactions. The study of industrial organization adds to the perfectly competitive model real-world frictions such as limited information, transaction cost, of adjusting prices, government actions, and barriers to entry by new firms into a market. It then considers how firms are organized and how they compete. Perhaps a most appropriate term is the "Economics of Imperfect Competition". The development of industrial organization as a separate field owed much to Edward Chamberlin, Edward S. Mason and Joe S. Bain.

There are two major approaches to the study of industrial organization: the first approach is primarily descriptive and provides an overview of industrial organization. The second, price theory, uses microeconomic models to explain firm behaviour and market structure.

STRUCTURE, CONDUCT, PERFORMANCE

According to the structure-conduct-performance approach, an industry's performance (the success of an industry in producing benefits for the consumer) depends on the conduct of its firms, which then depends on the structure (factors that determine the competitiveness of the market). The structure of the industry then depends on basic conditions, such as technology and demand for a product. For example: in an industry with technology that the average cost of production falls as output increases, the industry tends to have one firm, or possibly a small number of firms. A competitive market structure has the performance outcome of lower costs and lower prices, (Shepherd, W: 1997:4).

The subject has a theoretical side and a practical side. According to one text book: "On one plane the field is abstract, a set of analytical concepts about competition and monopoly. On a second plane the topic is about real markets, teeming with the excitement and drama of struggles among real firms" (Shepherd, W.; 1985; 1).

The extensive use of game theory in industrial economics has led to the export of this tool to other branches of microeconomics, such as behavioural economics and corporate finance. Industrial organization has also had significant practical impacts on antitrust law and competition policy.

Input-Output Model

In economics, an input-output model uses a matrix representation of a nation's (or a region's) economy to predict the effect of changes in one industry on others and by consumers, government, and foreign suppliers on the economy. Wassily Leontief (1905-1999) is credited with the development of this analysis.

Francois Quesnay developed a cruder version of this technique called Tableau economique. Leontief won the Nobel Memorial Prize in Economic Sciences for his development of this model. And, in essence, Léon Walras's work *Elements of Pure Economics* on general equilibrium theory is both a forerunner and generalization of Leontief's seminal concept.

Leontief's contribution was that he was able to simplify Walras's piece so that it could be implemented empirically. The International Input-Output Association is dedicated to advance knowledge in the field input-output study, which includes "improvements in basic data, theoretical insights and modelling, and applications, both traditional and novel, of input-output techniques."

Input-output depicts inter-industry relations of an economy. It shows how the output of one industry is an input to each other industry. Leontief put forward the display of this information in the form of a matrix. A given input is typically enumerated in the column of an industry and its outputs are enumerated in its corresponding row. This format, therefore, shows how dependent each industry is on all others in the economy both as customer of their outputs and as supplier of their inputs.

Each column of the input-output matrix reports the monetary value of an industry's inputs and each row represents the value of an industry's outputs. Suppose there are three industries. Column 1 reports the value of inputs to Industry 1 from Industries 1, 2, and 3. Columns 2 and 3 do the same for those industries. Row 1 reports the value of outputs from Industry 1 to Industries 1, 2, and 3. Rows 2 and 3 do the same for the other industries.

While most uses of the input-output analysis focuses on the matrix set of inter-industry exchanges, the actual focus of the analysis from the perspective of most national statistical agencies, which produce the tables, is the benchmarking of gross domestic product. Input-output tables therefore are an instrumental part of national accounts. As suggested above, the core input-output table reports only intermediate goods and services that are exchanged among industries. But an array of row vectors, typically aligned below this matrix, record non-industrial inputs by industry like payments for labour; indirect business taxes; dividends, interest, and rents; capital consumption allowances (depreciation); other property-type income (like profits); and purchases from foreign suppliers (imports).

At a national level, although excluding the imports, when summed this is called "gross product originating" or "gross domestic product by industry." Another array of column vectors is called "final demand" or "gross product consumed."

This displays columns of spending by households, governments, changes in industry stocks, and industries on investment, as well as net exports. In any case, by employing the results of an economic census which asks for the sales, payrolls, and material/equipment/service input of each establishment, statistical agencies back into estimates of industry-level profits and investments using the input-output matrix as a sort of double-accounting framework. The mathematics of input-output economics is straightforward, but the data requirements are enormous because the expenditures and revenues of each branch of economic activity has to be represented. As a result, not all countries collect the required data and data quality varies, even though a set of standards for the data's collection has been set out by the United Nations through its System of National Accounts (SNA): the replacement for the current 1993 SNA standard is pending. Because the data collection and preparation process for the input-output accounts is necessarily labour and computer intensive, input-output tables are often published long after the year data was collected—typically as much as 5-7 years after.

Moreover, the economic "snapshot" the benchmark version of the tables provide of the economy's cross-section are taken only once every few years, at best. Although many developed countries estimate input-output accounts annually and with much greater recency.

Usefulness

In addition to studying the structure of national economies, input-output economics has been used to study regional economies within a nation, and as a tool for national and regional economic planning. Indeed a main use of input-output analysis is for measuring the economic impacts of events as well as public investments or programs as shown by IMPLAN and RIMS-II.

But it is also used to identify economically related industry clusters and also so-called "key" or "target" industries—industries that are most likely to enhance the internal coherence of a specified economy. By linking industrial output to satellite accounts articulating energy use, effluent production, space needs, and so on, input-output analysts have extended the approaches application to a wide variety of uses.

PRICING BEHAVIOUR IN OLIGOPOLY MARKETS

The behaviour of firms in oligopoly markets is one of the mainstays of IO research. NBER researchers have made considerable progress in better understanding firms' pricing decisions, particularly with reference to price dispersion.

Although competitive models tend to assume that consumers are perfectly informed about each firm's single price, many markets deviate substantially from this description. The ability to price discriminate — charging different prices for a product either across firms or to different customers of the same firm — may enable firms to extract greater consumer value from a transaction or to expand the set of customers they serve. This phenomenon appears ubiquitous in the economy.

Consumer search costs may be an important source of sustained price variability in a market. For example, cash prices for a given prescription drug vary widely across pharmacies within a particular geographic market.

The magnitude of price dispersion is correlated with attributes that appear related to the costs and benefits of consumer search, for example, greater price variation for drugs prescribed for one-time use to treat an acute condition, relative to those prescribed for ongoing purchase as maintenance therapies. Alan Sorensen (8548) uses information on retail price dispersion and prescription attributes to analyse the distribution of consumer search costs for these products.

His estimated model of consumer pharmacy choice suggests that search intensities in this market are relatively low — implying that, on average, only 5 to 10 percent of prescriptions are comparison-price shopped.

One way to increase search intensity is to lower its cost. Internet retailing often has been cited as intensely price competitive in large part because of easy consumer search for low-price vendors.

Joel Waldfogel and Lu Chen (9942) argue that this reduces the price advantage of brand-name retailers. They find that consumer exposure to price comparison sites such as DealTime.com reduces Amazon purchase shares for those consumers, and that reductions are roughly twice as large for sites that include retailer reliability information (which may substitute for retailer brand reputation) in addition to item price.

Goolsbee and Judith Chevalier (9085) develop a method of estimating price elasticities for online booksellers using publicly available data on Amazon and

Barnes & Noble.com, and conclude that consumers are quite sensitive to prices, particularly at Barnes & Noble.com.

Glenn Ellison and Sara Fisher Ellis on (10570) show that Internet retailers respond strategically to the increased pricing pressure imposed by these price comparison sites, though.

Their analysis of the online computer components market demonstrates that retailers engage in a variety of practices to mitigate the extreme price-sensitivity that price comparison sites may induce, allowing firms to mark-up prices at least enough to cover fixed as well as marginal costs for efficient retailers. Glenn Ellison (9721) provides a theoretical model of one such practice, "add-on pricing" — for example, advertising low prices for one good in the expectation of selling additional (or higher quality) products to consumers at a high price at the point of sale. His work shows that this practice can sustain softer price competition as a competitive equilibrium.

A rich body of research by Florian Zettelmeyer, Fiona Scott Morton, and Jorge Silva-Risso uses data on individual consumer automobile purchases to explore the interaction of retail auto pricing, consumer information, and Internet information and referral services.

These researchers first document significant reductions in average automobile purchase price associated with using an Internet referral service (8667), on the order of 2.2 percent after controlling for selection effects in who uses the service.

They then show that Internet referrals disproportionately benefit minority buyers, offsetting the average 2 percent price disadvantage these groups incur because of their personal costs of search or negotiation for purchases made through traditional dealer channels (8668). In research that matches consumer survey and transactions data to explore the mechanism underlying these price effects, these researchers conclud e that increased transparency of dealer invoice costs combine with greater negotiating clout of the online referral service to reduce a customer's price by an average of 1.5 percent (11515).

Consumer information appears to be particularly important in extracting value from auto price negotiations. For example, Megan Busse, Zettelmeyer, and Silva-Risso find that purchasers obtain 80 percent of the value of auto manufacturer promotions in the form of heavily promoted customer rebates, but only 35 percent of the value of promotions that are paid as dealer discounts (10887).

This research agenda has provided unparalleled insights into pricing determinants in a significant consumer market, and generated important new findings for the role of the Internet in changing outcomes in conventional retail channels.

Auction Markets

While Internet retailing in general has attracted considerable attention and interest, the icon of Internet selling may well be eBay. Its popularity as a mechanism for matching buyers and sellers has spawned a rich economics literature as well as numerous competitors; much of this is described in Patrick Bajari and Ali Hortacsu's survey of Internet auctions research (10076).

The seeming ubiquity of auctions, for goods ranging from fine art to Beanie Babies, and in settings that range from government procurement to pollution permits, has prompted several NBER researchers to model the benefits of auctions over alternative market transaction mechanisms.

Alexandre Ziegler and Edward Lazear (9795) analyse the choice between retail store-based and auction markets. They describe the relative benefits of each, and characterize the conditions that lead to more efficient market organization through retail stores relative to auctions.

Eduardo Engel, Ronald Fischer, and Alexander Galetovic (8869) analyse Demsetzian auctions for exclusive rights in settings that range from procurement to royalty contracts, and conclude that "competition for the field" through ex ante auctions welfare dominates duopoly competition whenever marginal revenue is decreasing in quantities sold. Bajari, Robert McMillan, and Steve Tadelis (9757) highlight limitations of auctions relative to negotiations in procurement settings, particularly those dominated by incomplete information.

With Stephanie Houghton, Bajari and Tadelis estimate adaptation and renegotiation costs to procurement contracts awarded by auction mechanisms (12051).

As Susan Athey and Philip Haile point out (12126, p. 1), "auctions have provided a fruitful area for combining economic theory with econometric analysis ... to understand behaviour and inform policy." Athey and Haile describe methodological innovations, many by NBER researchers, which have facilitated estimation of more realistic models and provided significant insights into auction market operation and performance.

A significant thrust of this work has been to allow the data more freedom to drive results by relaxing parametric and functional form assumptions.

For example, Haile, Han Hong, and Matthew Shum (10105) develop nonparametric tests of one of the key valuation questions in auctions: are bidders' valuations generated by independent private values for the good, in which case bidders need not be concerned about the "winner's curse," or by common values, in which case bidders must optimally shade their bids knowing that winning means they had an excessively optimistic estimate of the good's true value. They apply this test to different types of U.S. Forest Service timber auctions, and find support for its ability to distinguish between settings in which common values are likely to be more or less significant.

Another approach to allaying concerns about constraints imposed by structural model estimates of auctions looks to experimental data. In this spirit, Bajari and Hortacsu (9889) use experimental data to calibrate the quality of structural estimation based on four alternative theoretical models of bidder behaviour. Andreas Lange, John List, and Michael Price (10639) develop an innovative combination of field data and lab experimental data to evaluate the impact of secondary resale markets for timber on bidding behaviour in timber auctions.

Improving the models and methods available to analyse auction markets can yield important economic insights into these markets, and can aid participants in developing appropriate bidding strategies. But an important policy goal is also to understand the performance of these markets.

Mireia Jofre-Bonet and Martin Pesendorfer (8626) develop a method of estimating a dynamic model of behaviour in repeated highway construction procurement auctions with firm-level capacity constraints, and then quantify efficiency losses that result in this setting.

In many repeated auctions settings, the potential for collusion among bidders may also be a significant concern. Ken Hendricks, Rob Porter, and Guofu Tan (9836) develop a theory of collusion in affiliated private value and common value auction environments, and use their model to test for bidding rings in federal offshore oil and gas lease auctions.

They show that the winner's curse in common value settings works against bid rigging for marginal tracts. Bajari and Fox (11671) analyse potential collusion in FCC spectrum auctions; Orley Ashenfelter and Kathryn Graddy (10795) provide a case study of price-fixing in auctions using the Sotheby's/Christie's art auctions case, drawing out the lessons for auctions and competition policy from details of this case.

THE NBER INDUSTRIAL ORGANIZATION PROGRAM

The NBER's Program on Industrial Organization (IO) celebrates its fifteenth anniversary this year.

Researchers in the IO program explore a wide range of topics within the field. Rather than attempting to skim the full scope of program activity, this report highlights work in three broad areas: regulation and antitrust policy; pricing behaviour by firms; and auctions markets.

Discussion of the substantial body of research on technology and technical change is deferred to reports of the Productivity Program and the NBER Project on Industrial Technology and Productivity. Those interested in learning more about the IO program may visit the NBER website for links to the full set of Industrial Organization Working Papers: here

Regulatory and Antitrust Policy

When markets deviate from competitive ideals, assessing the desirability of government intervention requires a careful assessment of the costs of market failures relative to the benefits of imperfect regulation.

The recognition that even imperfect markets may be preferable to regulated outcomes accompanied a dramatic transformation in the nature and extent of government intervention across a broad range of markets over the past thirty years.

Many industries long subject to price and entry regulation in the United States — among them airlines, trucking, railroads, and banking — were deregulated. Telecommunications and electric utilities have been vertically disintegrated and structurally competitive segments were opened to market-based outcomes.

Privatization of state-owned enterprises outside the United States has substantially increased reliance on market outcomes in many sectors, although regulators in some cases have replaced government managers in providing oversight.

Where government intervention ha s been maintained, various forms of incentive-based regulation increasingly have replaced state ownership or traditional cost-of-service rate determination.

IO program members are among the leading scholars of antitrust and regulatory policy, and many have been directly involved in the design or implementation of reforms through their government service, advice to regulatory agencies, or consulting to affected firms.

In the face of continuing policy debates over regulatory reform, highlighted more than a decade ago by Paul Joskow and Roger Noll in the NBER's 1994 *American Economic Policy in the 1980s*, the NBER recently sponsored a research project designed to leverage this expertise.

Project participants were asked to identify key issues in economic regulation, assess the impact of regulatory reforms across a variety of industries, and evaluate significant contemporary concerns about these reforms.

Two dozen scholars assembled for a September 2005 conference in Cambridge to discuss the results of this project, to be assembled in an NBER volume on "Economic Regulation and Its Reform: What Have We Learned?" This project complements a substantial body of primary research by NBER associates on regulatory and antitrust policy. A selection of research from the conference and from NBER working papers is described below.

ECONOMIC REGULATION AND ITS REFORM

Telecommunications

The telecommunications sector similarly has undergone a dramatic transformation over the past quarter century. Although telecommunications regulators adopted various incentive-based policies early, "forward-looking" cost-based regulation still plays a prominent role in setting prices for unbundled network elements (UNEs) that must be leased by local telephone companies to their competitors.

As noted by Robert Pindyck (10287, 11225), the typical pricing formulas used to set UNE lease rates induce substantial investment and entry inefficiencies by failing to account properly for the substantial sunk costs of telecomm investments.

Jerry Hausman and Gregory Sidak compare the outcomes of regulatory approaches in the United States, the United Kingdom, and New Zealand. They conclude that in both the United States and the United Kingdom, unbundling may have caused an increase in competition if one measures competition by market share of entrants, at the cost of adverse investment effects by both incumbents and new entrants.

They argue that emerging facilities-based competition should allow the end of telecomm price regulation and the regulatory burden that it creates for both consumers and the economy. If the nature of local exchange competition during the 1990s is a guide to the future, then Shane Greenstein and Michael Mazzeo's (9761) research suggests that we may see increasing product differentiation as a result of local competition.

Cable Television

Greg Crawford's analysis of the cable television industry highlights the impact of economic regulation on product quality and innovation. Regulation in this industry has varied greatly over time, as federal legislation has deregulated, re-regulated, and deregulated consumer cable prices.

More recently, penetration by Digital Broadcast Satellites raises questions about the need for regulation to constrain cable prices.

Crawford analyzes the interplay of price regulation and firm quality choices, with attention to the implications of satellite competition for performance in cable television markets. His work highlights ongoing concern over horizontal concentration and vertical integration in the programming market, and bundling by both cable systems and programmers, the latter being the subject of current policy debate at the Federal Communications Commission.

Airline Deregulation

In general, the empirical evidence on deregulation of structurally competitive industries suggests considerable gains from removal of price and entry regulation, although the transition from regulated to competitive markets may be longer and more costly than academics or policymakers originally envisioned.

Borenstein and I describe the significant consumer benefits from reduced fares and increased flight frequencies and from nonstop service subsequent to airline deregulation, while acknowledging the industry's considerable financial volatility.

We argue that market power concerns have diminished as growth by low-cost carriers now challenges legacy airlines in virtually all parts of the country. Recent research by Goolsbee and Chad Syverson suggests that even the threat of entry by carriers such as Southwest may reduce incumbent prices (11072).

This surge in competition, combined with adverse demand shocks, high fuel prices, and high labour costs, has contributed to current financial distress among many legacy airlines, though. Financial distress and accompanying bankruptcies have been costly for shareholders, high-wage workers, and the Pension Benefit Guaranty Corporation, although many costs and dislocations may be transitional.

For example, Borenstein and Rose (9636) show that schedule disruptions associated with airline bankruptcies are largely transitory; where they are more permanent, they appear to be modest relative to background fluctuations in flights and destinations served, and to be isolated to medium-sized airports.

Overall airline investment and consumer benefits continue to be substantial. The greater long-run challenge may be the performance of government-controlled airports, air traffic control, and security infrastructure, which have not in general kept pace with the growth and changes in the industry.

Electricity Restructuring: Competition and Incentive Regulation

NBER researchers continue in the vanguard of research, market design, and implementation of electricity restructuring.

Much of the empirical work to date has focused on restructured generation markets, in which prices generally are determined through a competitive bidding process. Frank Wolak describes the evolutionary nature of the restructuring process, emphasizing the tension between an imperfectly competitive market and an imperfect regulatory process in providing incentives for least-cost supply at various stages of the production process. In one of the first empirical analyses of restructuring supply-side benefits (11001), the potential for these incentives to reduce costs is highlighted: Kira Fabrizio, Catherine Wolfram, and I show that restructuring is associated with increased productivity, documenting generating-plant efficiency gains in the use of labour and materials input from replacing a regulated monopoly with market competition.

As Wolak points out, though, the technical characteristics of electricity supply and demand suggest that market power may be of particular concern, limiting the benefits of restructuring. Joskow (8442) discusses the role of market power and other contributors to the 2000-1 California electricity crisis; Ali Hortacsu and Steven Puller (11123) measure efficiency losses from strategic bidding in the Texas ERCOT market; and Dae-Wook Kim and Chris Knittel (10895) compare direct measures of markups to those inferred from oligopoly models of market power in California generation markets.

Wolak also describes market design and regulatory policies that limit the ability of suppliers to exercise unilateral market power — such as forward contracting, horizontal divestitures, demand-side participation, and local market power mitigation — and uses examples from worldwide wholesale electricity markets to illustrate the importance of effectively addressing each aspect of the market design process to ensure the maximum benefits of electricity restructuring.

While early empirical electricity research focused predominantly on generation markets, researchers increasingly have turned their attention to retail markets and demand-side policy.

Peter Reiss and Matthew White (8687, 9986) use data from San Diego households to measure consumer responsiveness to changing electricity prices and conservation programs enacted during the California electricity crisis. They argue that consumers may be more responsive to price fluctuations than previously thought.

Severin Borenstein and Stephen Holland (9922) suggest that substantial efficiency gains could be obtained from shifting even modest shares of relatively price-insensitive customers from fixed retail electricity prices to those that reflect time-varying wholesale electricity prices. Borenstein (11594) provides insight into continued res istance to real-time pricing, highlighting substantial distributional effects of real-time prices across heterogeneous industrial and commercial customers that may make it difficult to gain political support without some system to compensation losers.

For services such as transmission and distribution, which typically remain subject to regulation even in restructured markets, innovations have shifted the focus from cost-based price setting toward incentive mechanisms. Joskow provides a comprehensive review of the theory and complexities involved in applying incentive-based regulation. He then discusses applications of incentive mechanisms to the regulation of prices and service quality for "unbundled" electricity transmission and distribution networks. Further, he assesses the evidence on the performance of incentive regulation for electric distribution and transmission networks and describes challenges for future policy and research.

Among those challenges are determining the role of competition in electricity retailing and transmission. Joskow and Jean Tirole (9534) analyse the likely performance of competitive merchant transmission markets, and conclude that this model is likely to yield substantial investment inefficiencies.

While their prognosis for retail electricity competition is more optimistic (10473), they note a variety of challenges and efficiency limitations of competitive outcomes.

In their work on "Reliability and Competitive Electricity Markets" (10472), they analyse the complexity involved in integrating economists' approach to market design with engineering system design for reliability across the entire electricity network.

Finally, they highlight the implications for system investment, operation, and reliability of interactions among competitive markets, operational constraints, and regulatory and administrative practices.

Pharmaceutical Regulation

Pharmaceutical regulation has long generated concern over its effect on innovation incentives and product launch delays. Patricia Danzon and Eric Keuffel tackle these and other issues in their analysis of pharmaceutical safety, price, and marketing regulations on a variety of industry performance measures.

They note that regulatory reforms such as the adoption of user fees, fast track, and priority review may have reduced review-induced delays, especially for priority drugs. For example, Ernst Berndt et al. (10822) finds that implementation of performance goals and user fees for FDA drug applications substantially reduced approval lags — by an average of roughly six months. They estimate a net savings of more than 125,000 life-years from these reforms.

Discouragement of innovation also can be a significant hidden cost of price regulation. Price controls present in many countries may reduce the price of existing pharmaceuticals, but also appear to discourage the development and diffusion of innovative new treatments.

In their work on Medicaid prescription drug purchasing, Mark Duggan and Fiona Scott Morton (10930) highlight another indirect effect of price regulation: government rules that base Medicaid purchase price on the average price of that drug across private-sector purchasers increase equilibrium drug prices for non-Medicaid purchasers, and increase a firm's incentives to introduce new versions of a drug at higher prices.

Antitrust Policy

In regulated industries, firms may be subject to overlapping jurisdiction by both regulators and antitrust authorities. Dennis Carlton and Randal Picker analyse the tension that this produces, describing the historical origin of antitrust and regulation policy and the ongoing struggles to define the appropriate mechanism and substantive scope for regulating competition.

They note that debates over the role of antitrust and regulation continue with particular prominence in today's network industries, whether telecommunications, transportation, or electricity.

Moreover, core issues such as interconnection and mandatory access have increased in salience as reform-induced restructuring has led to vertical disintegration of firms and increased competition with incumbents in many industry segments, while the Supreme Court's decision in *Trinko* leaves open substantial questions about how these relationships will be governed.

For most sectors of the economy, interactions among firms are governed by court interpretations of antitrust policy rather than by economic regulatory agency decisions.

NBER researchers have explored a variety of aspects of antitrust policy, from theoretical and empirical analyses of merger policy to consideration of vertical restraints.

The appropriate role and application of antitrust policy in innovative sectors has attracted particular attention, both as a matter of principle and in the context of high-profile cases such as U.S. v. Microsoft.

In these sectors, the tension between encouraging competition through entry and maintaining profit incentives for dynamic growth and efficiency is particularly acute. Ilya Segal and Michael Whinston (11525) focus on this tension in research that analyzes a number of specific policies, highlighting those that benefit both entry and innovation.

Carlton and Robert Gertner (8976) argue that dynamic efficiency requires coordination of antitrust policy with intellectual property laws in an attempt to resolve tensions created by the tendency for network industries to evolve toward closed systems. Michael Katz and Howard Shelanski (10710) argue that traditional merger analysis, based on static welfare analyses, may miss important dynamic efficiency implications of mergers in highly innovative sectors. Carlton (11645) emphasizes the importance of dynamic barrier-to-entry analysis as one component of this.

Financial Services

Randall Kroszner and Phillip Strahan analyse the evolution of banking regulation of prices (interest rates), entry, capital, and investment decisions from the 1990s. to the last part of the twentieth century. They note that while industry adaptations to constraints partially reduced the costs of regulatory distortions, banking efficiency improved following the removal of most price and entry controls, generating substantial real benefits for the economy as a whole. Patrick Bolton et al. (10571) show that opening the banking sector to price and product-offering competition also may improve information provision and consumer-product matching, given the superior information that financial services sellers may have about product suitability for buyers of those services.

Eric Zitzewitz analyzes the implications of such asymmetric information for the regulation of non-banking financial services firms. He argues that agency conflicts created by information asymmetries and consumer behavioural biases may impede market efficiency. For example, asset management and financial advisor firms may have incentives to discriminate according to customer sophistication or search ability, offering low-price, high-quality products to sophisticated clients and high-price, low-quality products to the less sophisticated. Ali Hortacsu and Syverson (9728) provide some evidence of this phenomenon in research on product differentiation and search costs in the mutual fund industry. Zitzewitz too discusses the implications of these factors for regulatory and antitrust policy in this sector, with particular attention to recent interventions by the New York Attorney General and the SEC.

Bibliography

Alberto, P., & Troutman, A.: *Applied Behaviour Analysis for Teachers*, Columbus, OH, USA: Prentice-Hall-Merrill, 2003.

Allport, Gordon : *Pattern and Growth in Personality*, Holt, Rinehart and Winston, New York, 1961.

Amos Tversky.: *Choice, Values, Frames*, The Cambridge University Press, 2000.

Asch, M : *Abnormal and Developmental Psychology*, Ivy Pub, Delhi, 2003.

Baran, Paul A.: *The Political Economy of Growth*, New York, Modern Reader Paperbacks, 1975.

Brain, Christine: *Advanced Psychology: Applications, Issues and Perspectives.* Cheltenham: Nelson Thornes, 2002.

Brown, L. and Gilligan, C. : *Meeting at the Crossroads*, Ballantine Books, New York, 1992.

Burke, Frank M., *Valuation and Valuation Planning for Closely Held Businesses*, Englewood Cliffs, NJ, Prentice Hall, 1981.

Carkhuff, R.R.: *The Art of Health Care: A Handbook of Psychological First Aid Skills.* Amherst. Massachusetts: Human Resource Development Press, 1976.

Case, R.: *Intellectual Development: Birth to Adulthood.* New York: Academic Press, 1985.

Commons, J. R., *Institutional Economics-Its Place in Political Economy*, The University of Wisconsin Press, Madison, Wisconsin, 1934.

Cushman, P. : *Constructing the Self, Constructing America, A Cultural History of Psychotherapy in America*, Reading, MA, Addison-Wesley, 1996.

Damon, William : *Social and Personality Development, Infancy through Adolescence*, New York: Norton, 1983.

Dimson, Elroy: *Stock Market Anomalies*, Cambridge University Press, 1988.

Dubey, K.C. : *Experimental and Developmental Psychology*, Omega Pub, Delhi, 2009.

Ellis, A. :*Humanistic Psychology, The Rational-emotive Approach*, Julian Press, New York, 1973.

Freeman, A.: *Cognitive Therapy of Personality Disorders*, New York : Guilford Press, 2007.

Fruhan, W. E.: *Financial Strategy, Studies in the Creation, Transfer and Destruction of Shareholder Value*. Homewood, 1979.

Gabbard, Glen: *Psychodynamic Psychiatry in Clinical Practice*, Washington, DC : American Psychiatric Press, 2005.

Georgi, A. : *Psychology as a Human Science*, Harper & Row, New York, 1970.

Ginsburgh, Victor A. : *Economics of Art and Culture*, Contributions to Economic Analysis, Elsevier, 2004.

Homans, P. : *Symbolic Loss,* University Press of Virginia, Charlottesville, 2000.

Horney, Karen : *Feminine Psychology,* Norton, New York, 1993.

Hunt, E. K. *History of Economic Thought, A Critical Perspective,* New York, HarperCollins, 1992.

Jack Murrin, *Valuation: Measuring and Managing the Value of Companies,* New York, Wiley, 1994.

Jalan, P.K. : *Industrial Sector Reforms in Globalization Era,* Sarup, Delhi, 2004.

King, M. : *Existential-phenomenological Alternatives for Psychology,* Oxford Univ. Press, New York, 1978.

Kumar, Arvind : *Industrial Pollution and Management,* APH, Delhi, 2004.

Lipinski, B. : *Heed the Call, Psychological Perspectives on Child Abuse,* Sojourner Press, Los Angeles, 2001.

Loomes, G.: *Current Issues in Microeconomics,* New York: St. Martin's Press, 1989.

MacDonald, K and R. L. Burgess: *Evolutionary Perspectives on Human Development,* Thousand Oaks, CA: Sage, 2004.

March, J. G.: *A Behavioural Theory of the Firm,* Englewood-Cliffs, Prentice Hall, 1963.

Rathod, P B : *Dynamics of Political Psychology,* ABD Pub, Delhi, 2008.

Roach, J.R. : *Cities of the Dead, Circum-Atlantic Performance,* Columbia University Press, New York, 1996.

Rogers, A. : *Adults Learning for Development,* London, Cassell, 1992.

Roth, A. E.: *The Handbook of Experimental Economics,* Princeton, Princeton University Press, 1995.

Snygg, D.: *Individual Behaviour: A Perceptual Approach to Behaviour,* New York: Harper and Row, 1959.

Suri, R.K. : *Dynamics of Industrial Relations,* Pentagon Press, Delhi, 2007.

Taylor, D. : *Disappearing Acts,* Duke University Press, Durham, 1997.

Taylor, F. W.: *The Principles of Scientific Management,* New York, 1917.

Tinbergen, Jan.: *On the Theory of Economic Policy*; Amsterdam, North-Holland 1952.

Tutu, D. (1999). *No Future without Forgiveness,* Doubleday, New York, 1099.

Verhelst, T. : *No Life without Roots, Culture and Development,* Zed Books, London, 1987.

Weber, M.: *The Theory of Social and Economic Organizations,* New York, Oxford University Press, 1947.

William B. Jr. : *Theories of Personality,* Macmillan, New York, 1974.

Williams, R.: *Critical Issues in Psychotherapy : Translating New Ideas into Practice.* London : SAGE, 2001.

Yegge, Wilbur M., *A Basic Guide for Valuing a Company,* New York, Wiley, 1996.

Index

❑❑❑